MECCA IN MY WAKE
A Pilgrimage to Christ

By Dr. Ahmed Joktan

© 2020 by Dr. Ahmed Joktan
Printed through Proclaim Publishers, Wenatchee, Washington

Library of Congress Cataloging-in-Publication Data

Joktan, Ahmed, 1991–
    Mecca in My Wake: a pilgrimage to Christ / Ahmed Joktan.

        p. cm.

    ISBN: 978-1-7345462-2-4 (print)

    ISBN: 978-1-7345462-3-1 (ebook)

    1. Joktan, Ahmed, 1991- 2. Evangelists – United States – Biography I. Title

First Printing, 2020
Manufactured in the United States of America

PROCLAIM PUBLISHERS

WENATCHEE, WASHINGTON

To all who are still on the journey taking a rest, come and drink from the only true fountain of Living Water

Endorsements

for Dr Joktan's story, as told in his memoir, From Mecca to Christ

Dr. Ahmed Joktan has told a story of God's grace in action. He gives insight into present-day beliefs that will give understanding to the non-Islamic reader. More than this, his book is a rehearsal of the kindness of God extended to everyone. I hope his journey toward God's love will be your story, too.

—Chris Fabry, Chicago, Illinois

Host, Chris Fabry Live on Moody Radio

Author of "War Room: Prayer Is a Powerful Weapon"

Abandoned in the hot Saudi desert for hours at the age of four by a father who wanted to make a man out of him, flogged before reaching puberty for making the smallest error in reciting the Quran, trained to hate and terrorize the infidels in his early teen years, being visited by Jesus in a dream, receiving Christ and committing his life to his Savior, facing horrendous persecution, Dr. Ahmed is now dedicating his life to sharing the gospel with his people and drawing them to a saving knowledge of Christ. These are but glimpses of Dr. Ahmed's life. But the book is more than a testimony. It is also an introductory course on Muhammad and Islam. The author, in graphic images, exposes the hardship of growing up in Saudi Arabia and the harsh persecution after his conversion. Dr.

Joktan is now a joyful, hopeful and passionate follower of Jesus with a vision for his people. Do not just read this book; take action to encourage this dear brother who has a God-given vision that we do well to support.

— Georges Houssney, Boulder, Colorado
President, Horizons International

The book *From Mecca to Christ* by Dr. Ahmed Joktan, born and raised in Saudi Arabia, is a compelling testimony of his conversion abroad and his harrowing experiences of persecution upon his return as he courageously shared the gospel with fellow Saudis and other Arabs in the Gulf area. It is also a shining example of the triumph of love in his heart for his lost compatriots, in spite of their cruel treatment of him. His founding of Mecca to Christ International is a tribute to his undying love for his own people. His book closes with a passionate invitation to join him in his ministries.

—Dr. Don McCurry, Colorado Springs, Colorado
Ministries to Muslims

I strongly recommend the book *From Mecca to Christ* by Ahmed Joktan. I lived through some of the experiences with Ahmed described in this book and can confirm first-hand the persecution he lived through! It was the highest honor to exalt the Lord Jesus Christ with Ahmed while he was in Riyadh and lead the homegroup of Bible discussions. Reading this book will give you an insight of what our Lord is doing in unreached places.

—Charles May, Riyadh, Saudi Arabia
Retired U.S. Air Force officer

Dr. Ahmed's book is heart-wrenching, and it truly demonstrates the power of God in a person to forsake all and follow Christ. Dr. Ahmed and I attended the same church when I lived in the Gulf States, and I walked with him through a lot of the persecution he suffered. I remember him driving 13 hours each Sunday just to get to our church in another country since churches are illegal in the Kingdom of Saudi Arabia. In *From Mecca to Christ,* you will see the power of God on display. I can testify that this book is true because I witnessed a lot of it.

—Andrew Stewart, Louisiana
Retired U.S. Naval officer

Undoubtedly the most dramatic conversion story in the Bible is that of Saul of Tarsus meeting the risen Christ on the road to Damascus. This story of the transformation of Ahmed Joktan has some remarkable parallels. From his powerful encounter with the risen Christ in a hotel room in Auckland one year during Ramadan, to the Lord's words to Paul that he would \"show him how much he must suffer for my sake", this book traces the journey of Ahmed through persecution and suffering from both family and state authorities. It's a page turner, and well worth a read.

—Murray Robertson
Former Senior Pastor, Spreydon Baptist Church, Christchurch, New Zealand

The phenomenon of Muslims turning to faith in Jesus Christ is the latest in a series of divine "surprises" that has marked the global move of the Holy Spirit over the last century. Most surprising of all is the extraordinary conversion of the son of the mufti of Mecca, Ahmed Joktan. This book describes his unexpected conversion and the horrendous suffering he experienced as a result. It is a story of the Lord's surprising grace and of the courageous witness of a Muslim background convert. That this should happen in my own country of New Zealand, so far from the heartland of Islam, is further tribute to God's surprises.

—Rob Yule

Retired Presbyterian minister, author, and former Moderator of the Presbyterian Church of Aotearoa New Zealand

This is the extraordinary journey from privilege in Islam to persecution for Christ, all through encountering Jesus in a dream in Auckland, NZ, in 2010. I met this modern Apostle Paul and first heard his stories, when Ahmed visited our church in 2017. More compelling than his stories of suffering, was his gracious Christ-like character and transformed life mission, with a special burden to evangelize his own Saudi people and equip others to reach them. Read his story – you won't want to put it down!

—Rev. Steve Jourdain, North, NZ

Senior Minister, St Alban's Presbyterian Church, New Zealand

Dr. Ahmed Joktan pens an excellent account of his personal story in his new book *From Mecca to Christ*. He documents his experience as a means to encourage and inspire his readers so that we can stand for what we believe. I can see this book changing many lives.

—Kevin Wayne Johnson, Washington, D.C.

The Johnson Leadership Group

Contents

Foreword: Letter from a Ghost 1

1 | Staring Down the Barrel 7

2 | A Time to Celebrate 9

3 | Allahu Akbar 15

4 | Shepherd Boy 21

5 | Reflections 29

6 | In the Footsteps of the Prophet 49

7 | A Man of Islam 57

8 | Dream 69

9 | The House of White Pillars and the Tall Man 81

10 | A Storm Before the Calm 133

11 | Outcast 149

12 | A New Beginning 159

13 | Conversion Therapy 181

14 | Thirteen Hours to Church 211

15 | Opportunity 245

16 | Collision 267

17 | Outcast, Part Two 301

18 | Refrigerator Rights 323

19 | The Letter 339

20 | Dictation 345

21 | Land of the Free 367

22 | Home of the Saved 389

23 | A Forever Family 405

24 | His Great Commission 419

Appendix 427

Foreword:
Letter from a Ghost

I will be brief—such are words those who know me well understand to mean either five hundred pages or at least three hours of one-sided conversation. To be honest, this is my third attempt at composing what truly needs to be a quick piece, twofold in its purpose: first, to comment on the unlikely pairing that is this ghostwriter with this story and its author; and, second, to lay bare how this text differs from its parent piece, *From Mecca to Christ*, and the reasons for these differences. As this is not a book about me, I will keep the sketching of my visage to that of a stick figure, rather than a Michelangelo.

I write.

(We might need a little more than that)

I write, and I arranged the words you are about to read.

However, I did not write this story.

Nor was I worthy to take part in this project.

An unlikely candidate am I even to have been asked. To put it simply, I was an agnostic skeptic, soured to the Christian faith, and a proud patriot with a clear memory of the day he watched as thousands of innocent Americans lost their lives by the hand of those under the black banner of Islam—

this was the man a Christian pastor approached for help writing a story about his friend, the former jihadist.

Unlikely, indeed; but, as you will find in the pages that follow this letter, being unlikely fits perfectly into this tale.

Needless to say, I was not immediately enthusiastic about the proposition; however, I did eventually agree to help edit the *From Mecca to Christ* manuscript, after which I was asked if I would be willing to capture the entire story in narrative form, something more like a novel, unlike the original memoir. To do so would be a great undertaking, and I was never remotely inclined to write any work other than my own, and had in the past turned down similar requests; but there was something about this story—something even about a grander change happening in my own life, of which I dared not speak—that I simply could not pass up the opportunity. However, if I was to get this right, I needed more than *From Mecca to Christ*; I needed to meet the man himself. And it was about this time I was finally introduced to Ahmed.

He looked nothing like I had imagined the subject of such a high-octane story would look. Save for the scars on his face and his uncommon affinity for smiling, he was about as ordinary as any other man I'd known; yet, one could feel the extraordinary work being conducted through him. My initial interest in his story when first presented to me was to simply help expose to the masses the evils of a religion I held in contempt. But I quickly discovered as I edited *From Mecca to Christ* and spoke more with the man who had lived it that while a lifting of the veil was necessary, this tale possessed something far more earth shattering.

Ahmed and I discussed the narrative version of his story, at which time he revealed to me hard evidences of a world of darkness like I'd never known. For several months following our conversations, I wrote nothing; my world had been irreparably shaken, and I would never be the same.

Still, as a stubborn skeptic, even with his stacks of documentation and the proof carved into the face gazing peacefully back at me, I could not take his word alone when it came to the core of his former life. I had to know this bedrock more intimately; so, I became a student of Islam, diving headlong into the Qur'an and its supporting texts, scouring the depths of its claims, giving ear to its most ardent and studied supporters and followers, seeking every stone that it might be overturned; and in so doing I have returned like the prodigal to the faith I had many years prior to meeting Ahmed rejected for a life of ignorance, self-fulfillment, agnosticism, even nihilism, returning now from the sty of pigs that had been the culmination of my wasteful path: there in the mud and filth of squandered time, self, and purpose. Christ was made all the more real, beautiful, and even necessary to and for me as I embarked on this journey, on which I had set out with the full intent of merely exercising the old muscle to deliver the highest quality work for a story that would change the world, but leave this heart of stone intact.

That, in probably still too many words, is my part in all of this; and I will happily now fade behind the lines.

So, with phase one of this letter now complete, let us saunter onto phase two.

There can be no reading of this narrative without also consuming the memoir from which it was derived: *From Mecca to Christ*. It is the raw account of the events as they happened, point by point and piece by piece, as well as a most enriching history of Islam and exposure of life as it is today in Saudi Arabia: the birthplace and hotspot of that religion.

Founded on Ahmed's story, that which was autobiographically dictated, the forthcoming composition is arranged and presented in such a way as to highlight and magnify, not exaggerate, its most compelling elements and to make he who is a stranger to the reader as one alive and speaking his story in an intimate, personal setting, as he did for me. The purpose of the narrative is to harness more than just the facts; it seeks also to bind your spirit to the people and events, to let the heart of the tale bleed before you; it aims to bring forth the colors, the sights, sounds, and smells; to let you taste the bitterness, to sup on the hope; to wrap you in the chill of the darkness and shower you with the rapturous warmth of the light. Above all, it seeks to break upon your soul the power of the living God, let your arms feel the weight of the cross Christians are called to carry, and point you to a glorious Savior.

Now, in order to properly convert the language of a memoir into that of a narrative, a translation is required. For the sake of full transparency and to ensure there is no wondering or misunderstanding of the facts as they stand in this history, these alterations I will list in an appendix at the end of the book. Review these however you like: before reading, after reading, while reading, on your lunch break, with a spot of afternoon tea, up a tree, on a boat, standing on your head—it doesn't matter. Our desire is for you to be as informed as possible about the facts of this tale, for, as you will read, there have been many (as yet there are) who doubt its veracity, in spite of its evidentiary backing. Remember, even I had been one such skeptic.

In this book you will find no exaggerations or fictitious events—fictitious as they relate either to events experienced by Ahmed as specifically recounted in the timeline of his memoir, in the full scope of his life thus far, or events as they presently happen in Saudi Arabia. Rather, the most prevalent changes come in the following forms: Firstly and most prominently, the majority of characters are presented under invented names for the purpose of protective anonymity. Some characters are dressed in metaphorical clothing, coloring the features or attributes of a person or persons to represent something larger than themselves, like a sentiment, a collective, or a belief. The text also includes some timeline modifications: the compressing of large passages of time into single moments or short periods, for the sake of pacing; and other times real occurrences or situations found in Saudi Arabia today are placed before Ahmed's character, making him a spectator in the narrative to things he's seen daily and knows intimately, but might not have seen or encountered in that specific moment in history.

I will not exhaust that list here—it's all in the appendix.

Again, however, I stress this point: do not consume this narrative and neglect to take in the meat of *From Mecca to Christ*—such would be akin to reading only the allegory and leaving unturned the pages of the text from which it was derived.

Having long overstayed my welcome, I will bring this "brief" letter to a close with this: It has been my honor and joy to compose this piece, as well as a most humbling and enlightening experience. I can't explain how it happened, but I think I'm beginning to understand *why*—and the answer to that has nothing at all to do with me, or whatever ability I might possess. Truly, the man presently staring back at me in the mirror was an inconceivable impossibility when this journey began. I simply cannot explain the *how*; but I'm coming to better understand the *who*.

The story penned by God through his servant Ahmed has been changing lives for many years. And if this narrative version is blessed to be yet another means by which lives will be touched, let me claim to be the first so impacted; for the man who laid the first keystroke is not the same man as lays the last, here and now.

As Ahmed says through that bright and beaming smile, For Christ and His Kingdom!

Yours Faithfully,

Ghostwriter
June 12, 2020

1
Staring Down the Barrel

Few things in life can compare to the sensation of having the barrel of a fully-loaded AK-47 rifle pressed violently against your forehead. For days, my body had bellowed tormented screams from the grisly bruises littering my beaten body; the hard ground in which I knelt gnawed mercilessly at the bones in my knees; and fear, like a shrieking, spectral choir, echoed its all-consuming poison through my veins and violently trembling frame. Yet, even with the chaotic cacophony of bruised body, gnawed knees, tumultuous terror, and a cold steel rod boring angrily into my skin, driving right between my eyes with so vicious a pursuit that it seemed only moments away from puncturing straight through to my skull—even with all these clanging together in what should have been a deafening death knell, I could hear only the rubbing of a rage-filled finger against a pristine, polished trigger, and the heavy snarls rumbling from the face behind that finger: my father's.

Many times had I trembled before this mighty Meccan Mufti, but the look on his face this day was one like I had never seen in all my life. Not even in those times as a boy when I had greatly offended him had I seen this wild, maniacal look of hatred—those times when he would loom over me, his voice booming like thunder, and repeatedly strike the palm of my hand with a round, wooden rod, pouring into my soul more terror than the arduous pain could overwhelm until the next day. I was, right now, in his eye, like a swine that has tracked filth through his house and gobbled up his sacred treasures. Whatever bond beyond blood that had tied me to this man had now been permanently severed. I was no longer his son; I was his despised and mortal enemy.

There was no turning back now. Even if I survived this moment, I knew my life would instantly become even more unfamiliar than I had already anticipated it would be. Call me crazy, but even though I knew full-well the cost, the reality of being forsaken by my own father and divorced from my own family—my mother, brothers, and all those whom I love dearly—seemed too extreme to come true, to actually happen to me. I had been called to forsake father and mother and this temporary family of mine, and take up a cross on a new road; only, they'd beaten me to the punch, casting me from their bosom and hurling me onto a road unknown with a burden I knew not if I could bear.

From this day forward, I would be a stranger in a strange land—if, that is, this Muslim son, now declared dead by his kin, would be found alive tomorrow.

His wide eyes gazing eagerly over the body of the rifle, my father parted his snarling lips.

2
A Time to Celebrate

"**C**OME!" screamed my father, thrusting his AK-47 rifle into my hands. "Outside, Ahmed! Our heroes have triumphed!"

It was Tuesday, just after one o'clock in the afternoon, making it a rather odd day and hour for my father to suddenly return home from his many travels. As a Mufti (an Islamic scholar who interprets and expounds Islamic law), my father is a deeply esteemed and respected man, whose path from having been a pupil studying directly under the Grand Mufti of Saudi Arabia to a distinguished leader in the holiest city of Islam, has elevated him to a position of high honor and placed great demand upon his words, making ours a most prominent and wealthy family. Being that he is also of the line of Joktan— the great-great grandson of Shem, who was the son of Noah, as in Noah's Ark—my father enjoys, as I did, the dignity of being part of a tribe known for being Allah's jihadist warriors, intensely committed to the beliefs of Islam. And, for my family, that's putting it lightly.

As I'd mentioned, he travels quite often from our home in the city of Mecca, usually to conduct his work of interpreting, applying, and expounding in lectures the holy books of Islam (the Qur'an, the Hadith, and the Sunna); but sometimes he's in the midst of dividing his time between his other wives and children, scattered about different cities.

Usually, a speedy, unexpected return meant someone was in trouble, *serious* trouble, which also often meant that blood would be spilt. You'd better believe I gave myself a light-ning-quick self-examination when I saw him skid into the driveway. However, on this September afternoon, I quickly came to realize that in him was nothing at all akin to rage or indignation—on the contrary, he was overflowing with bliss and shouting praises to the heavens; for in a distant land across the sea, the blood of three thousand infidels had been spilt in the name of Allah.

As I emerged into the streets, shouts of, "Allahu Akbar! America has fallen!" filled the air, playing together with the roar of AK-47s, showering the atmosphere with the blood-red streaks of flaming tracer bullets, in a song of chaotic jubila-tion; the midday sky was like a pale-blue canvas sprayed with a grisly crimson mist. My father, insane with glee, ordered my brothers and me to join the deafening circus with our rifles.

This would be a celebration for the ages, the likes of which few had ever seen; some even viewed this day as more of a celebratory occasion than a wedding. Certainly, in my ten short years, I had never seen such a jubilant uproar. There were shouts of triumphant joy and wild breast beating; sheep and camels were slaughtered by the dozens and tossed whole into giant vats of boiling water, each twice the size of a hot tub, before mountains of rice were dumped in after them. How like a picture of the paradise we truly believed our terrorist heroes were now enjoying was this sight of an extravagant feast, bubbling and overflowing in a wasteful demonstration of our wealth and unbridled prosperity.

"Light up the sky, my boy!" screamed my father, whose overly excited slap on my back broke my mesmerized gazing at the commotion, and emptied the air from my lungs. "Our heroes are looking down on us from heaven, right now! There, at the right hand of Allah—see how your cousins sneer at you for keeping silent on their day of victory! Honor your tribesmen by casting your bullets at their feet!"

My ears were ringing and the world around me was becoming an ocean of blurred streaks of light. But I was soon snapped back into the moment when the vibrations from my rifle began pulsing through my finger; and with every bound through my body, those vibrations awakened and emboldened within me a passion to be unto my father what these heroes were to him, to make him just as proud of me as he was of them. Indeed, I had never seen him look at me the way he looked toward heaven this day.

Having run out of ammunition, I slung the rifle over my shoulder and followed the crowd to a nearby tent, wherein a serving platter, ten feet in diameter, had been laid on the ground. In it, like a trough, was a sea of rice; and floating within the white, steaming waves were the various limbs and tender meats of the boiled sheep and camels.

The men of my tribe all gathered around the platter, while I waited just outside with the rest of the women and children, as it is customary in my Muslim culture for the men to first eat their fill and leave the remaining scraps for the rest of us. Slaves from my family and others' hurried about to ensure the preparations were in order, being careful to steer clear of their master's wives, or else suffer a severe beating. Most of the slaves in my camp had been sent here from Africa and castrated to ensure obedience. But there were a few that had come from other lands in search of service and construction work, only to be turned into their master's property.

Once the men had settled down from their hugging and laughing, my father rose and addressed our tribe.

"Our jihadist heroes," he cried in the same authoritative, commanding voice he used when teaching in the mosque, "blood of my blood, my own nephews, our sons from within this very tribe—they have raised the black flag of Islam in the United States! They have brought the Great Satan down to its knees!"

A roar of approval and applause, as one might expect elicited by a game-winning grand slam in the World Series, erupted in the tent.

It took more than a little while for the atmosphere to return to a calm adequate for speeches.

"How important it is for all of us to follow their examples!" my father continued, his words becoming hotter and sharp like razorblades. "We must destroy *all* infidels— *EVERY. LAST. ONE!* We must take down these contemptible unbelievers, until the name of Allah is exalted throughout the earth!"

The explosion of cheering, of a horde of wild men infected with a feral rush of elation and power, shook the ground on which I stood; and when they sprang to their feet to stamp the ground and dance, I was sure what Americans remained alive in that accursed land overseas could feel the tremors. And as the darkness fell over us all on that infamous day of 9/11, a smile grew onto my face, while in my heart was ignited the same flame that had filled my eyes.

Someday, thought I, when the blood of American infidels runs warm over my hands, my father will look to the heavens, his face filled with love and admiration, and whisper to me, "Well done, good and faithful servant of Allah."

3
Allahu Akbar

WHEN the men had at last finished eating, a great many rose to take one of his female slaves by the arm and lead her roughly from the gathering. It was no secret, their intent; nor was it any of my business, much less the business of the men's wives, by whom they quickly passed. But as I had been this night dwelling a great deal on my father, the words of his teachings in the mosque came to mind, when he would stand before young men and preach from Qur'an 4:3 about "what your right hand possesses."

"Muhammad teaches us that you may marry up to four women," I once heard him say. "See here he instructs, 'Marry such women as seem good to you, two and three and four.' Indeed," he quipped with a chuckle, "I have reached *my* limit; and let me tell you that a woman who bears you many children will quickly see her power to please you diminish. Muhammad goes on to say, 'If you fear that you will not do justice between them, then marry only one, or what your right hand possesses,' that is your slaves. So," he declared, "why not get yourself a few sex slaves and have unlimited sex?"

As these words filled my head, my thoughts turned to our local terrorist heroes, and I wondered what sort of pleasures they must have been enjoying at that very moment. Unlike the wives they'd left behind, who had but a reunion with their husbands to anticipate in heaven, these men had just received Allah's generous gift of many *houris*, heavenly virgins. In my daily life, I tried to apply all things to the Qur'an, and recite as I went, so that I might better learn and understand; and now, all the verses of the Qur'an read to me as a child, and that I had recently and diligently been memorizing, the ones regarding these very creatures, zipped through my mind; words like "lovely-eyed," "modest gaze," and "full-breasted companions of equal age"—promises of the great prophet Muhammad—danced about, forming strange and curious images of what they must look like. The very nature of it all struck me as both exciting and odd. A gift from above was surely a wondrous thing, but a boy of my age could scarcely comprehend and had yet little interest in the things about which the men around him seem so ardently passionate and insatiably hungry.

My thoughts turned then to heaven. The words given to Muhammad from Allah describe a magnificent place, filled with pleasures untold, where crowns of glory will be bestowed upon the faithful, and where those who give their lives in the killing of infidels are guaranteed a place for all eternity. Without the latter, there could be no assurance of entering through those golden gates above; but I was quickly becoming certain that someday, and perhaps soon, I would earn my guarantee, and in so doing bring honor to my father and see that he would be glorified in the next life. Surely, I would be there one day. The thought of going to hell was unbearable, for in my heart were the words of the one who had seen it firsthand.

"I was shown Hell," said Muhammad, as recorded in the Sahih al-Bukhari, Book 16, Hadith 12, "and I have never seen anything more terrifying than it."

Looking around the feast, I started analyzing each and every person, wondering which of them would make it to heaven, and which would spend an eternity in the fires below. Some of the young men I knew to be brave and upright; these would surely spill the blood of the infidels and be forever in paradise. I could be like them—indeed, I could! I was, at least, better off than some of my peers, like the ones struggling to memorize the Qur'an. More than that, I was a whole bound ahead of the game being that I am male; many of the women around me, I knew, would one day taste the fires of hell. As Allah explains, women are inherently fit for the fires, due to their ungrateful nature.

"And I saw that the majority of its people are women," said Muhammad. And the great Allah replied to the question of why this sex was the dominate group among hell's inhabitants, saying, "Because of their ingratitude…They are ungrateful to their companions and ungrateful for good treatment. If you are kind to one of them for a lifetime, then she sees one undesirable thing in you, she will say, 'I have never had anything good from you.'"

My heart shuddered to think what these women would one day and for all eternity endure. Still, if they were ungrateful and offensive to Allah, I thought, would they not deserve their portion?

About that time, my eyes caught sight of our Filipina housemaid, standing silently in the corner. The thunderous roar of nearby celebrations rumbled through the tent, and I was reminded of those nights when I was very young, when terrible storms would rage outside my window or through my dreams. I'd spring from my bed and sprint to her side like the lightning I sought to escape, there to be comforted in her warm and precious arms. My father was never one to soothe the terrors of the night, if he was home at all to do so; and my mother had never been willing to offer nurturing. But here was my faithful, beloved housemaid, always ready and eager to read me stories and recite the Qur'an until I slipped into a happy dreamland, deep within her embrace.

Watching her was peace.

Could such as she be bound for the fires?

Just then a great explosion was heard in the distance, accompanied by a bellow of celebratory cheers that split the night. My train of thought suddenly derailed, as several more explosions rang out, each carrying with it a verse from my nation's anthem—with every earth-shaking *BANG*, the next line in the series was thrust into my brain:

To glory and supremacy,
Glorify the Creator of the heavens!
And raise the green flag
Carrying the written light reflecting guidance,
Repeat: Allahu Akbar!
O my country!
My country,
Live as the pride of Muslims!
Long live the King
For the flag
And the homeland!

Allahu Akbar...Allah is greater. Yes, thought I; yes, he is—and at no time in history had he been more so demonstrated than on this day, when America was brought to its pitiful knees.

4
Shepherd Boy

STEPPING out of our immaculate, glinting, black SUV, my brothers and I walked slowly about the smoking rubble; an angry light glowed red within it, and a molten stream churned through its heart. As I continued forward, the smoke began to clear, and I noticed that several Sudanese shepherds had accompanied us, as often they did when we went to survey the fruits of my father's house. However, what struck me as odd was the fact that I seemed terribly small in comparison to my brothers, who strode beside me like giants, their heads lost somewhere in the thick dome of smoke and debris hovering over us. Though I could not see their faces, I knew their voices, which rang out in whispers, just as clear as if their lips were pressed against my ears.

"Every great man must be a shepherd," said the giant to my left, whispering like a hurricane wind. "Such are the words of Muhammad."

"Father would see this command fulfilled in you," said the one to my right, with a voice like a distant, raging storm. "See here that to which you must tend."

As he spoke, the haze cleared all the more; and I beheld before me a foreign city in devastation, its buildings razed and ablaze; a chorus of tormented wailing from distant shadows silhouetted in plumes of destruction filled the polluted air, and over them rained a hellish and furious barrage of blazing stones, like those jettisoned from a volcano. The ground beneath my feet was like embers painted white, and the night that engulfed this place was a suffocating shroud of endless death.

"A shepherd's work," declared the giant to my left; and I looked up into the blackened clouds and saw his massive finger pointing toward me, directly at my hands.

Turning my eyes downward, I gazed in abject horror at my tiny palms, from which all the ruination before me seemed to fountain and flow forth. My walking feet then trod upon a trail of blood; trembling, I followed it. There at it end, I discovered a torn and mangled mess of something, draped over a pile of simmering rubble: it was a once glorious banner, one I'd seen hanging beside the doorways of happy homes, flying high atop skyscrapers, and draped over the coffins of the honored departed. It was dying, its life essence oozing slowly from its muddied and distorted colors in a seemingly never-ending flow of white-crested blood and water.

These colors dripped from my fingertips.

Darkness then filled my eyes; like kerosene, it ignited my excitement and set my sight aflame.

Standing there in the carnage, my heart quickly began to pound; a rush of adrenaline surged through my body; and, clenching my fists about the scene of darkness, causing a miry sludge to leek through my fingers, I relished in the power of the great commission I had been given, and burned with gleeful anticipation of the praise I would soon receive from my father for having faithfully carried out this great work as a shepherd of Allah.

But before my excitement could reach a crescendo, there came a great roar from somewhere behind me. Turning quickly, my shoulders bearing forward, I beheld the SUV in which I'd arrived speeding away into the distance. Both giants, along with the Sudanese shepherds, had vanished—they had piled into the car and were abandoning me in that cold wasteland!

Every spark of power instantly drained through my feet, making me like limp and worn rubber. My tiny legs sprinted after them, but I went nowhere. I screamed and yelled and cried for them to return and deliver me from the darkness, of which I was now a victim, no longer a master; but they could not, would not, hear me. And it wasn't long before my struggling to reach the safety and salvation I sought in the arms of my family left me so thoroughly exhausted that I collapsed, weary and terrified.

Feet burnt and aching, I scurried on all fours to a cave in the rubble, and there curled up into a ball and sobbed. A mess of tears rained over my face, mucus gushed from my nose, and urine soaked my garment—for a time outside of time, I stayed hidden; until, faintly, in the distance, I heard the whimper of one whose misery eclipsed my own.

Crawling forth, I beheld a woman in ragged, tattered clothing, clutching an ever so tiny infant wrapped in white. Kneeling pitifully in the rubble, jagged stones and twisted metal piercing her knees, she guarded and covered the child, and sobbed as she whispered words that penetrated my heart like a javelin; for in them was a note of hope—even here, among the death and darkness, she spoke only of hope.

"We'll soon be home," she promised.

And then, a shadow of light filled the darkness, undoing what the darkness had devoured. I looked up for but a moment, as my eyes could not bear to gaze any longer at the overwhelming glory. The outline of what I saw seemed strangely familiar, and I could have sworn there stood beside it a staff like the ones carried by the Sudanese shepherds.

Just then, a voice thunderous, yet soft, fell over the world, saying, "I am the Good Shepherd. Gather unto me such as these."

Falling flat on my face, I begged, "*How*?"

No sooner had the words breached my lips did a new voice, like a wartime siren set right beside my ear, scream out, "PRAYER!"

A violent spasm and subsequent *THUD* later, I found myself lying face-down on my bedroom floor, with the pre-sunrise call to prayer blaring through my open window.

Fortuitously, I realized that my head was facing in the direction of the mosque; so, without moving (as I was also, double-fortuitously, on my prayer rug, which I always laid out beside my bed for morning prayer), I slipped into my first of five religiously-required and state-mandated prayers for the day.

I would never have said—at least, not out loud—that there was anything routine about my daily prayer routine. Just as I used a toilet without thinking about it, going as soon as the need struck, when the command to pray rang through all of Mecca, I was bent over and muttering to the floorboards.

Still, as I recited my usual morning script to Allah, there was a twinge of surprise and wonder sparking at the very back of my head: never yet, since the age of two, had I not been up and ready long before the call to prayer. Surely, the son of a Mufti could not forget the exact times of the day—the very position in which hung the sun—at which one was expected to pray. Being startled by the call and even a moment late to set my prayer in motion...this was not like me; and all at once an ocean of guilt sprang up all around, pulling me quickly through the surface, there to sink to the depths and be drowned.

As I repeatedly, fervently begged Allah for his mercy and forgiveness for my having been so careless as to neglect this second of the five pillars of Islam, visions of the unfaithful filled my head. Once, while in the heart of the city at midday, I began moving with others of my religious kin toward the mosque before the second call to prayer was announced. Shopkeepers locked their doors, all dealings in the city were halted, and a great horde of us all began the short trek to our place of prayer—except one man, who sat perfectly still along the side of the road, perched on a corner curb, gazing with unblinking eyes toward heaven.

For a moment, I wondered if he could not walk, or was deaf; but his body was full and healthy, and he carried no cane or other tool that would suggest a disability. And I could tell he wasn't deaf, for when the call finally cut through the streets, I could plainly see his body twitch, reacting ever so slightly to each siren syllable that broke upon him.

Then came the feral shouts of the religious police.

I could tell he'd heard these, too; yet, his gaze broke not from the clear sky above.

Unresponsive to their command to fall in line with the rest of us, he was viciously ripped to his feet, shackled hand and foot, and then dragged down the dusty road.

What fate I knew awaited him was confirmed when, roughly a week later, I saw him in the very same spot—only, this time, his once healthy body appeared slightly less so. A whip's bite marks could be seen around the collar of his neck, hinting at what lay beneath his shirt.

Again, the midday call rang out.

I stayed not to see how the man's tale would unfold.

A vacant corner curb greeted me the next day, and every day thereafter.

Once my petitions for forgiveness had come to an end, I took a moment to praise and thank Allah for the gift that had led to my staying up until only three hours before the first call. How glorious, thought I, and how poetic that Allah would raise up men so faithful as to execute the justice of the one true god, and to do so in perfect alignment with the holy Qur'an, right down to the numbers of the book and verse!

"Indeed," I recited joyfully, "you, oh mighty and blessed Allah, have purchased from the believers their lives and their properties in exchange for that they will have Paradise!" My fists clenched and I pounded the floor in triumph. "They have fought in the cause of Allah; so, they killed and were killed! It is a true promise binding upon him in the Torah and the Gospel and the Qur'an. And who is truer to his covenant than Allah? So, rejoice in your transaction," I exclaimed, "which you have contracted! And it is that which is the great attainment!"

Qur'an 9:111—a perfect verse for a glorious day, forever and poetically cemented in the pages of Allah's history, for his justice was by our heroes carried out on the date 9/11 at 1 PM Saudi time: a beautiful, exquisite reflection of 9:111.

The purposes of Allah are perfect, thought I, as I heaved a spirit-filling sigh; and he who acts that those purposes might be executed paints by the blood he both sheds and leaves behind a glorious portrait, standing forever as a testament to the greatness of the one true god.

My prayers concluded, I climbed back into bed, there to muse on the celebration past and the glory of the future to come; however, my thoughts quickly shifted back to the most vivid dream that had preceded my faceplanting onto the floor. While there were a great deal of images therein that puzzled me greatly, I knew exactly from where the whole ordeal with my brothers and the shepherds had come; and living it again in my dream had spawned a twisting in my stomach, the twinges of which rippled into my mind, there to jostle back into the mental mix, as settled sediment rattled from the bottom of a glass of water, long-buried wounds of old.

5

Reflections

MY father was firm in his belief that every great man should be a shepherd of sheep or camels; this he took from Muhammad's words in Sahih Bukhari, Book 55, Hadith 618: that every prophet was a shepherd in some way. He, therefore, ordered two of my elder brothers to take me, not yet four years old at the time, out into the desert near Mecca, to the place where his sheep and camels were kept. Along with several Sudanese shepherds, we all piled into a gleaming, black SUV and rode in a cloud of dust into an ocean of scorching sand: The Empty Quarter, Saudi's vast Rub' a Khali desert.

The vibrations rumbling through the car as we traversed the barren terrain could not contend with those dancing through my bones, as my wildly thumping heart slammed against my ribcage. I was extremely nervous for my first day of training as a shepherd, but all the more excited that my father had seen in me something that told him I was ready for a man's work. I knew whatever lay ahead would not be easy, but I was so eager for the chance; and with my brothers and the shepherds there by my side to guide and train me, I knew I would make my father proud.

After driving through much of the early morning, the car at last came to a halt. It was just about midday, and I scurried from the car as fast as I could, relieved to finally be free of the cramped quarters, and ready to get to work. Once I'd shaken the stiffness out of my legs and popped the cricks out of my back, I looked about for the sheep and camels. Only sand, rolling dunes, sand, waves of heat, sand, and more sand met my eyes.

Turning around, I saw my brothers and the shepherds slowly exiting the car.

"Where are father's camels?" I asked, feeling a bit disappointed and confused. "Where are my father's sheep?"

My brother gave a snort and smiled; towering over me, he tousled my air, turned me around, and together we began walking up a nearby dune.

"Come," he said palliatively, draping his arm over my shoulder. He seemed to sense my confusion and unease, for he added, "Don't worry about a thing—father is confident you'll do well. Just over this dune; you'll see."

With my other brother walking on my other side, I was led to the dune's peak. Before reaching it, however, I glanced back at the shepherds; they were all standing by the car watching us walk—they weren't even gathering the supplies we'd brought. And that's when it dawned on me: I could not recall loading any supplies!

No sooner had this thought leapt into my mind did my brother shout, "Here we are!" And before my eyes could fully register the sight of a camel- and sheep-less, empty desert below, a great burst of pain exploded through my back and the desert set off in a sprint toward my face and into my mouth. When at last I'd lifted my head and spewed the sand from my throat, I spun around and watched terrified as my brothers dashed down the dune, back toward the car, into which the shepherds were piling quickly.

The tidal wave of fear that fell over me in that moment rendered my world like the deck of a tiny boat on a turbulent ocean: my feet could not find the ground, and I staggered and stumbled, my head dizzy in a cyclone-like whirl, collapsing and getting no closer to the vanishing safety of my father's car. Head over heels I tumbled down the dune, screaming and gasping plumes of dust and sand all the way, until at last I reached the bottom; and through sand-filled eyes over tearstained cheeks, I watched a pair of taillights fade into the cloud rushing forth to envelop me and muffle my desperate, throat-shredding shrieks.

I was going to die.

Death had ever been an incomprehensible given, a reality I had been unable and too blissfully ignorant to grasp. This day, however, it grasped me, and did so like a mighty hand, squeezing me from all sides; and I knew Death intimately by its presence, its taste, and its noisome stench.

How stubborn was the sun that day, reluctant to forfeit its place in the sky to the waiting night, and offering no mercy whatsoever. The longer it refused to fall behind the horizon, the hotter it burned, as if aggravated by an impatient evening trailing behind it.

Equipped with nothing but my ankle-length garment, a head covering, and my sandals, I wandered aimlessly about the scorching Rub' a Khali, dumbstruck and traumatized. I had not developed a single survival instinct in my four years of living, and not one mental or bodily reaction helped me in the slightest. Screaming loudly served only to sear my throat and kill my voice, while my cries were quickly absorbed into the surrounding sand, swallowed up into the vast, droning silence. Crying and wetting myself only further depleted my stores of hydration and strengthened the mounding exhaustion. My bodily resources were rapidly diminishing, but food and water were the furthest things from my mind— not that I would have known how to find either. And, so, I stumbled about in utter shock, lost and confused, unable to grasp what was happening to me.

Eventually, after walking all through the blaze of the day, my thoroughly exhausted body collapsed, muscles quaking and seizing and cramping. There would be no rest this night, nor would I have allowed myself to sleep, even if my body wasn't screaming in pain; for who knew what wild beasts lay just over the next dune, waiting to devour a helpless child like me? With the sound-trapping nature of this ocean of sand, there would be no detecting an approaching threat until after its lethal strike; though, even if approaching footsteps or the scraping of a scaly belly slithering forth, hissing its telltale hiss, could have been perceived in this gigantic, soundless tomb, the symphony of madness flooding my ears and bellowing through my brain, was more than enough to drown even the noisiest metropolitan streets.

The darkness was like nothing I had ever experienced; it devoured my body, making me like a formless ghost. Just as I had been abandoned, so too had the earth: completely stripped of its light and warmth, as well as all its features, leaving a void of emptiness that taught me the chill of nothingness.

I moved as little as possible, afraid to wander into a bottomless pit, a pond of quicksand, or meet some other unfriendly visitor in the darkness. Often had I heard my brothers talk of killing vipers for sport; and the deeper the darkness became, the more my eyes perceived ripples in the blackness, until I found myself in a pit of vipers, completely surrounded by their dreadful chorus, their born fangs gleaming brightly and dripping venom like water from a leaky faucet. Sometimes I even caught the sensation of their boiling bane dribbling like acid on my ankles, or a long, salivating tongue sampling the sweat running the length of my cheek.

By the time the midnight moon was at its full height, I was at my wits' end, nearly permanently out of my mind. There were no more tears to cry, and nothing left in my bladder to further stain my garment. The icy atmosphere of the night had embedded itself deeply into my bones, and I lay curled up in a violently shivering ball, eyes protruding so far from my skull they were at risk of falling out.

And that's how they found me.

A set of mighty hands fell roughly upon my shoulders; the impact was like being hit blind- and broadsided by a semi truck racing along at a breakneck speed.

"Get up!" yelled a disgusted voice.

My head whipped around.

There stood my brother.

His face was filled with darkness and by darkness defined, framed by the gleam of headlights, which cast about him rays of brilliant light, making him like a dark angel. His hands held me up by the arms; behind him stood a pack of shadows painted against the headlights of the SUV—none other than the pack that had deserted me were they.

Heart-stopping relief flooded my body, while a fiery rage burned through my veins. Had I have had the strength and energy to do so, I might have kissed my rescuer, then spat in his face; I'd have hugged him with all my might, then beat his chest until my hands were reduced to bloody pulps.

"Look at you!" snarled my eldest brother, looming over me—his only offered mercy being that his fiery words had so heated his breath that it rained over my frozen face a cloud of soothing warmth. "Curled up like a baby, quaking like a *woman*—and you've wet your garment! *Pathetic!*"

Never in my life had the thought of talking back to my eldest brother crossed my mind; but, in this moment, I was short only a voice and the power to wield it to break that tradition.

I was lifted from the ground and dragged to the SUV, which took us to an encampment they'd established that afternoon shortly after abandoning me. There I was set firmly into a chair opposite my eldest brother, who demanded I look him in the eye, or be made to do so.

He glared at me.

"A true man doesn't cry!" he scolded with a finger in my face. "He doesn't pee his undergarment! A true man is NEVER scared of anything!"

Utterly petrified and so enraged that I thought my whole body might erupt in flame, I gazed back at my brother; and, in my mind, I replied, "If this is what it is to be a man, I want no part of it!"

"Father will be most disappointed when he hears how you've fared," he continued. "How hopeful he had been when

34

he'd instructed us to perform this test. His faith in you will be utterly shattered."

It was as if the exhaustion, rage, and madness that had swept over me suddenly passed; even the intense thirst and hunger I'd felt were banished.

My *father* had arranged this?

"Lamentable, to be sure. This night was supposed to be your first step toward becoming a fearless man! Instead, you are a weak and feeble woman! We have much yet to do with you."

Having spilled all his disgust, my brother left the tent, and I was presented with water and a few dates. One might think I'd have inhaled both the moment they were within reach, but I took my fill very slowly. The revelation that my father had organized the traumatizing ordeal was, perhaps, the most traumatizing element of it all, and the weight of that reality made me so heavy I could hardly move, much less chew and swallow.

I eventually succeeded in finishing the water and dates.

Immediately thereafter, I moved toward the bed, where I collapsed into a deep sleep.

***

The next several months would see me trained in the ways of a man by my brothers, deep in the Rub' a Khali. I learned how to hunt, make a fire, set up a tent, shepherd a flock, and was even taught how to drive. It would end up being a most valuable time, in which I did indeed grow as a man and gain a wealth of essential skills. But, even now, in the present, as I lay on my bed and reflected on the events that had trickled into my dream, I contemplated the cost of becoming a man worthy of being called my father's son. Fear and suffering had been my introduction into the path toward his heart, and the terrorists of 9/11 had showed me how favor is won and the title of "blessed hero" is obtained.

Though I still puzzled over some of the other imagery in my dream, it seemed, in light of all I had just called to mind, a rather simple reminder: that the road to favor and glory in the eyes of my father and in the hand of Allah would require a price.

That price, I was now, more than ever, willing to pay.

With a deep and soul-filling breath, I leapt from bed and set out to accomplish my task for the day: to run into the market on an errand for my mother. The house was still high on the joys of the day past, as were the streets ever so lively; the party, I thought, might never end. But, being that my father was home, and a tad worse for wear, it seemed, following the night prior, it was imperative that there be no hint that life was in any inconvenient or disruptive way out of the ordinary; so, I operated quietly and made sure to take at least twenty seconds to latch the door on my way out, before sprinting down the street.

Mecca was still buzzing with people scurrying to and fro, many of them cheerful, and many more wild; some of the shouts coming out of blind corners and alleyways hastened my feet into new directions. There were yet a great many foreigners about—whether they had merely lingered long after the most recent hajj, or had somehow lost their way home, I could not tell; not all pilgrims make it back to their homelands. Though I hadn't been there, at this year's hajj in Mina, just east of my city, a great many pilgrims were trampled to death in a stampede during the stoning of the Devil ritual. A symbolic reenactment of Abraham's hajj, during which he'd stoned three pillars representing temptation to disobey Allah, it has a reputation of getting out of control. A foreigner's ignorance always puts them at a disadvantage, regardless of how devoted to Islam they think they might be.

Rounding another corner, my speeding foot kicked what looked like a stick, though it was far more dense than something simply plucked from a tree, and it made a bizarre clanking sound as it tumbled about the alley.

I came to a swift halt and turned to take a quick look at the curious thing.

Long and wooden, my initial thought of it being a stick was very nearly on the mark; but it was expertly carved, seemingly by hands wielding perfection. My eyes searched about the dusty road for something with which to poke the strange object; I found a sturdy piece of garbage, and began to tease it this way and that.

The top and bottom were plated with a decorative metal, their faces bearing intricate, swirling designs, etched as very fine lines that formed what looked to me like a rush of billowing smoke. These plates had been screwed to a rectangular piece of wood, into which, on either long edge, had been cut a series of smaller, rectangular holes. And along one of the short edges of this wooden piece had been inked the words, "Made in China."

My mind could conjure no name for this curious object, nor had I anything with which to compare it. Throwing a careful glance in either direction, I tossed aside the piece of garbage and reached for the object.

"Don't touch it!" roared my father's voice.

My head zipped around.

I saw no one.

Then, turning back, I perceived before me a Russian pilgrim, extending forth a trinket of some sort, brought from his homeland.

It was a plump woman, her head covered and her body draped in colorful, floral attire. She wore a strange smile, but what was most intriguing was the fact that she bore within her two identical copies of herself—three in one was she; each piece was wholly its own, and yet they came together to make a single whole. I had never encountered anything quite like it.

"An idol!" growled my father, throwing a nasty look at the pilgrim before grabbing my hand and tugging me away.

The vision was so vivid and powerful that I fell backward there in the alley.

After a series of blinks and a thorough rubbing of the eyes, I looked and saw that both my father and the Russian were gone, had vanished back into to the past from which they'd come.

Once again, it was just this strange object and I.

And it didn't take long for curiosity to get the better of me.

Reasoning that something without a face could not be an idol, I took up the piece of metal-sandwiched wood and, rising to my feet, began to examine it. As I did so, those same feet unwittingly began to walk right into the middle of the street; and as I held the object before my face to peer through the holes, a great wind rushed through the streets and passed with great force through the thing in my hands.

As if from the parting clouds above, into my face was blasted a most beautiful, glorious sound like never I had heard in all my days.

But before I could savor the enrapturing joy and momentous experience of hearing wind produce the sound of a glorious sunrise, a sea of enraged hands grabbed me from all sides, one of which snatched the object from my grasp and smashed it on the ground.

"Stupid, disobedient boy!" one screamed.

"Purchaser of idle talks!" yelled another.

"Humiliating torment be yours in the hellfire!"

Petrified to my core and screeching at the top of my lungs, I was dragged away past thousands of disgusted, merciless faces to the mosque, where I was thrown to the floor and held down, while one man snatched my legs, holding them high in the air, and another ripped off my sandals.

I could see nothing through the tears flooding my eyes. I pleaded and begged and shouted my father's name, but there came no mercy—only a rain of hellfire upon the soles of my feet.

A roar of rage was answered with a mind-shredding shriek of tormented agony from my tiny lungs; shouts of approval filled the air, urging the rain to fall unceasingly upon the faithless child.

When at last his strength had been spent through beads of sweat bleeding from his brow, the man cast aside the rod and hurled my legs to the ground, leaving me in a cold puddle of tears, while every muscle in my body quaked uncontrollably.

The *falaka* (foot-whipping) had been severe, the kind a grown man and heinous criminal might expect to receive. My eyes could but gape at the long, wooden rod used to torture my feet, lying helplessly, harmlessly on the floor in the distance, painted with the blood of my small, terribly cold feet.

Music, as I had been taught, was forbidden, as such was a means by which sinful, disobedient wretches like myself would lead people astray from Allah. I was so ashamed, so fearful of my sin, that, though still burning in agonizing pain, I rolled onto my face and begged Allah not to destroy me. I cursed music and my folly, and vowed to never again touch what I had quickly come to realize was a musical instrument, nor allow these ears to hear even one note of music ever again. And in my fear and rage, as I crawled through the dusty street, I spat on the accursed object that had exploited my curiosity; and for decades thereafter I knew that thing only by the vilest of names my child's mind could conceive—the rest of the world, as I have recently come to learn, knows it by the name harmonica.

I crawled most of the way home, walking only the last leg of the journey, as the swelling in my feet had by then subsided just enough to do so.

My mother ferociously stained her opened hand with the tears running over my weeping face when I returned empty-handed. For the life of me, I couldn't even remember what my errand had been.

"Let this be a lesson," snarled my father, after I explained the cause of my condition and reason for being late coming home. "Allah grants nothing but punishment for those who would disobey him."

After a thorough beating of my palms, I was sent to remain the rest of the day in my room without a meal. I hadn't eaten since that morning, but I was so paralyzed by the pain gripping my entire body, not to mention the terror in my heart, that neither hunger nor thirst had any sting whatsoever.

***

No part of me had any desire to venture back into the city; just thinking of the shame of showing my face after such a great disobedience was unbearable. A week passed, and my luck held out still—that is, until it died in a most thorough fashion two days later.

After my morning prayers, I began preparing for my usual Friday routine; but before I could get started, my father burst into my room.

"Ahmed!" he bellowed; that large, commanding voice of his filled the room. "Come," he said, swiping at the air with his hand. "You will accompany me into town today."

Per my decade of conditioning, I hopped right into action and hustled out to his giant, black SUV, glistening in the hot morning sun, while a cold dread covered me with goosebumps. I had always enjoyed accompanying my father on whatever business of his needed attention in town; it was an honor to be called specifically to join him. But bringing shame or embarrassment on my house was a serious offense, and I wondered if perhaps the ripples of my wrongdoing had yet a few more rings that were soon to break upon me.

Parking his car at the mosque, my father took me by the hand and led me to the town square. There was quite a commotion. I couldn't tell if the shouts I was hearing from the mass of bodies up ahead were celebratory or enraged or frightened; strangest of all was the way the sun reflected upon the dust of the street, casting streaks of crimson amid the familiar bright amber.

As we approached, many in the crowd beheld my father, and the sea of people began to part. I was so amazed by the power of his presence that it wasn't until he'd come to a halt and very calmly stated, "Proceed," that I looked up from my fascination with the parting crowd and realized where I was.

Before me knelt a young man, maybe ten years older than I; his face was drenched in sweat and stained with dirt, and it was wide-eyed and contorted in a most unnatural fashion. A pair of officers each held one of his arms, pulling them wide, while another viciously lashed his exposed back with a leather whip.

"Blasphemer," muttered my father coolly, as if he were telling me the man's name. "One hundred lashes."

He must have received ten times his sentence; the sound of cruel cracking against raw, mangled flesh, punctuated by his desperate cries, seemed to go on for hours and hours, piercing my skull with its madness.

Several more like him there were, male and female, of all ages. I dared not let my father see me look away from any of it, nor betray upon my face any of my heart's alarm.

"Allah is not without mercy, son," said my father somewhere amid the series of lashings; his calm voice hit me as if he'd bent down and screamed into my ear. "These," he continued, motioning to a new group of chained individuals, "will bear a more pressing reminder of their sins and Allah's undeserved mercy."

A screaming man was brought forth and forcibly restrained, while another man grabbed the prisoner's hand and extended it over a wooden stump.

"The hand of a thief," my father growled, "is a worthless abomination."

And no sooner had the words breached his lips was the right hand of the condemned sliced from his wrist.

I can still hear his traumatized screams.

The men who had held him in place continued to do so; beads of sweat poured down their faces, for the dismembered man had become like an animal possessed and deranged.

One man in particular kept screaming, "Still! Keep him still!" He was the one designated to hold firmly the now stumped arm, while a doctor from a nearby hospital, as casually as any other day on the job, quickly tended to the wound. Another mercy of Allah's, performed also to the footless ankles of a handful of others.

"See how mercy is exercised this day, son," my father whispered, placing his lips against my ear. "But the one true god will not hinder his instruments of justice for long."

About that time, another group of condemned individuals were marched forth; these were lined up against a nearby wall, one at a time. Among them, as my father would inform me, were those convicted of treason, atheism, murder, and adultery, the latter offense exclusive to the women of the group. I could not distinguish which sinner had committed which sin; all I could see was a collection of wretched, beaten, weary, and frightened individuals, all with cries for mercy or vile curses on their tongues, eyes weeping desperate pleadings or shooting stony defiance, as they stared down the roaring crowd that began to encircle them in a half-moon arrangement. The tumultuous chaos was so loud and the otherworldly rush of the situation so overwhelming that my body went numb and the earth fell silent.

Just then, as my gaze moved through a world caught in slow motion toward a condemned face bleeding with rage, my reality was snapped back into the wild, as a large stone impacted the person's forehead, splitting it wide, and causing the head to whiplash violently. My last memory of that person is the circle of blood their head left on the stone wall behind them.

Mighty hands grabbed my shoulders, and I was pulled against my father's thighs, as the crowd, overflowing with feral mania, rushed forth, hurling stones with all their might until all who had been lined up to die had fallen. It was then that I realized my senses had been deceived, for so great was this rattling of my world, so jarring, unprecedented, and unnatural, that my heart, it seemed, had begun to project its internal reaction onto my external reality—my very soul seemed to be painting over my world that which lay buried beneath the physical presentation set before me; for where I had perceived great roars from the crowd, there had actually been only grave silence; where I had seen mania, insanity, and madness painted on the faces of those bearing stones, there were but casual expressions, coldness, and indifference, very much like those seen on faces in supermarkets when inspecting produce; and where I had felt the tremors of burning rage and hatred issuing from the horde, I now sensed clearly a sentiment of good riddance and stiff-necked pride. Those who were to face Allah's just wrath begged for mercy or cursed their accusers in ways devoid of dignity, in ways those on the opposite end of the stone would call inhumane, animalistic. But, in this moment, it was the pack of cold-blooded, merciless dealers of divine justice, clutching in their hands a stark representation of that which sat encased in ice beneath their chest, who appeared to me as something other than human, something foreign, something animal. Yet, I would have wished for no other place in which to make my stand than right there in the jaws of justice, clamping down upon the reviled of Allah.

As the mangled bodies were dragged away—some lifeless, others convulsing—I looked down at my feet and beheld a stone. It was smaller than the others I had seen hurled, and must have been kicked by a falling body, or had ricocheted after completing its work. There was no thinking in this moment; I stooped down and picked it up. And after turning it about idly through my fingers, I noticed what I had neglected to see: one face of the stone had been painted red, as were now my tiny hands.

My eyes turned up to my father.

He was gazing down at me, smiling.

As the next round of stoning commenced, I turned my attention again to my bloodied palms and the stone therein.

How like our heroes, thought I, to be washed in the blood of Allah's justice!

A wave of tremendous excitement began to stir within my soul, and my fist clenched about the stone; I felt as though I could crush it to dust. With my father's large hand proudly massaging my shoulders, and the perceived presence of Allah racing about with the whirling wind, I grit my teeth and lifted my fiery eyes.

The stoning had ended.

I felt as one who had slept through a great gathering of joyous revelry.

But the day was far from over, for another man was brought forth.

Appearing as though he had been lashed by a thousand officers for one thousand days, hobbling, as if walking on two stumped legs, and swinging his twisted torso, as if he'd just survived a brutal bombardment of stones, this man had all the symptoms of condemnation; yet, his weeping eyes gazed at the officers and the crowd with what I could not help but recognize as pity—but, surely, I thought, this could not be. His gaze reflected the light of the sun; it was not consumed with flame; his lips, defiant of a broken jaw, did sing a joyful song I did not know. His every note seemed to touch the once stoic crowd as the live end of an electrical cord, sending the people quickly into a wrathful rage; and though his words were drowned, the tune and its spirit could not be hindered. Not a single curse or plea breached his lips by the time he was made to kneel; and there in the dirt, he raised his eyes to the sky and whispered softly as his eyes sealed. He looked ever so peaceful.

The mighty hands that had been on my shoulders shoved me aside, and I watched my father march angrily toward the officers, shouting violently. I could not hear a word; I was lost in great puzzlement, looking at the strange, broken man, as he, kneeling with head erect again, continued to mumble toward the sky.

After much saliva-laced berating, my father returned to my side, where he stood silently, watching the broken man intently; his breathing was hurried and heavy, and it produced the sound of a hungry lion.

The crowd became restless in this time; some broke out and began beating on the man, screaming at him with seething hatred dripping from their teeth. Then, from a corner of the crowd there came a jubilant cheer, and bodies parted as large iron pipes were brought forth through the hurricane of hatred.

"Hang him like the dog he serves!" screamed someone from the crowd, as the broken man was dragged toward the pipes, while men bearing great lengths of wire approached from either side.

My heart pounded harder and faster with every second, wondering what was about to happen and still unaware of what heinous crime this sinner must have committed to deserve such a severe punishment.

I watched his body glide along the dirt.

"See how he smiles, father!" I cried—I could hardly believe such an expression could be found on anyone so condemned.

But I received no answer.

The man's broken body was forced into a seated position; and as his shredded robes were stripped, his arms pulled outward, and his legs extended to full length, while the cords were bound tightly about his wrists and ankles, peeling away the tender flesh thereon, I saw his shining eyes seal; and as a final tear fell along his dirty face, I knew his soul had already departed.

That night, through my bedroom window, I looked at a bright light in the distance. Held atop the highest point of a gigantic crane, the star-like glow illuminated a silent corpse, swaying in the midnight breeze, bound by wire to an iron contraption. I was many miles away, and yet I could see him; I could see his smiling face, as well as the Arabic writing hung about his neck: the letter N, an infamous symbol indicating a "Follower of Jesus of Nazareth."

A Christian.

He'd gotten what he'd deserved, I thought, and was now rightfully getting all the more beneath the wrath of Allah.

With that consoling thought, I turned toward my bed; but not before taking one last gaze out my window, there to look upon the condemned, swaying for all to see in the midnight air, perfectly framed in the reflection of my face, there in the window.

6
In the Footsteps of the Prophet

THE very air I breathed in the days of my youth was Islam. Even before I could walk there on my own, I was a dedicated attendee of the mosque. From age two, I prayed more than five times a day, adding extra prayers before and after every required prayer, just to be assured that Allah might be convinced that I was his pious servant. I fasted from food and water two days every week, and each year performed the Umrah pilgrimage to Mecca; I had completed the more detailed and holy Hajj pilgrimage to Mecca five times. I even bore intense loyalty to my denomination of Islam, Sunni, harboring an increasing and intense hostility toward those of the Shiite denomination—a tradition perpetuated for hundreds of years by both sides, rooted in the division of the Islamic people over the issue of the proper successor to Muhammad, following his death. But above all these, there was no greater demonstration of my allegiance and steadfast devotion to Islam than my having memorized the entire Qur'an with the ability to recite it perfectly in Arabic, sans even the tiniest mistake or mispronunciation, all by age 13.

Never in all my life had I beheld such pride in my father's face, as it related to me; for I had won for him a crown of glory, per Al-Haakim, Book 1, Hadith 756. How excited he was at my accomplishment, and all the more so to one day have that crown of glory set upon his head in heaven, that all might know that he is the father of one who has memorized the holy text.

An occasion like this could not go uncelebrated; so, my father threw a most extravagant ceremony, at which I was presented with a coveted certificate, one of high honor and confirmation, as well as national recognition, naming me as one in a long line of Muslims who have memorized the Qur'an: a line dating all the way back to Muhammad himself.

At the ceremony, my proudest of proud fathers allowed me to lead the entire worship service at the mosque. My whole family was in attendance, and I saw in their eyes as I spoke that day—petrified though I was, and doing everything in my power to maintain clear and concise speech and not pass out—something like the water that fills an empty cup. This was my family; their honor and respect were being showered upon me; and I knew there was but one way to have this water fill and overflow from within my cup for all eternity. On the flipside, there was, too, a way for me to ensure that the cup remained forever desert-dry; but such was so ridiculous a notion, it actually never once crossed my mind.

Indeed, it was a glorious day, but it had not come easily. Cramming into my teenage brain 114 chapters (or, *Surahs*, as we call them), over 6,000 verses, and well over 77,000 words takes more than just effort, more than just a daily, hourly obsession with the words; more than just ceaseless meditation, occupying every waking moment—it takes fear, as well.

With only seven verses in the first Surah, my classmates and I breezed through our reciting without a problem.

Chapter two was a different story.

Staring down the barrel of 286 verses, one of us children was bound to slip up somewhere along the way. I would not be the first to do so; nevertheless, I was a fast study in the lesson that quickly followed a classmate's misquoting of Qur'an 2:10.

"In their hearts is disease," he chanted, "so Allah has increased their disease; and for them is a painful punishment because they lie."

He should have said, "*used* to lie;" and so did he learn, when our teacher ripped him from among us and pulled him before everyone gathered at the mosque, where he was made to remove his sandals and lie on his back in a most humiliating manner: with his legs set against a chair and his bare soles facing the sky. Stepping forth, our teacher gave us a nonverbal lesson in *falaka*, when he began to savagely beat the child's bare soles with an electric wire; the soles of my feet ached at the memory of my own encounters with such torment. The terrified, agonized screams that filled the air made the words of Qur'an 2 very clear in our minds; and no matter how loud or painful the boy's shrieks became throughout his torture, there was no sympathy for one who would misquote the Qur'an—none.

For the rest of us, it was but a matter of time. I was once asked to recite Qur'an 8 before the entire congregation in the mosque, with all my neighbors present.

Up until verse 60, I had been flawless, despite quaking knees and a surprisingly well-masked weak and terrified voice.

"And prepare against them whatever you are able of power and of steeds of war by which you may terrify the enemy of Allah," I said with 59 verses down and only 16 to go, "and your enemy and others besides them whom you do not know, but whom Allah knows. And whatever you spend in the cause of Allah will be fully repaid to you, and....and you...wi— you will—"

My face went white.

The words disappeared.

My head went blank.

I couldn't conjure a single word to complete the verse!

Struck mute, my trembling lips began to babble incoherent sounds; then, from the corner of my eye, I could see a tall figure in white float into view.

Stepping forth with a scowl on his face and a rubber hose clenched in his fist, my teacher ordered me to lie on my backside and put my feet up into the air.

My eyes darted about the congregation, but not one friendly face could be found.

"DOWN!" screamed my teacher when I'd failed to respond to his first command.

I couldn't believe this was happening, not again, here, in front of all my neighbors.

Once more my teacher screamed, igniting in me a flash of fury, which saw a scream of my own bellow forth through my throat and my tiny body shove him aside and sprint into the street. This, at least, was the fantasy replaying in flashes of lighting through my head, as I, obedient to my teacher's command, lay crying in agony as vicious hellfire rained down upon my naked soles.

When at last the torture had ceased, I rose to my thoroughly bruised and bleeding feet, feeling as though I were standing impaled on white-hot spears, and, through silent tears and trembling knees, I finished reciting.

I was so humiliated; I couldn't even look my neighbors in the eye. And when it was all done, I collapsed to my knees and, like an animal, crawled back home, while my feet swelled and all passersby cast looks of disgust upon me, refusing even to help me walk. They hadn't exactly been Samaritans when I'd picked up a harmonica, and misquoting the Qur'an is an offense far more shameful.

In all, my feet would know roughly twenty thorough beatings before my brain knew thoroughly the Qur'an.

But there remained yet the final test.

Now, aged thirteen, wearing a beard to match the one worn by Muhammad and toting a head lined from end to end with the sacred words Allah as given to his final prophet through the angel Gabriel, it was time for my dedicated cramming and devoted memorization to become officially certified. Three, terribly long days lay before me, in which I would be reciting the Qur'an from sunup to sundown, stopping only to use the bathroom and grab the minimum handful of hours for sleep. But such was required; and, being the devout and increasingly adamant Muslim that I was, I took a deep breath and began with verse one: "In the name of Allah, the Entirely Merciful, the Especially Merciful."

Hours passed.

"Indeed, the penalty for those who wage war against Allah and his Messenger and strive upon earth to cause corruption is none but that they be killed or crucified or that their hands and feet be cut off from opposite sides or that they be exiled from the land."

The sun was reaching its peak, and my stomach began to grumble.

"Fight those who do not believe in Allah or in the Last Day and who do not consider unlawful what Allah and his Messenger have made unlawful and who do not adopt the religion of truth from those who were given the Scripture."

But there would be no relief.

"It is he who has sent his Messenger with guidance and the religion of truth to manifest it over all religion, although they who associate others with Allah dislike it."

For my teacher believed that filling my stomach would make me lazy.

"They say, 'You, O Muhammad, are but an inventor of lies.' But most of them do not know. Say, O Muhammad, 'The Holy Spirit has brought it down from your Lord in truth to make firm those who believe and as guidance and good tidings to the Muslims.'"

He said I would need to be treated like an Arabian horse: fed little, lest I become fat and lack speed enough to win the race.

But, thankfully, a break did come. I was permitted to use the bathroom, fed a small handful of dates, and given a sip of water.

Then, it was back to business.

The rush of dizziness that swirled about my head when at last the three days had come to a successful conclusion was not unlike the feeling that came over me when my father gazed proudly down upon the son who had won him an eternal crown of glory, and invited this honored offspring to borrow his place as the worship leader in the Mosque. And that feeling kept right on giving, and was compounded when, fresh off my great achievement and overflowing with the words of the Qur'an, I proudly stepped off the bus and into jihadist training camp.

7
A Man of Islam

EVEN with my overabundant ardency for the faith—praying more than five times a day, fasting, annually performing Umrah and making several Hajj pilgrimages to my hometown, not to mention all I have just related about winning for my father and mother a crown of glory, Allah and his prophet offered me no assurance that I would dwell forever with them in paradise. There was but one way to secure a guarantee: jihad.

If my father had been ecstatic about my memorizing the Qur'an, how much more over the moon would he be if I were to attain the highest of all honors in dying while killing infidels? He adamantly encouraged me to pursue jihad, saying, "There is no better time to learn how to wage holy war for Allah than *right now*," referring to my recent certification.

I didn't need much convincing: to die amid the slaughter of infidels had been my wholehearted desire since childhood! It was a very superhero-like dream for a Muslim youth. Odd though it may seem, it had never occurred to me to wonder why my father, or a great many other passionate men of Islam, had been ever so encouraging toward me and my peers to acquire this great honor and guarantee of salvation, yet were themselves still alive. Regardless, I was determined to see my father exalted, to purge myself of the many sins I feared I could never crawl out from under, and to buy for myself a room in the halls of Allah—being also that I was now a teenager, getting a horde of *houris* to boot sounded better than ever it had.

In line with a number of my peers, I stepped proudly off the bus and into a realm of soon-to-be-heroes for Allah. Several had come to this jihad training camp from my city, but I met a great many people from around the world; and on the grounds of our common desire to spill blood for our god, we bonded. I came to feel for these dedicated souls a deep sense of kinship; they were, to me, and in no great span of time, the best of friends. And what better kind of friend to have, I thought? Here, I have not only those with whom I share a faith and calling, I have also true, forever friends—these bonds would be eternal, our deaths ensuring it. And, so, we lived passionately in every moment, our zeal for Allah growing by the second; waking and sleeping, eating and breathing, we let surge through us this great commission to purge the world of lies and disbelief and dishonor to the highest of the high. Every day was our last, and tomorrow we would bask in the splendor and pleasure of our eternal reward, together.

I could hardly sit still through orientation. A man of many years spoke to us of the path to guaranteed favor and the unmatchable glories to come.

"Jihad is the highest honor a Muslim can achieve!" he declared. "Great is the reward of Allah's successful soldier— riches untold, honor and fame, pleasure beyond comprehension!"

My ribs received a nudge from one of my new European friends; a wink followed.

But I paid this little attention, for with his next breath the man before us said, "And your every sin erased: perfect favor with Allah!"

I did not understand it then, but, as he spoke, the image of my father flashed before my eyes.

Though I knew this truth—that all my toil and praying and petitions to cancel all my misdeeds, even those of which I had no knowledge, would be wiped away and I made blameless in the eyes of Allah, if I successfully carried out the killing of a wicked infidel—hearing of this reward acted as a steroid for my determination. Oh, that I could gather all the infidels of the world into one place and spill their bowels with my righteous demise! Dedicated though I had ever been to Islam, even beneath the shadow of a Mufti and in the very footsteps of Muhammad, even with Mecca on my doorstep, deep down I feared some buried, unknown wickedness of mine—worse still, something even my father might not have known to be a sin—might in my last day be brought to light, and so disqualify me from entering through the gates of heaven, and send me tumbling into the eternal void of torment.

With this guarantee set before me, I sunk my teeth into every facet of my training, readying myself to be the greatest bringer of death my god had ever known.

**

"Boy!" said one of my foreigner friends with a deep yawn, as he shuffled into our training room the next morning. "Here already? How long have you been up?"

"Since my morning prayers. You went back to sleep?"

"Never got up," he chuckled.

"You missed your morning prayers?"

A soon-to-be soldier of Allah missing the first prayer on his first day of training?

I was dumbfounded.

Heaving a dismissive shrug, he yawned again and said in his rather lazy, broken Arabic, "Eh, just one more sin to be wiped away by the blood of the infidel, right?"

Before I could form a response, the classroom's idle chatter evaporated, and to the front of the room stepped our instructor.

"*Sabahu Al-khair*," he said.

"*Sabahu An-Nur*," we replied—an Arabic exchange of good-morning salutations.

"Jihad is not a suggestion," he began. "For every follower of Allah, it is a strict command. Sharia demands that we must be *active* in our pursuit to destroy the unbelievers—at the very least to pray for such destruction. We!" he shouted, pounding the podium by which he stood. "We are those active pursuers, foot soldiers for Allah; we leave the praying for the women," he added with a derisive chuckle that trickled through us all.

He went on to briefly introduce an instructional video we were to watch, then wheeled before us a projector and cast the film onto the wall behind him. Much of the video was devoted to an inordinate amount of Islamic propaganda; it was silly, most of it, but we ate it up with great, gluttonous mouthfuls. This must be like those superhero movies from America, I thought as I marveled at the jihadist heroes racing triumphantly across the wall. And here I am: a real superhero.

From there, the video turned to basic field tactics—nothing too exciting, at first; not until we got to the part about executions did my attention become laser-focused.

Though I had seen many Friday executions in the town square, this was my first time witnessing a beheading with something other than a long sword. In those cases, as once I'd witnessed, the bound victim is made to kneel, their blindfolded head tilted forward to expose the neck. All those observing are silent, like people watching ducks swim aimlessly about a tranquil pond. Then, after a quick reading of the crime, the executioner raises high his blade and swings downward in a single, swift motion. The hot razor passes through the flesh and bone as through air, seemingly without resistance, while the head drops suddenly with a chilling *THUD* into the sand, and a burst of crimson erupts from the neck. The body falls away like the slack of a taught string when cut, and the person he had been is thereafter dragged out of memory.

It's a quick, quiet, and extremely easy process.

The knife method, as I observed, is not.

If there was one thing I could not do, it was betray upon my face the feeling in my heart. If my eyes watered, I opened them wider; raising a hand to them, even to scratch a legitimate itch, would send a terrible message. There was no touching of the face at all, in fact; and though my entire body was engulfed in the scene playing before me, my mind was working double time to both process the video and steady my breathing. My teeth acted as the last line of defense against the contents of my stomach; if they failed, I was determined my mouth would not leak a single drop.

Shot on what gave the impression of a cheap, home video camcorder, a man in black read his poorly crafted but ominous words over the kneeling body of a man dressed in orange. When he had finished speaking, the man in black, of whose person I could see nothing but a set of lidless eyes, unsheathed a large knife from his hip, while the cameraman stepped forward.

Brandishing high the knife, the man in black took hold of his prisoner's hair with his free hand and violently yanked the head backward; by this point, the camera loomed over the condemned man, holding in focus only the area between his head and his waistline. And then, as my mouth ran dry and my throat tightened, the blade fell across his neck, on the protrusion of his throat, where it began to glide back and forth in a frantic sawing motion.

The moment the cold steel toughed his tender skin, the man flinched and whimpered through his mouth gag; then, with the first cut and burst of blood, his entire body convulsed and thrashed; everything within him was screaming to run, desperately grasping at delusional, phantom hopes that he could escape his fate.

Barely through the first layer of flesh, the victim let out a gut-twisting, muffled wail through his covered mouth and nostrils; the sound wrapped itself around my insides like a string of barbed wire. That cry lasted but a moment before his throat was exposed; and through that opening came a raw sound: it was the cry of a human stripped of all humanity, for it passed no longer through vocal cords: the unique mark of the man soon to be no more; rather, it blared a single blare into the empty desert, before the bubbling contents of severed arteries filled the opening, creating grotesque gurgling, choking sounds as blood flooded his throat.

Crimson mists burst forth as the knife sawed further and further. These mists, like sprays from a bottle of window cleaner, hastened in frequency with every cut, mirroring the tremors rippling through the victim's body, until they, along with those tremors, began to subside; those tremors slowed into fewer, more violent spasms, coming at greater intervals.

By this time, three quarters of the head had been removed. The victim's body suddenly fell limp, robbing the knife of the last quarter of its work, for the remaining lifeless flesh ripped away with a sound like fingernails scraping along carpet, leaving the blood-soaked executioner standing proudly, clutching by the hair his grisly prize.

My mind was far from blank, but of the jumbled mess that whirled about it like the contents of a blender, there was one crystal-clear element that rose amid the noise, lifting from within the part of the mind wherein lie those basic functions, such as walking and breathing; and this was presented to me as an engraving, carved before my eyes into the wall set before me: "Slay the idolaters wherever you find them, and take them, and confine them, and lie in wait for them at every place of ambush" (Qur'an 9:5).

***

Whereas punctuality had been the presumed key for getting through this training with all favor and understanding, it became apparent to me that perseverance and adaptation were needed first and foremost. The more beheadings I watched, the easier it became—more effective than conditioning through repetition, however, was a tactic offered by my instructor.

"What do you see here?" he asked one day, sticking his finger angrily against the beheaded face projected against the wall. "What do you see? Now, ask yourself this: through whose eyes are you seeing? Your own? Don't let it be so! Such is a foolish way to view the world, for in so doing you are liable to be deceived! And if you *are* deceived—if you see with your own eyes and see the infidel as a human, like yourself—your only mercy would be to have never been born! No!" he screamed, slamming his palm against the wall, slapping the disembodied head, "See this creature as Allah sees it! A *dog*! A filthy *swine*! Less than the lowest creature is the infidel, for he spits in the face of god! Never forget the words of Allah in Qur'an 24:2: 'Let not compassion move you!'"

These words became my daily recitation. Eventually, I could not only watch a knife beheading, I could also and intimately feel the very sawing blade projected on the screen, as if it were in my hand. My fingers ached to clutch such a knife and feel the life of the infidel tumbling over my palms, as I banished it from its body and cast it into the pits of hell.

"The only reward for those who make war upon Allah and his messenger, and strive after corruption in the land," my instructor would often recite in closing from Qur'an 5:33, "will be that they will be killed or crucified, or have their hands and feet on alternate sides cut off, or will be expelled out of the land! Such will be their degradation in the world, and in the hereafter theirs will be an awful doom!"

In response, we would chant loudly the final line from Qur'an 47:4: "And those who are killed in the cause of Allah— never will he waste their deeds!"

The remainder of my initiation was rounded out with hand-to-hand combat and firearms training, bomb making, and daily reciting of the Qur'an with my friends, with whom I also started memorizing portions of the Hadith, until we had finally become this world's most ruthless weapons of destruction. We knew neither pain nor mercy; we could not be bought nor bargained; and with our eyes set upon the prize of death, we stormed out of that camp with hearts ablaze for jihad and souls committed to the glorious grave.

**

Upon my return, I took an extended walk through the streets to absorb the sights and smells of home. Though I was eager to show off to my father the new man I had become and see a look of pride swell in his eyes, I just had to take in the atmosphere and be washed with the holiness that was the home I had missed more than I had realized.

"There has never been a more glorious day!" I exclaimed to myself; and, unable to contain it, I stopped abruptly, sealed my eyes, threw my hands to heaven, and let fly a long and powerful, "*ALLAHU AKBAR!*"

No sooner had these words breached my lips did a drop of rain fall upon my cheek.

I smiled broadly as the drop ran sluggishly along my face.

Allah is good, I thought, beaming brightly; his sun and his rain are proof of his many mercies!

Just then, a man touched me on the shoulder.

I was so startled that I missed his hasty words, gathering only that he wanted me to take the rag he was offering me. Having done so, he began frantically pointing to my cheek whereupon the rain had fallen, and then shot his finger to the sky.

Throwing him a curious look, I dabbed the rag to my cheek and simultaneously looked up. There, high above the buildings and directly over me, hung three thoroughly bloodied men, crucified and suspended from a giant crane.

It was Friday.

Lowering the rag from my cheek, I beheld upon it a streak of crimson.

The man ushered me away from the spot, and I returned his rag with thanks.

Scraping the bloody sand from my sandals, I assured myself that I was not shaken—startled, is all; surprised by the suddenness of the moment.

Indeed, just surprised.

But as I paused to draw a calming deep breath, I heard a woman's cry coming from the main square just around the corner. By the sound of it, she was either in the jaws of a wild beast or the clutches of a madman with libidinous intentions.

Without a second thought, I hastened to the square; and there I beheld a woman, her body writhing in the dirt, while three men struggled to grab a solid hold of her.

All at once I stopped.

My feet walked no further.

And into the gathering crowd encircling the scene I stepped.

Her screams scraped violently against her throat; they were coarse and sharp, as if the air with which they were lifted was coated in splintered metal. Covered head to toe in her black burka and niqab, she was like a cloud of smoke racing about the ground.

Eventually, the executioner found her arms; the woman's screech cut through the square and shook the dust at my feet.

"*Rahmah!*" she screamed. "*Rahmah! RAHMAH!*"

Every time she yelled, her plea for mercy became longer, more desperate. She knew no sadness; only the unbounded terror of facing unprepared a god of judgment could be heard in her tears.

Her hands bound, another man fashioned a noose and wrapped it around her head, while another held her body in place. Though her airway was now partially obstructed, her feral screams projected all the more. And when the noose had been pulled tight and the length of its rope extended, forcing her neck into place, the executioner raised and quickly threw down his blade.

Whether he'd missed his mark or her burka had prevented a clean cut, I cannot say; regardless, out of this woman came a roar of unparalleled agony, one that reached a peak of eternal revelation that the living know not. It was a ghostly scream, very much and very literally like one who suffers with undivided, living consciousness the full extent of the deathblow delivered against their life.

Frantically, the executioner, who I had ever seen swing his sword with balletic elegance and robotic precision, began to frantically hack at the woman; she wailed all the while, until the man pulling tight the noose fell backward onto his bottom.

The head had finally broken free.

Judging by the reaction from the crowd and the misty evaporation of their departure, it had not been much of a rousing show.

Everyone simply went about his or her business.

For those who'd missed it, a full recap, along with footage of the execution, would be played on the evening news, along with that of three condemned individuals being cast off a high building for the crime of homosexuality.

My walk commenced, carrying me into the last leg of my journey home. As I went, passing through the quiet, residential streets, I happened by a police officer engaged in what looked like casual conversation with the man of the house before which they stood. There was very little commotion, and, any other day, one might have dismissed this as a simple chat between friends. However, both stood in a pool of blood that trickled like a lazy river from the head of a young man at their feet. I then noticed the gun in the homeowner's hand, as well as a small, leather-bound book, torn in half beside the dead youth, its pages stained red.

The officer shook the hand of the homeowner, who then retired into the house, while the officer made a phone call.

Another father judging apostasy, I figured.

Good riddance.

Rounding a few more corners, familiar territory met my eyes, all set beneath a blood-red sunset.

I was home.

8

Dream

MY life on this earth would be saved by a great contradiction, when, upon finishing high school, there was born in me a desire that began to quickly and persistently push my ardency for jihad onto a proverbial bucket list. Some might say I had been bitten by the bug of scholarship, that my recent academic achievements had instilled in me a desire to scale the heights of mental expansion and scour the depths of understanding. Indeed, education had increasingly become a passion of mine; my thirst for knowledge, my need to grasp the mysteries of this world, was indeed great. But I know of no bug born of any earthly persuasion that could turn around a young man so filled with devotion to his god and zeal for his mission in jihad, and make him pursue the exact opposite of destruction: healing.

No. It was certainly no bug.

The field of medicine had captured my fascination and had so dominated my thinking that all the promises offered through jihad that I had stored up in my heart—all the glory and honor waiting at the other end of a detonator—were, if you can believe it, effectively shoved aside and into a dark corner. Yes, my eagerness for jihad was still there...but I really wanted to try my hand at medicine first. And this, I reasoned, seemed not unprecedented! For I'd had jihadist instructors, had I not? Meccan scholars preached the fame and prestige of so honorable a sacrifice, did they not? Of course! Well, I said to myself, if *they* weren't exactly rushing off to die, there must be at least *some* value in living—theirs, it seemed, was to pass onto others their knowledge and training in the art of righteous death; mine, I decided, was to practice medicine and preserve life. A great contradiction, indeed.

This, as I had anticipated, turned out to be a rather difficult discussion when I brought it to my father.

"*WHAT*?" he cried upon hearing that I was planning to enroll in medical school. "And waste your life? What honor is there in such a path?"

"Father," I replied, doing my best to brew a tone of both respect and resolve, "I do not wish to upset you with this decision. But—"

"And yet you have!" he barked. "Have my words meant nothing to you? Do you count my instruction as refuse to be trampled underfoot?"

"Of course not, father!"

"Then, why this foolish talk of medicine? To serve Allah— *this* should be your wholehearted pursuit! Do I not wish for you a good thing?"

I restrained my reply to let a brief but nonetheless tense pause pass between us.

"Father," I said, wetting my lips, "since my youth, you have been my example, my standard by which to measure my devotion to Allah and Islam. I want only to bring you honor."

"Then devote yourself to the study of the Qur'an!" he shouted. "Not those medical texts, which are written by men and altered year after year! What knowledge can you gain from something so fickle and fluid? Of what quality is an understanding that changes with the wind? The Qur'an *doesn't* change, Ahmed! You can have no greater education than the one it provides!"

"You wish me to be a scholar?" I asked, anticipating the conversation three steps ahead. "You would rather I follow in your footsteps, to be a judge?"

"Yes," he huffed, "and to have you dedicate your life to the study and application of the Qur'an for everyday life!"

"But father," I replied, adding a touch of innocence to my voice, "was not al-Razi both scholar and physician?"

My father eyed me crossly.

I persisted.

"Was not al-Tabari the same? Even Zakir Naik! Father, this you already know, but have not some of the most respected Islamic scholars often first pursued the study of medicine?"

This would be not the last conversation he and I would share on the matter, nor was it the last of those one might call "heated." In the end, however, my father, albeit reluctantly, relented and even blessed my chosen path; though, he made it decidedly clear (in more ways than just verbally) that he was most unhappy.

***

I did my best in the days leading up to my departure to assure him that my medical studies would be always second to my study of the Qur'an and devotion to Allah. There would be no laxity in my duties—this I emphatically reiterated.

My following in the footsteps of other Islamic scholars hadn't exactly been the tipping point for him. Rather, he was most persuaded by my attending a specialized medical college that carried an Islamic emphasis. Basically, my education would not only prepare me for a career in medicine, it would also lay the foundation for my thereafter becoming an expert in Islamic law.

"You will see when I return," I said to my father before parting, "the same man of Islam you see here today—only with a new head for healing and a deeper respect for his god!"

The college I attended is one of the highest-ranked medical schools in Saudi Arabia, administered by the Saudi government (another point to sway my father). However, upon entering, I was shocked to discover that medicine is taught in the English language (a counterpoint to negate the one earned by the former). If my father had known I would be occupying my time also with the learning of this foreign tongue, which he called "the language of the unfaithful" and forbade in our house, he and I would surely have had a handful of additional lively discussions about my life choices.

Nevertheless, I was excited for the challenge—and what a challenge it turned out to be! Though my first year consisted of preparatory classes in physics, mathematics, pre-med, and so forth, for one who could gather just as much meaning from the words "Hello! How are you?" as he could from the braying of a donkey, it was enough to trigger more than a few sleepless nights and lost hairs. I couldn't even recite the English alphabet! Had it not been for the wonderful world wide web, through which I decoded all my textbooks via free language translator sites, I wonder if my sanity could have endured the long road ahead.

To be perfectly honest, though, the internet was not exactly an ideal study companion, as translations were often quite inaccurate, even laughable. For someone who might one day be making incisions into human bodies by these foreign directions, something much more comprehensive and immersive was needed to ensure my degree would read "Doctor," rather than "Butcher." So, just before the summer holiday arrived, I commenced a search for a college-level English as a Second Language course to take during the break; however, in order to reap the greatest value, I knew I would also have to study in an English-speaking country, wherein I would be constantly surrounded by the language and have there the necessity of adaptation to further motivate and educate me.

As this was the post-9/11 world, and still less than a decade removed from the world-changing event, finding an English-speaking country welcoming of a Muslim was challenging; therefore, my search honed in on countries carrying a low level of reported violence against Muslims. It wasn't long before my scouring unearthed New Zealand: a place rather open to my kind and one that didn't even require a visa application for individuals carrying a Saudi passport. And, so, having enrolled in my desired class at a reputable Islamic center in Auckland, I packed my bags for a long stay on what I quickly declared the moment my foot stepped forth onto New Zealand soil must truly be an alien planet.

The culture acted upon me less like the shock one gets from static friction, and more like the live end of a severed power line. Not surprisingly, it was the female culture that first sent me searching the ground for my dropped jaw—their bodies were on full display! As one who had just emerged from a world of face-coverings and burkas, short-sleeves, exposed knees, and discernable facial features were more than enough to send my eyes screeching into the pages of the Qur'an, where they might be shielded by the words of Allah. Food was also a challenge. Not only were the selections, in most cases, rather bizarre, I had to approach each item with great scrutiny, so as to not violate the Halal food laws of Islam. This collection of laws, similar to Jewish kosher laws found in the Old Testament of the Bible, place many restrictions on foods and even require a life-long abstention from alcohol. It was for this reason I had elected to live out my stay in a hotel, rather than with a host family—more expensive, yes; but it afforded me the opportunity to hand-pick my meals, rather than risk offending a non-Muslim family by refusing what food they might provide. Even the classroom setting in which I participated rocked my world and served up its share of firsts. For one, males and females were being taught together! Divisions between the sexes in such situations were to be strictly observed in my culture; thus, I made a point to never sit beside a female, and worked to place as much distance between myself and any person of the opposite sex. But, if this co-ed setting wasn't enough, I discovered that my instructor was a female! No male in my culture had ever received instruction from the opposite sex, and my being made to do so here in exchange for the attaining of a necessary skill brewed in me a silent dilemma. Lastly, as if this class had been designed to test the limits of my cultural tolerance, the instructor would often play music during class! Given my convincing lesson in the forbiddance of music, and the thorough manner by which it had been delivered, I had taken to shutting music completely out of my life; I had even set my cellphone to chant an Islamic poem in place of ringing. Often I would request the studying music played in class be silenced, and often I was simply ignored.

My introduction to Western culture acted as a propellant toward and an intensifying of my devotion to Islamic culture; I could see no way to serve Allah while participating in such a carefree way of living. Thankfully, I would go on to make many Muslims friends during my stay, who plugged me into the Islamic culture and made my stay on this alien planet a great deal more familiar.

If there was one thing my English as a Second Language class had in spades, aside from culture shock, it was diversity. Including myself, we had students from Saudi Arabia, France, Italy, South Korea, China, Japan, Germany, Holland—you name it, we'd probably had a representative. And I found myself growing a great deal more comfortable with this new world; though, I nonetheless kept myself positioned as an outsider, a enchanted observer, who could appreciate the cultural and lifestyle differences, even find them charming, but would never adopt any of them as his own.

The summer progressed rather fruitfully, seeing my English comprehension and oral application advance most promisingly. Great things seemed to be on the horizon and my future looked bright; so, when at last came the holy festival of Ramadan, I gathered with my Muslim friends and performed by duties with more joy and thankfulness than ever before.

As the festival drew nearer to a close, I selected my Night of Destiny (also called the Night of Power, or Laylat al-Qadr), which can be taken at one's discretion any time during the days of Ramadan. On this night, any request to Allah, whether glorifying to him or not, will by him be granted, and good works will be multiplied by one thousand. As one so enticed by the promise of jihad to have all of one's bad deeds erased in a single act, this night, since my childhood, had always been one of utmost importance, for with just one good deed I could have one thousand bad deeds canceled out, expunged from my eternal record. Thus, I had ever held the words of Qur'an 97:3 to be some of the truest ever spoken: "The Night of Destiny is better than a thousand months."

Laying down my prayer mat, I knelt and chanted Qur'an 1:6: "Guide us to the straight path."

From there, I commenced my list of extensive and rather exhausting rituals.

My face to the ground, I chanted one hundred times the prayer of forgiveness, taken from Qur'an 112:97-98.

"I seek the forgiveness of Allah," I whispered into the floor, "and repent before him."

Being that I was one to go the extra thousand miles to have my slate washed clean, upon completion of the prayer of forgiveness, I performed several other rituals, such as the remorseful remembering of ten sins from my seven main members and organs (eyes, ears, tongue, hands, mouth, stomach, and reproductive organs). Thereafter, I confessed to Allah all my repeated sins, vowing never to commit them again, as I actively recalled and acknowledged the just punishments he had for these sins set in place.

As my eyelids began to droop heavily, saturated with sleep, I chanted from Qur'an 4:110, "And whoever commits an evil or wrongs himself, but then asks for Allah's forgiveness, he will find Allah forgiving and merciful!"

By all accounts, it seemed my Night of Destiny had drawn to a close.

But I was wrong.

The night had only just begun.

***

It began with a *BANG*.

Hurling my body upright in bed, I threw my eyes in the direction of my balcony. There I saw that the balcony doors had been violently thrown open, and through them rushed a tempestuous wind, carrying with it the cool, midnight air, as would a speeding freight train cart along a hapless pedestrian who'd bypassed the crossing guards while sauntering over the tracks. The force of the wind projected my body backward, pinning me against the headboard, while its imposing presence and earth-shattering essence filled the tiny room. All the air I sought in response to cast forth in the form of a terrified scream was thrust back down my throat, both by the magnitude of the moment and the curious revelation of the mighty force's essence: a voice, majestic and lovely, one so inviting and beautiful beyond what the power of the most skilled wielders of art's finest instruments could ever dream of capturing. So loud was this voice, so thunderous and piercing, that its very resonance broke upon my body like waves on a storm-tossed ocean crashing against mighty cliffs. And yet, though I had initially reacted in terror, I could find in my heart no trace of fear for the single, soothing note singing through my balcony doorway.

In almost the same moment that the doors had blown open and the booming voice had entered did there follow after the tempest a raging fire of pure light, which banished every speck of darkness and scattered every shadow into a distant oblivion, as it burned a cleansing flame that painted all the room a pristine white. And through this spectacular display, there stepped forth a glorious figure, the very source of this supernatural light, whose radiance appeared so much grander than ten thousand suns that I dared not look upon it.

The thundering voice that yet filled the room could be now clearly perceived to be issuing forth from the figure before me; and as the whirling note it sang condensed, I could both hear and feel deep within the most sacred realm of my humanity my native tongue of Arabic laying within me these words: "Come to me."

In the midst of what should have been a permanently blinding glow, I suddenly dared to look up; and there I was granted to see him, standing before me in divine clarity, draped in a robe of sunlight. He was so near, right before my very eyes; yet, he was so infinite and glorious—he both filled and extended far beyond what my feeble eyes could see!

"Where?" I begged, my body trembling like one standing on the head of a pin, overlooking an endless drop. "Where must I go to find you?"

Something within me yearned to reach out to him, but he seemed so distant.

"Go to the house of white pillars," he replied; "there you shall find truth."

As if compelled by a silent urging, I snapped my head to the left, where I beheld the entire half of the room, right up to the edge of my bed, transform into the very house of which he'd spoken, rising impossibly but in perfect alignment with the small space, keeping its true size and scope.

And then, just as suddenly as this whirlwind had begun, it ended. The room had been restored, the figure vanished; the heavenly light had been replaced with darkness, and both the voice and the rushing wind had instantly dissipated. Even the balcony doors had been neatly closed, as if nothing had happened at all.

Heart racing and clothes soaked, I found myself awake, drenched in wonder and terror.

What had happened?

Who was that?

And why...oh, no.

A dark and terrible thought entered my mind: I was so very far from home, literally at the other end of the world; and, thus, well outside Islamic territory. It was an indisputable fact to me at the time that Muslims living for more than three days in such places are extremely vulnerable to demon attacks and assaults from other forms of black magic and evil. Had I just beheld the Devil? Had al-Shaitan himself come to torment me?

Immediately, as I had been taught to do, I fell on my face and frantically began to pray, repeating over and over the verses from the Qur'an believed to ward off evil. Though I had been so careful to remain faithful to Islam while in the belly of Western influence, to lag not even a little in my duties as a Muslim while away from the precious holy city that was my home, I feared now that he who was known to the West by the name Satan had set his sinister gaze upon me.

Utterly petrified, I wept and prayed and pleaded and screamed there on the floor of my tiny hotel room, until a stale, empty darkness overtook me and carried me swiftly into the morning.

9

The House of White Pillars and the Tall Man

COMPELLED by this urgent need to return to the land of Islam, there to find protection from the flaming eye of the evil one, I called the travel agency first thing in the morning—the very second their office opened—and attempted to book the next plane back home to Saudi.

"I don't care what it costs!" I shouted, well past my wits' end, and as such rather lax on my manners. "Whatever sum you want, it's yours! I'll pay anything up to purchasing the entire airplane! I must return to Saudi Arabia immediately! Can't you understand?"

"Sir, I understand completely," said the extremely patient woman on the other end—which, by the way, was no small statement to make for someone listening to panicked screaming coming over a landline hotel phone in woefully broken English. "Unfortunately, we have no flights currently available for passage to Saudi Arabia, and we probably won't have one for another week, at least."

"That's unacceptable!" I cried. "I must leave this treacherous place! How much do you want? Name your price!"

"As much as I'd like to rattle off a random number with a bunch of zeroes tacked to the end of it, not one dime of your money would reach my pocket, nor could anyone here be by any price swayed to put you on a plane that doesn't exist. I'm sorry."

I was stuck.

Sliding the receiver down my cheek, I hung up the old phone and dazedly slid it back to the hotel check-in agent who had connected me to the travel agency, and was at present regarding me with eyes the size of ostrich eggs, as I slinked away, mumbling verses from the Qur'an I had hoped might bring some comfort and encouragement to my thoroughly frightened and traumatized mind.

There I sat, alone in my room, chanting and praying, but I could find no comfort in any of the words I was saying. Truly, I thought, I must be terribly far from Allah.

Eventually, I decided it was not a good idea to stay in the hotel alone; the Devil might return. So, I quickly packed up my books and hustled off to school. Perhaps there I could find some blessed diversion until I could make my escape.

I didn't.

And I quickly found myself, day after day, growing increasingly paranoid and desperately afraid of being alone—I would even sit up through the night in the hotel lobby, many times being very kindly asked to leave. Day and night began to blur into one. I paid no attention to the times of my daily prayers, because I was bowing down every hour on the hour, and a handful of times in between, begging Allah to send his

angels to protect me from the evil one. But the fear only compounded, to the point where I was even using extreme caution
rounding blind corners.

Amid this haze of horror that had become my obsession, I
stepped into class, only to be reminded that this day we would
be doing a language lab, wherein we were to stand in front of
the class and, speaking in only English, recount a recent experience. Even though I was about as collected and focused as
a man on his fifteenth cup of coffee, I do remember hearing
some rather pleasant speeches. Some spoke of parties on the
beach, hiking in the wilderness, going to the movies with
friends—and then it was my turn.

"So, Ahmed, what have you been up to recently?" my
teacher asked.

Aside from losing my mind, not much.

I tried desperately to work up some sort of simple, composite experience, an amalgamation of things I had done since
arriving—*anything*, really! But my mind refused to unlatch its
talons from the death grip it held on my dream.

No! Anything but that!

"Ahmed?"

My wide, reddening eyes snapped onto my teacher, who
gazed back with a look that seemed to say, "Any day, now."

I had to speak.

Taking a deep, trembling breath, I wet my lips and looked
out at my peers, before hastily throwing my eyes to the floor
and spewing out every detail of my dream, as quickly as my
developing English would allow.

"I think," I said, having at last reached the end, "I think I
was attacked by Satan, and that is why I'm leaving for Saudi
Arabia as soon as possible."

Like the rest of the students sitting with brows furrowed and lips parted widely in thick, heavy silence, my teacher just stared at me in amazement. All through my speech, instead of taking notes as she had with the other students, she'd just stared. No longer was she a teacher; she was like a fully attentive and transfixed child.

At length she broke through the palpable quiet and exclaimed, "You have seen Jesus!"

We hadn't yet covered that word in class.

"What's that?"

The astonishment on her face intensified.

"Not *what—who*!"

"Who?"

I'd never heard that name in all my life.

"Yes, Jesus! You've seen Jesus!" she said again.

"Do...do you mean Satan?" I replied, quite confused. "Is Jesus what you call the Devil? I'd thought you called him Satan."

"No!" she cried. "Jesus is holy!"

"You mean Satan?" I really could not grasp the concept being presented here, as I could barely understand English and had no clue what she was trying to say.

Appearing frustrated, she repeated loudly, "No! *Jesus*! Jesus is holy!" No doubt due to the dumbfounded look I was giving her, she heaved a sigh, smiled, and said, "Come to my desk after class."

A sinking feeling fell through my stomach. I thought I had greatly offended her and wondered if she was planning to bring me before the school director to have me kicked out.

Then a light bulb went off in my head.

This is wonderful, I thought!

This could be an even faster way to get home to Saudi Arabia!

Looking back, I am almost certain my teacher had been a newly converted Christian, for when we spoke after class she employed what I see now as a rather limited knowledge of the Bible in an effort to explain to me who is Jesus. Either way, it was a rather futile endeavor, as her limited knowledge of the Bible mixed with my limited English yielded a pair of people talking past one another, exchanging a lot of words and yielding no real understanding.

About the time we began our third turn on the repeating-ourselves-merry-go-round, she sat back in her chair and said, "I want to introduce you to a man who will tell you more about your dream."

She then took out a pen and wrote down on a slip of paper a man's name, along with an address.

This could be one of Satan's tricks, I thought, a tactic to lure me into a trap.

Sensing my uncertainty, my teacher reminded me of the story of Joseph the dreamer, whose tale is featured both in the Bible and the Qur'an.

"You are like Joseph," she said. "He had dreams given to him by God, just like you."

Dreams and their interpretations are very important to Muslims, and the story of Joseph is revered in part for that reason. But I didn't trust her; so, after briefly examining the address she'd written, I angrily crumpled it up and tossed it into a trash can as I stormed out of the school, mumbling as I went, "I am in *no* way like Joseph!"

***

The travel agency had contacted me days earlier to offer me a spot on a flight to Saudi Arabia, departing a week from the present day. I took it, of course; but having yet to wait—even now with a definite date of departure, rather than endless wondering—it did nothing to ease my tortured mind. And, so, lost in this crushing anxiety, grinding me ever deeper into the bedrock of hopelessness, compounded now by the worthless answers and confusion gifted by my teacher, I wandered from campus in a daze, turning over questions, fears, and echoes of despair and cold isolation, until, hours later, I found myself shuffling about a foreign neighborhood.

Spring had just begun in New Zealand; yet, as I looked about me, lost in the bustling streets while drifting through the deepest, unknown recesses of my mind, I felt as though the winter had taken my body for its hibernation hole, here to linger while it regained its strength before it again covered the land. Bright and cheery faces reflected the sun raining from its peak all over the budding, bubbly world, bursting with color; but I shuffled beneath the curved wings of a stalking shadow, my sun suffocated by cloud, and all the world muted, grey, and threatening.

About the time I'd come to realize that I was probably very far from my hotel, as well as any of the Islam-friendly zones my Muslim friends had shown me, my feet, which had seemingly been compelled by something more powerful than their usual master, decided it was time for me to turn around at the approaching street corner; but, just before I got there, from behind the building by which I passed there leapt a sight that nearly knocked me onto my backside.

There before me, rising out of the ground and hurling itself at me from between the buildings that had like a great, concrete cloak concealed it, was a magnificent structure, bearing the likeness of a museum or ancient Grecian monument; for it carried a presence of strength and power, mixed with a most elegant beauty, as evidenced by the exceptional hand-crafting stonework, namely that which could be found atop six, towering white pillars.

"This is it!" I shouted, completely unaware that there might be more people than just me in the world. "From my dream! This is it!"

And so it was, to use my phrasing, it—and in more ways than just being the very structure I'd seen in my dream, for as I approached, I noticed the building's address, as carved into a stone plaque near the door. Indeed, it was the very same address my teacher had written on the slip of paper I'd discarded.

"It can't be," I mumbled through a dropped jaw; but, as I'd already declared, it was—this was it.

But, how?

Though the reasoning I had recently been employing should have sent me hightailing away from the very spot Satan himself had commanded I meet him, I found myself slowly inching closer. This was certainly not for the sake of curiosity, nor did I creep nearer because of any doubt in my assessment of the dream. I simply went.

Above the pillars were giant letters carved from dark stone, reading, "Baptist Tabernacle," whatever that meant.

There were no other signs or symbols that I saw this day to signal to me what might lie within this incredible house—had it have born a cross anywhere, I would have known right away this was no place for a Muslim, much less one presently besieged by demons, and promptly departed for safer territory.

Slowly, I climbed the stairs to a set of gigantic, wooden doors. Pushing carefully against these, I peeked my head into the strange place, while the creeping doors announced my presence with a long, high-pitched squeal. The smell of old wood filled my nose, and all around were artifacts of an ancient, alien world of sorts, from the terribly long, wooden seats stacked one after the other along a massive, open space, to the truly bizarre collection of towering, silver pipes lining the back wall. I had never seen an organ before, and therefore could never have identified it as a musical instrument. Thankfully, I treated this piece with distant respect and awe, and touched none of the keys—had I have done so, I don't wonder if I would have sprung into action and leapt through a window.

After a great deal of exploring, a young man entered the room.

"Welcome to the Baptist Tabernacle, sir!" he said with a sunny smile and an outstretched hand.

Surely, seeing the look of stunned confusion on my face, as well as my reluctance to take his hand, he examined me quickly and with a knowing, "Ah!" and added, "Please wait here—I'll have someone with you in just a moment."

His definition of "moment" seemed not to match my own, as I ended up waiting quite a while in the silence of the giant room; and I had just about had enough waiting, and had turned to leave, when a door behind me slowly opened and through it burst forth a cheerful, *"As Saalam a'alaikum!"*

Turning quickly around, I saw a very tall, very white man extending his hand toward me.

"Wa alaikum assalam!" I cheered in reply, snatching his hand and shaking it giddily, as I was so overcome with a feeling of relief and security to hear in what had become so dark and treacherous a place this beloved Arabic greeting of "Peace be upon you." It was a desperately needed slice of home, and I instantly felt a sense of bonding with the man.

But before any more pleasantries could be exchanged, the tall man, with his very next breath, said, "Tell me about your dream."

Though he'd continued to speak in Arabic, that wonderful, warm feeling of safety and familiarity that had wrapped me like a child's security blanket was instantly ripped away, leaving me once again shivering and vulnerable in a foreign wilderness. How could this man know about my dream, I wondered? Was this knowledge given to him by heaven or hell? My brain was proving a tad sluggish at connecting the dots.

"Who are you?" I asked, eyeing him with fearful amazement.

"Forgive me," he said with an air-expelling chuckle. "I guess I got a little carried away by the excitement."

The second he said his name, a spark ignited in my head, and I saw clearly the slip of paper my teacher had given me. Above the address she had penned this very name.

"I'm one of the pastors here. Your teacher phoned and told me you might be stopping by—so, how about it?" he continued eagerly, after asking my name. "What did you see?"

Apprehensive and afraid, I did not speak immediately; rather, I debated frantically in my head, arguing the merits of everything from spilling my guts to running away screaming. My eyes scanned every detail of his face—it was pallid; gaunt might even be a good word; yet, there was a rosiness in its manner that, while it did not appear on the skin, seemed to be the life that animated his gangly frame. I scanned every detail, every pore and blemish, every curve and valley, looking for a sign of malice buried beneath what could very well have been a most clever veil, woven by unfriendly otherworldly hands.

He remained patient through it all.

Eventually, having turned up nothing particularly frightening in my search, I began recounting my dream.

Though slow at first, I soon found myself rattling off every little detail. I told him about the doors of my balcony flying open, about the rushing wind, the thunderous voice, the blinding light; I told him about the glorious man: his magnificent robes, his fiery form, his beautiful voice, and his compelling words, commanding me to come to him and to find the house of white pillars. All of this, it seemed, I had expelled in a single breath, for I was quite winded and sweating profusely by the end.

"And this was not a vision from god!" I explained, once all had been related. "This was Satan! All hell is breaking loose in my life!" Gasping for air, I continued, "But I will be leaving for the sanctuary of Saudi Arabia; there, at last, I'll be safe and free of this demonic torment."

The tall man, who hadn't once broken eye contact the entire time I'd been speaking, offered me a warm smile and, with a shaking of the head, responded, "No, Ahmed; you've seen Jesus!"

There was that name again!

"Satan, you mean?"

"No, no!" he chuckled. "Not Satan—Isa!"

Those words hit me like a baseball bat to the gut from a major league slugger.

Isa?

The prophet of Allah?

The one Allah carried up to heaven, confounding those below who'd sought to crucify him?

How could it be so?

Given all I knew of the man, Isa would *never* appear to *anyone* in a dream, for his next appearance will be only the day of his Second Coming, when, according to the Hadith, he will destroy all the infidels. Furthermore, why would Isa call me to follow him? I was already following him! Any faithful Muslim who follows Allah follows his faithful prophets.

I was thoroughly confused.

"Are you a Muslim?" I asked the tall man.

"I submit wholly and only to the one, true God," he replied. "In that, you may call me a Muslim, as does the Qur'an. However," he added quickly, "neither Allah nor Islam do I follow; I am a Christian, a servant and follower of Isa, whom we call Jesus."

"A *Christian*?"

A sworn enemy of Allah?

My lifelong Islamic indoctrination and jihadist training roared at the back of my mind. But there was something about this man that gave me pause. By all appearances, he was a perfect representation of the Christians I'd been trained to behead; yet, his words and actions painted a picture of the condemned unfaithful that I never could have imagined. He spoke Arabic and seemed to know something of Islam! More than that, though, I'd told him while recounting my dream that I was a Saudi Muslim; yet, his manner hadn't changed one bit. Thinking back, I realized he hadn't even flinched when I'd told him! Rather, his care and concern for me and my situation seemed only to increase by the moment; there was not a drop of fear, disdain, or dislike—much less hatred—in his conduct toward me. He treated me as no one other than my Filipina housemaid had ever done. It was, though I dared not let the idea last long in my mind, something akin to...something like...well, love.

Whatever mental images I'd formed over the years of Christian pigs and dogs, like this man was supposed to be—they looked nothing like what sat patiently and attentively before me.

Something deep within bade me indulge curiosity rather than hostility.

"Yes," he said again. "A follower of Isa."

"But...how is that possible? A person cannot follow Isa and *not* be devoted to Islam. He was Allah's prophet, after all."

"'And in their footsteps,'" he began, speaking in Arabic from Qur'an 5:46.

"'We sent Isa the son of Mary,'" I interjected, completing the verse, "'confirming the Law that had come before him!' Yes! Isa, may peace be upon him: a prophet of Allah!"

"Peace, indeed," he said with a smile. "And so great a prophet was He!"

"Very much so!" I agreed, delighted to see we were getting along, yet completely puzzled as to *why* we were getting along, as this man had already declared his rejection of Islam.

As he and I took a seat, I poked at this very point.

"You say you follow Isa," I began; he nodded; "yet, you also say you are a Christian. But, Christians do not follow Isa; they have rejected the words passed down to him from Allah, corrupted his teachings, of which Isa was a messenger. You speak with knowledge of the Qur'an: that is truth; so, why do you count yourself among those who reject truth for corruption?"

"Well," he said, throwing one leg over the other and relaxing his hands upon his knee, "why don't we investigate that? But let's not lose sight of this dream of yours. You say it was Satan who'd visited you; I say it was Isa, Jesus. I claim to be Jesus' devout follower, a servant of Him who bears the true identity known by that name—I should, therefore, know Him pretty well, no?"

"Not if you know him outside the words of Allah."

"Very well; let's see what Allah has to say about Isa."

It was only now I came to realize he was holding a Qur'an.

"So," he said, licking his thumb and flipping through the pages, "where should we begin?"

The Qur'an makes plain the twisting of the truth that is the Christian belief, but I had never encountered someone who actually claimed to hold fast to that perversion, especially one who demonstrated a knowledge—though, perhaps not a clear understanding—of Allah's unchanging words, as I had ever known them to be. He was, in my eyes, the culmination of Qur'an 5:18, wherein Jews and Christians claim, "We are children of Allah and his beloved." This verse continues with an example for Muslims to act as ambassadors, to question those who so claim to be what Allah clearly says they are not, to test their faith and so prove Islam to be the truth. Likewise, in Qur'an 10:94, we read that Muhammad is told that if he is in doubt about the revelation given to him by Allah, he should ask those who have been reading the Scripture that came before him.

And, so, I did.

"How do you Christians claim Isa was born?" I asked.

"Of the virgin Maryam," he replied without hesitation. "We call her Mary."

"As you have said."

"Yes—Qur'an 19; a most interesting read. You can really see how special Mary is to Allah, in that the entire chapter is named after her, and she is the only female mentioned by name in the entire Qur'an."

"Ah!" I cried. "But she is not equal with Allah, as is your claim!"

"No, indeed!" he answered with gleeful concurrence; his balance was unshaken. "Qur'an 5:116: Allah asks Jesus if He'd told the people to worship even His mother as a God."

"'It was not for me to say that to which I have no right,'" I quoted.

"True followers of Jesus," he continued, "do not take Mary as a god; they do not elevate her among mankind, nor put her on equal footing with God; for she is but a human being—one very much blessed by God, yes; but a human being, nonetheless, with just as many sins as everyone else, in just as much need of God's mercy and forgiveness as you and I."

I eyed him carefully, and then readied to pose my next question; however, he tapped slightly at my footing when he suddenly posed a question of his own.

"How does Jesus compare to the rest of the prophets in this respect?"

"What do you mean?"

"Well," he said, "who among the twenty-five prophets is the greatest?"

Never had there been a more juvenile question about Islam!

"Muhammad, of course!" I declared, in such a manner as I would have done had he asked me the color of grass. "Peace be upon him—he is Allah's great messenger!"

"It would stand to reason, then," he continued on beat, "that all the rest of the prophets, from Adam to Joseph to David and Solomon, all the way through Jesus—it stands to reason that the first twenty-four would, next to Muhammad's position as the greatest, be unable to compare with his deeds and message. Is that not so?"

There was no need to think about the answer.

"Indeed, it is! He is the prophet given the final revelation, sent to restore the people to Islam, to the worship of Allah and Allah only, to turn them away from their corrupted teachings before the final day."

My eyes fell quizzically and perplexedly upon him.

"But you demonstrate knowledge of this final revelation, the noble Qur'an," I muttered, almost breathless by his seemingly upside-down perspective and position. "How, then, do you claim first to serve Isa over he who came after, bearing a greater message, uncorrupted through the years?"

"Do you believe in truth?" he asked, his eyes penetrating my very being.

The enigma of this man was both twisting and attracting.

"I do."

"Why?"

"*Why?*"

No man had ever posed such a question—I hardly knew how to respond.

He waited.

At length, I answered softly, "I must."

"As must I," he replied, "for even to declare there is no such thing as truth would require truth to exist for the statement rejecting its existence to be valid."

Naught but the blinking of my eyes could answer this assertion.

"What, then," he continued, "is truth?"

"The Qur'an."

Though confident was my reply, firm in the foundation that was my life up to this point, there began to tingle a strange sensation in my footing.

And just as I began to wonder what the ground on which I had staked my life had ever felt like beneath my feet, the tall man leaned forward and skewered a sharp eye through my gaze—his was a searching stare; it called me with the voice of a man to rise to a man's task.

"Are you willing," he said, speaking slowly, deliberately, softly, "to search that truth for understanding, to examine the words and deeds of the latter prophets, and so know them? Are you willing to know the truth, to learn why you were called to this place in a dream, and who it was that sent you?"

I had no breath by which to lift a reply; the sheer force that was the magnetism in his words, in their beckoning and great call to examine truth for truth's sake—had I any power to make a sound, I would not have known which to make. And, so, in a mere instant, I assessed my curiosity of this man and situation, and the cause of my being in this place. A dream so vivid—it had shown me a place my eyes had never seen, in a town to which I'd never been, and grabbed me with a touch no vision had ever the power to possess. This was no accident, no wild chance—I had seen and heard things of which there had been no previous reference from which a slumbering mind might draw inspiration; this was real, and I could find nothing more than folly in my following the inclination to abandon this pursuit. If for no other reason than I feared to go the rest of my days wondering about the cause and reason for my dream, I had to remain; and with my firm grounding in the Qur'an, its infallible word cemented into my mind, I was sure no corruption could shake the foundation I had forged in the Saudi sand that was my heritage and destiny.

Silently, I filled my lungs.

"I am."

Straightening up in his chair, the tall man tickled the pages of his Qur'an, smiling at me—not as one salivating for the triumph of which he was confident to discover in a challenge laid before him, but rather as a patient, loving friend.

It was a most foreign look.

"You really believe it was Isa who came to me that night?"

"Do you still believe it was Satan?"

Silence again passed between us.

"I don't know," I replied at length; my words had never before held a more transparent representation of my being.

"What do you believe of this book?" he asked, holding up the Qur'an. "Does it bring clarity or confusion?"

"Clarity."

"To which book, then, would Satan seek to lead you, and from which teach you—the book of clarity, or the book of confusion?"

"The book of confusion."

"Which will you choose?"

Hours passed like minutes, until all the daylight had been expired, quite unlike my ever-blooming questions. Where one question was answered, three more would sprout in its place; and he'd had replies for them all, leaving not one unexplained. His great knowledge and gentleness of spirit, as well as his willingness and kindness to spend so much time guiding me through the mystery of my dream and indulging my curiosity, made me want to go on conversing with him, day after day, and never stop.

There seemed no topic untouched, from high and heavy to small and light—light, but as significant as life itself; the infinite and all the way down to the finite, wherein I did take a second look at what quickly became a most curious claim. Qur'an 51:49 states that of all things Allah has created two mates or pairs. Now, I had ever been taught that the Qur'an was a vast storehouse of scientific knowledge, things Muhammad in his time would not have been able to invent; only an all-knowing god could have revealed such wonders. But if these words were as concrete and divinely bestowed from the highest wisdom, how could there be within the pages such a stark scientific fallacy, for in my medical studies I had come to learn about parthenogenesis, wherein reproduction occurs without fertilization; no pair is required to multiply, and no pair exists. Had man's understanding of nature through science been a blind walk, or could this be a tiny, but in perspective gargantuan, crack in the unshakable foundation of my faith?

While any curious contradiction pointed toward the refuting of the claim that the revelation of the Qur'an was infallible, making me question (albeit penitently) its reliability, we spent relatively little time on such topics; our conversation centered mostly about the uniqueness of Jesus, as he was presented in the Qur'an, measuring him up against all the prophets, but mainly against Muhammad; for if indeed Muhammad was the greatest of Allah's messengers, Jesus would surely fail even to match Muhammad's standard of excellence.

It was clear that Jesus had come to bring peace, never once fighting or killing, or encouraging anyone to do so; while Muhammad, though he spoke of peace early in his career, ended with a much different tune, becoming akin to a war lord when he settled in Medina, pushing forth a "fight them all" doctrine. Night and day contrasts, for sure; but these differences ran far deeper.

"So," said the tall man after a great deal of back and forth, "we can see that Jesus was rather unique, wouldn't you say? Being one of only two prophets without a human father, but unlike Adam, being born of a woman."

I nodded thoughtfully, musing on Qur'an 3:59, which states that "the similitude of Jesus before Allah is as that of Adam."

"Unlike any other prophet," he proceeded, "Jesus had power over life and death and even creation itself—Qur'an 3:49, in which Jesus states, "'I have come to you, with a Sign from your Lord, in that I make for you out of clay, as it were, the figure of a bird, and breathe into it, and it becomes a bird by Allah's leave: And I heal those born blind, and the lepers, and I quicken the dead, by Allah's leave.'" Much more authority," he said, "is shown to be given to Jesus than to any other prophet. He heals the sick, raises the dead, and before the eyes of many forms the figure of a bird and breathes life into it. He even possessed speech as an infant, according to Qur'an 93—He states clearly that He is a prophet, making it plain that He never *wasn't* a prophet. Could such a person have the power to come to someone in a dream to, as He says in Qur'an 43:63, come in Wisdom to make clear that which is in dispute?"

I thought long and hard, reciting verse after verse in my head, searching for even a single miracle Muhammad had performed to demonstrate his authority over, well, something; but I could find none.

"But Allah sent Muhammad the Qur'an," I argued. "Just as he sent Isa the Injil and Moses the Torah; but only the Qur'an remains uncorrupted."

"The Injil," he said, "the Gospel, was, as you say, given by Allah to Jesus—twice we read this in the Qur'an: in 5:46 and 57:27. And what was Jesus' response to this Gospel He had been given?"

"He came as a witness to the Torah and to proclaim the revelation Allah had given him!"

"And what did He command?"

"Obedience!"

"Yes; Qur'an 43:63—He says, "'Therefore fear Allah and obey me.'" He sounds rather sure of His message, no?"

"How could he not be so? Given all that he was and had received!"

"Was Muhammad so sure that his way was the right way?"

"Of course! Why, he is the one who set straight the wayward; he—"

My mouth stopped; Qur'an 34:50 suddenly popped into my head. And I looked and saw the tall man had already opened to the page.

Probably seeing in my eyes that I was reviewing it in my mind, he read, "Muhammad said, 'If I go astray, I go astray to my own loss.'" How could he do so, if indeed he possessed the truth, divinely bestowed?"

This was beginning to hurt.

Then, still in his soft, tender voice, the tall man asked, "Why did Allah give the Qur'an to Muhammad via the angel Gabriel?"

Like an automatic Rolodex in the mind, my mental fingers flipped to Qur'an 42:51.

"And it is not for any human being that Allah should speak to him except by revelation or from behind a partition or that he sends a messenger to reveal, by his permission, what he wills. Indeed, he is most high and wise."

"We agree that Muhammad was human?"

I nodded.

"As were the other prophets? As was Jesus?"

Two nods.

"This is probably one of my favorite marks of the uniqueness of Jesus," he said, flipping through the Qur'an again. "What do we see starting at Qur'an 5:110?"

Having turned to it in my head, my eyes shot wide open, and I grabbed the Qur'an from his hands to be sure I hadn't somehow misremembered.

"Allah is conversing with Isa," my words exhaled from my lips.

"Is this the only time?"

I didn't need to think.

"Quran 3:55—'Allah said: "O Isa! I will take thee and raise thee to myself.""

I shook my head, my stomach turning.

On and on we talked, my heart all the while aching under this strange sensation that it was being squeezed in the midst of an ever-tightening grip.

"Why do you Christians want to believe Isa died?"

"Do you believe in sin?" he asked.

"Of course!"

"What does sin do to you?"

"Well," I said, "if I have too many sins, I will not achieve paradise in the next life—my good deeds must outweigh my bad by the time I die."

"So, your sin separates you from God?"

"Yes—now, what about *my* question?"

"I'm answering it," he said with a big smile. "Is sin part of our nature? Would you say you were born perfect?"

"Certainly not!"

"Sin comes easily, then?"

"Does it not for us all?"

"Indeed, it does. Now, if we need not be taught how to lie or cheat or steal or hate—all sinful things; if no one has to teach us how to do sinful things, and sin makes us unfit to be before God, our very nature is in opposition to God. We are unholy before a holy God; we are unjust before a just God; therefore, we cannot hope to stand before Him and live, unless our sins are taken away."

"By our good deeds."

"Wait a minute, though," he interjected. "We just established that God is just. Say your neighbor broke into your house and stole your belongings, even killed someone in the process—a family member. Would you expect a Saudi judge to pardon his crime?"

"Of course not!"

"What if he could irrefutably establish a host of good deeds, more good deeds done than most men *ever* accomplish, displaying an uncommon devotion to Islam and the religion?"

"That's..." I began with a burst of eager energy; but, as I heard the words I was intending to speak, all the wind was taken out of my sails. "That's irrelevant," I said softly.

"We've also established that our very nature is sinful," he continued. "How did you get to New Zealand from Saudi Arabia? Did you pay with Saudi money?"

"No. I had to exchange it for New Zealand money."

"Your native money is worthless here?"

"Yes."

"How much more worthless would the deeds of a sinner by nature be as payment for paradise with a sinless God? Think of yourself as a rag stained with dirt, your sin—no matter how hard you scrub, nothing you touch or produce will be clean; everything will be stained, as you are stained."

"What does this have to do with Isa?"

"Jesus came preaching the Good News that He, sinless though He was, would stand in our place before God, bearing our stains, our sins, upon Himself; He would put His holiness over us, make us clean before God; and in Him we would have salvation. This He would do, and did, by dying on the cross and absorbing the full wrath of God, poured out against sin, dying as the propitiation and giving us eternal life, if we would but believe in Him."

I did believe in Isa—but only as a prophet; he was not god.

"Well, Ahmed," said the tall man, some time long after the cleaning staff had packed up for the night, as it was now well into the fourth hour of the morning, "what do you say we pause our discussion here and pick it up at my house?"

The sun would soon be rising, but sleep was not the concern urging caution at this invite, for while I was deeply curious and unwilling to halt our talk, even more reluctant to reject his warmly offered hospitality, this was my first encounter with a Christian; and, if Christians were anything like me, I could be in deep trouble, I thought. Given that Islam provides only one way to guarantee a trip to heaven, namely killing an infidel, I feared maybe a follower of Isa might have a similar guarantee after which to strive.

Truly, I thought, this man may just kill me if I go with him.

The decision, as you may expect, was an easy one.

"No, no," I stammered, "thank you, but I really should be getting back to my hotel."

"I completely understand," he said with a chuckle—though, I seriously doubt his understanding was all that complete. "My wife might have already let loose the dogs to find me. What do you say we talk again tomorrow, here?"

It seemed wiser to operate with a potentially murderous Christian in public places, and to be sure to do so when people are present—I wasn't about to again test his bloodlust by losing track of time, as on this occasion.

Agreeing, I accepted his card and scurried off into the dark streets back to my hotel room, where I would lie awake until the dawn, turning that card about in my hand, contemplating the risk/reward ratio of discovering the purpose behind my dream and scratching this deep itch that was this new perspective on the very book I had memorized. Had it all been merely liturgical, or had I actually studied what I could recite by heart? Did I know what I knew? A sound like the crumbling of a world rippled through my ears; and as I seemed to be slipping off into a void, tilting off of the plain that was my existence, my eyes shot open, and I realized, far too late to help the matter, that the crumbling sound was the creaking of my bedsprings, and that tilting was my rolling off the mattress.

WHUMP

About the time I managed to get the circling birds dancing about a halo of stars to fly off to other dazed and confused places, my gaze focused on the name of the tall man, staring me dead in the eye.

Peeling his card from my forehead, I looked at my watch; it was nearly six o'clock in the evening.

My head was still reeling from the hours upon hours we'd spent tearing the Qur'an to shreds (not to mention my little tumble)—and there was still so much ground left to cover! Petrified though I was, and though ardent were my pleas to Allah, begging for forgiveness for having missed some of my prayers due to this unexpected pursuit, and begging my god to send forth the truth to blot out all the lies, to secure me in my foundation; though I trembled from the ends of my hairs to the ends of my toes, this booming command to "Come" and to "find truth" pounded endlessly through my head and heart.

I could find no rest.

I *had* to know what was this truth I had been commanded to find.

And, just like that, I rushed to my phone, called up the tall man, and broke all kinds of land speed records getting back to the house of white pillars.

As on the previous days, I found no comfort, only what felt like a scaly skin being peeled away one scale at a time.

"Why did he say that, though?" I asked, tugging slightly on my beard and running a hand through my hair.

"All right," said the tall man, repositioning himself in his chair, as we had been several hours sitting and were again creeping through the early morning hours, "we've already determined the first part of what you'd heard—the figure in your dream said, 'Come to me;' after which you begged to know where to go."

"Then I saw this place."

"Right—and the figure then told you to come here."

"And he said I'm supposed to find truth here! Well, I did!" I exclaimed, tapping on the Qur'an in the tall man's hands. "It's right here—but I already have that truth," tapping my head, I added, "up here."

"Do you think the figure just didn't know you have the Qur'an? Given all He was able to do—come in a dream, fill the room with light, show you a place you had never seen before in all your life, and tell you to go there; and now you're here, in a foreign land with a foreign man who speaks your tongue and knows the book of your faith; given all that, does it stand to reason that He made this trip to you for nothing, because He didn't know something about you? Why not first ask you if you knew the Qur'an, rather than assuming and sending you on a needless errand?"

I had become almost entirely convinced that Satan had not been my glorious visitor. Truth belonged to Allah, and anyone pointing me toward truth must be sent from above; but this was a haunting, terrifying feeling; for it suggested I was lacking something true—the word "truth" being so firm, concrete, and whole a word that I knew it was meant to carry more reference and weight than what merely one single misconception could carry.

No, I feared, this meeting on my Night of Destiny was the first tremor of a great quake, readying to shake the foundation of all I'd known and to which held fast all my life.

"If the Qur'an is truth," the tall man continued, "it will not fail the test of fire."

We had already struck some matches against it the other day; that imperishable book was looking curiously flammable.

But there had to be some sort of concrete truth in there! Surely! There just had to be!

After some discussion, we came to the creation of man.

"How was it done?" he asked.

"Referring to Isa, Qur'an 3:59 says Allah created him from dust, likening his creation to that of Adam."

"And if we read further?"

"Where?"

"Qur'an 15:26."

"'And we did certainly create man out of clay from an altered black mud.'"

My head shook in frustration as I spoke—then, I started to scour my brain for every reference I could find regarding how Allah creates man: Qur'an 16:4—Allah created man from a sperm-drop; Qur'an 19:67 and 52:35—created out of nothing, created by nothing; Qur'an 96:2—from a blood clot, a clinging substance.

By the time I had run through them all, there rested a clump of beard hair in my fist.

"Come, Ahmed," said the tall man, tenderly placing a hand across my shoulders. "Let's take a break—why not go back to my place, where we can talk some more in comfier chairs, with tea and some snacks?"

The mouse is lured to the trap with the pungent smell of a tasty morsel.

Again, I refused, and we continued.

"Allah commanded Muhammad to be the first of those who submit themselves to him through Islam—is that true?"

"Yes," I replied with a sigh; it was a most obligatory sigh. "Qur'an 39:12."

"What then of Isa? Does the Qur'an say He was not a devout follower of Allah, a Muslim preaching Islam?"

My head fell into my hand.

"Then there's Moses," he continued. "In Qur'an 7:143 he gives glory to Allah and declares that *he* is the first to believe."

Eyes lifting over my fingers, my hands gently pressed against my pursed lips.

"And let's not forget Abraham—even earlier than Moses! Qur'an 2:132 tells us Abraham left the legacy of the faith of Islam to his sons. If he'd given it to them, surely he must have had it first."

Patterns were emerging left and right—not the least of which was the fact that we were again but a few hours from sunrise, and the tall man was wetting his lips to pose his favorite question.

"Let's not stop," he said; "this has been a most fascinating experience. You could come stay at my place for the night—

or, morning," he chuckled. "After a good morning's sleep, we could begin again right away. What do you say?"

He must really be desperate to kill me and get to paradise, I thought! Or, I wondered, as I stared at his pleasant smile, maybe he's older than he looks, or has a terminal disease, and wants to be sure he ends it well—goes out with a bang, taking me with him.

Kindly, he insisted.

"We have a guest room," he said, "and my wife is there— she'd love to meet you."

Taking out his wallet, he showed me a picture of a lovely woman and many children.

"These are my grandkids," he smiled, his eyes reddening a little as he gazed rays of brilliant light over the photos.

It was so heartwarming a sight, and he had been so kind up until this point, giving up entire days to sit and talk with me, that I began to feel sick in my stomach; for I had more than his generosity compelling me in this moment. There is a rule of three, of sorts, in my culture, which demands acceptance by the recipient of an invite, if that invite is offered thrice.

So, caught by the quality of the man before me, and the command of the culture, I accepted his offer; and together we walked to his car and drove along the dark and empty streets to his home. I made sure to note all my escape means and routes, plotting after every turn into a new area which way I would run in the event he should move to kill me.

Upon arriving, I scanned the neighborhood and quickly identified a route with the least number of running obstacles.

He opened the door to his home; I tiptoed in, looking both ways—left, then right, then left again, and then a quick right-left-right—and testing every floorboard for traps. I permitted him never to see my back; I walked pressed against the walls, eyeing the hallways and stair system, plotting and re-plotting how best to flee if and when the big moment came.

"What would you like for midnight breakfast?" he asked as he strolled to the refrigerator.

"WATER!" I blurted, quite unaware of anything other than my impending doom, much less the volume of my voice.

My nerves were teetering on the edge of a cliff, so much so that when he returned with a glass of water, placing it before me with that same, genuinely pleasant smile, I refused to drink it—for all I knew, it was poisoned!

"So!" came an angelic voice from the other room. "This must be your night owl friend!"

"Ahmed," said the tall man, standing and ushering into the room a very friendly looking woman, "this is my wife."

She took my cold and clammy, dead fish of a hand without so much as the batting of an eye.

"It's so wonderful to meet you!" she cried. "I've heard you two have been doing some serious studying—touched on one of his favorite topics, you have."

Whether I was much for conversation, I cannot say; but I can suppose—and I do suppose I was rather dull, awkward company, what with my bouncing knees, chattering teeth, and sharp glances every which way, throwing sweat from my brow like a dog shaking off water.

Before long, the tall man said, "Well, what do you say we turn in for the morning, eh? Let's rest the ol' noodle so we can have a fresh go at it tomorrow."

"Yes!" declared his wife. "And I'll be sure to have a warm, midday breakfast ready when you wake up! Goodnight!"

Having been escorted to the guest room, all neatly prepared just for me, I pressed my ear against the closed door until I could hear that they'd gone away; then, as quick as a flash, I began darting about the room, collecting whatever items I could find heavy enough to barricade the door. Snatching the space heater, I rammed it against the base, before whipping off my belt and wrapping it around the doorknob, anchoring it to a dresser pinned to the wall. I scurried then to the windows, closed and locked them all, then tied the curtains into an impossible knot. Having burned now about three thousand calories, I set in place the final defense: a decoy—I took all the pillows and arranged them under the covers to look like a human body, then crouched down into a corner beside the bed, wondering if I had done enough.

"How foolish!" wept this trained jihadist. "Surely, he'll be down in an hour, maybe two; he'll find a way in here, some passage he knows that I don't know—he'll kill me for sure!"

So great was my madness that I didn't even notice the jaws of Sleep creeping up on me.

I was devoured into a coma-like state until long past midday.

"Good afternoon!"

A familiar, angelic voice broke through the blinding light streaming down the hallway along which I slunk.

"Sleep well?"

I knew that voice, too.

My eyes focusing, I saw the tall man seated at the kitchen table, while his wife prepared a meal and I stood dumbfounded, gaping at the both of them—I was alive! It seems

Christians are either really patient about killing non-Christians, or murder is just not their style.

A great, internal wall was suddenly razed, crumbling into a silent mist, and I felt strangely at ease.

"Eat up!" said the tall man as I took a seat opposite him, and a plate of the finest aromas a nose could smell was placed before me. "We'll need all the strength we can get!"

A steaming cup of coffee slid before me.

My eyelids slipped slowly shut as the glorious fragrance rippled through my nostrils, and when they opened again, the room seemed to have changed color—it was a fantastic array of brilliant, bold hues, stark and powerful like a bowl of delectable candies.

The tall man nodded with a smile, then attended to his newspaper and glass of water while I ate.

After a fantastic meal, the tall man and I retired to his office, where we resumed our talk; this time, we each held a copy of the Qur'an; he kept three among his library.

As soon as he'd answered one question, I'd hit him with another—slowly, though I knew not what it was, there came over me a feeling like a mighty river, pouring through the gates of my soul, which were beginning to open.

"But you Christians claim Isa was crucified!" I posed. "See here, Qur'an 4:157," I said, flipping the pages and pointing to the verse: "it says the Jews boasted that they'd killed Isa—but the verse continues to say that they surely killed him not!"

"That's right!"

His reply was like the blunt side of a hammer.

"*What*? You agree?"

"Of course! See what the verse says—what are the words? It says *they*, the Jewish leaders, did not kill Him; yet, they believed they had done so. Jewish law had no provision for execution; therefore, they needed the Romans to sentence and kill Jesus at their urging. So, we can see that it was the Romans who actually killed Jesus, while the Jewish leaders boasted that it had been by their power that He was put to death."

I nearly fell out of my chair.

Reciting the verse in my head, chanting the pure Arabic revelation I had memorized, I could find no cause to refute this interpretation; however, this was not the only way to look at it.

"No, no," I said after a moment spent regaining the ground beneath my feet, "the verse doesn't say Isa was killed by *anyone*; it was made to appear that way to those watching the crucifixion—these words refer to another who bore his likeness. Whether they had taken Simon of Cyrene by mistake, or Allah had placed the resemblance of Isa on another, like Judas Iscariot, Isa did not die—the Qur'an is very explicit on this point."

"We agree that Jesus stood trial before the Romans, correct?"

"Condemned by the testimony of false witnesses, liars in opposition to Allah!"

"History concurs. The documentation preserved even unto today makes the consensus unanimous that Jesus faced crucifixion; and, as such, He would have faced all that crucifixion entailed—most significantly, scourging, which preceded one's being nailed to a cross. Are you familiar with Roman scourging?"

I shook my head.

Taking a large text from his shelf, he began to flip through the pages. A peek at the spine revealed the text to be a college history book. After a few moments, he turned the book upside down, facing me, and threw his finger on an image.

"It's called a flagrum," he said, as I stared spellbound at the cruel-looking instrument.

At first glance, it looked like a multi-corded whip; but the winding throngs of leather bore within them something far more sinister.

"Lead balls affixed to the tips," said the tall man: "these would beat and bruise the skin, causing vasodilation; the blood would well up into the back, while the shards of bone woven beneath them," he pointed to these on the diagram, "would shred the flesh, ripping off massive chunks and causing severe bleeding."

"Hypovolemic shock," I muttered, clutching the book.

"Exactly—the rapid decrease in blood volume rendered a victim exhausted, to say the least; they would no longer be able to put up a fight or resist the nailing to a cross; as such, they would die sooner on that cross, having no strength to lift their body to draw air as their lungs collapsed. Many condemned to crucifixion died long before meeting their cross."

"Such pain..."

"Excruciating." His tone was dark and low. "That word was invented because of crucifixion—*ex crux*: Latin for 'of the cross;' *excruciat*: tormented."

The hands that had ached to hold the knife of beheading trembled as they handed the tall man his book.

"Do you find it logical," he proceeded, slipping the text back onto his shelf, "that a man thoroughly lashed into a bloody mess by the savage Roman cord, driven mere steps from death, could be mistaken for Simon of Cyrene, an otherwise healthy bystander forced to carry Jesus' cross? Would not the blood, at the very least, have been a dead giveaway?"

As one studying to be a doctor, it would have been disingenuous to argue in favor of the mix-up.

"Well, then," I persisted, having gathered myself, "we see that it was Allah's intervention—he placed Isa's likeness on another!"

"All right," he said, nodding; "let's take that point as a sure fact: Allah put the face of Jesus on another; thus, he tricked those who sought to kill Jesus into thinking they had. Allah is even called the best of schemers—or, planners—in Qur'an 3:54, where, in the next verse, Allah foretells the departure of Jesus from this world, saying, 'I will cause you to die and raise you to myself.'"

"Okay," I interjected. "As you say, Qur'an 3:54 tells how the disbelievers plotted against Isa, but Allah was one step ahead—he had planned for this, planned to raise Isa to himself. Verse 55..."

I stopped.

Qur'an 3:55 and 4:157 stood side-by-side in my mind; one fit not with the other, and the other not with the one.

"It's metaphorical," I muttered at length, barely able to lift the words.

"Was it also metaphorical when Jesus himself declared He would die and rise again?"

"*What?*"

I had memorized the Qur'an, had I not? Why were its words and what I knew to be true seeming like foreigners to one another?

"Qur'an 19:33," he began, turning to the verse: "Jesus said, 'So peace is on me the day I was born, the day that I die, and the day that I shall be raised up to life again!'" Does He use the word 'die' in this instance to metaphorically refer to His being taken up to heaven?"

I could not speak—had it have been as the tall man had suggested, there would have been no need to mention raising up to life a second time.

"After Jesus departed," he continued, "whether by death or being snatched to heaven by the hand of Allah, what became of the disciples?"

Blinking into space, I mumbled from memory part of Qur'an 3:55: "'I will make those who follow thee superior to those who reject faith.'"

"The apostles of Jesus, according to history, died proclaiming Jesus as the risen Christ, the Son of God and God Himself—why?"

My eyes widened, then, slowly, they turned to the tall man.

"Because even they saw who they thought was Jesus die on the cross."

"If what they had seen was the product of Allah's planning or trickery to confound the unbelievers, he confounded them as well, sparking into life the thing for which these 'superior' or 'uppermost' followers would die: the unforgivable sin of Christianity."

The words would never have breached my lips, but my mind was now seeing Allah as the founder of the forbidden faith.

Could Allah be a deceiver, even a liar?

Would he trick those he had declared superior, to lie and say they would be uppermost, only to kick them into the unforgivable sin?

"These superior men," he continued, "didn't come to the conclusion that someone had stolen Jesus' body, or that He'd somehow survived crucifixion and had just walked off somewhere—that's too stupid a conclusion for those named 'superior' by a god. Nor did these uppermost followers steal the body and then go off to lie and preach polytheism in contrast to the faith they were said to be upholding—such is not an 'uppermost' thing to do. Rather, they saw Him die and later found the tomb empty and, like you, were visited by the risen Jesus Himself."

We had been looking at many historical texts, most of which had no Islamic or Christian bend, and it appeared that all accounts of the apostles had them dying for the Christian faith.

"Christianity holds that Jesus is God, as its text demonstrates His claiming to be. In death, He took the punishment for our sins, satisfying the wrath we deserve, and in raising from the dead—as Christian texts demonstrate Him claiming He would do—He fulfills His claim, defeats Death forever, and offers us salvation. History shows us these men who died believing and defending this: the death, deity, and resurrection of Jesus. Now," he said, "if they were willing to die preaching and believing this, was it because they were deceived by Allah, or was Jesus so incompetent a prophet that He could not manage to convince His followers that He, though miraculous, was not God, and so sabotage His entire mission and message?"

The Qur'an elevates Isa and makes no claim that he in any way failed. So, the very fact that the disciples preached and died for an unforgivable sin, though Allah himself had called them blessed...this was mind-boggling.

"But," I mumbled, reading Qur'an 4:48 and 4:116 in my head, "Allah does not forgive those who take other gods before or beside him."

"Except in Qur'an 4:153," he added, as if he were reading the same mental text as I.

"What?"

I hadn't yet gotten to that verse in my head.

"Allah says he forgave those who worshiped the golden calf: the god the Israelites took in the time of Moses."

Gripping my head, I let out a moan—the contradictions were piling! And as the hours continued to mount, so too did my frustrations. We had been exclusively scouring the Qur'an; yet, for every challenge I raised for the man's Christian faith, he was answering me using *my* faith's book! And that very book, which had once been called noble and clear, was looking more and more like an ignoble book of confusion!

Onward still ticked the hours, carrying us well past midnight, at which point the tall man floated a simple question.

"What is meant by 'the Word of God,' as stated in the Qur'an?"

"Isa," I replied.

Flipping through the Qur'an, we read together Qur'an 3:45.

""O Mary, indeed Allah gives you good tidings of a Word from him, whose name will be the Messiah, Jesus, the son of Mary.""

"Then again in Qur'an 4:171," he said, turning to that page: "'The Messiah, Jesus, the son of Mary, was but a messenger of Allah and his Word.' Qur'an 3:39 talks of John the Baptist, who comes as a confirmer of 'a Word from God,' and Qur'an 19:34 calls Jesus a 'Saying of Truth.' We see that the Qur'an clearly puts forth this point of Jesus being called *the* Word. Do you agree?"

"Yes," I replied—there had never been any contesting this; as he'd stated, the Qur'an was clear on this point.

"Now," he continued, "if I speak, my words represent who I am; they are a manifestation of my being. Do you agree?"

"I agree."

"If you speak, then, your words are a representation of who you are—correct?"

"Yes."

"If, then, God speaks, His Word is a representation of who He is—and God's Word is perfect; it's holy. Do you agree?"

I nodded.

"So," he said, "God's Word is perfect; it is a representation of who He is; and the Word of God, according to the Qur'an, is Isa, making Him a direct representation of the image of God and perfect."

I could feel a heavy rain pouring over me; it but pooled on the surface, growing in breadth and weight over a field of stone.

"God is complete; His word must support that truth. God is sinless, perfect—so too must be His Word."

We stared at one another blankly for a moment; then, he reached beside him, opened a drawer and pulled out a book: a Bible.

He might as well have drawn a gun.

"NO! NO!" I screamed, leaping from my chair and pointing as if at a vicious, venomous serpent. "That book will make you *crazy*! It's corrupted! No good can come of it! Put it away, *NOW*!"

"Please," he said, very calmly; he hadn't even flinched at my outburst, "sit down; this book is very important to our discussion."

"HOW?" I yelled, backing further away. "You Christians are *deceived* by these corrupted *lies*! Everything in that book has been blackened—what truth can we find in there?"

"In this book are the revelations the Qur'an states were given to Moses, David, and Isa: the Torah, the Psalms, and the Injil. They will help us better understand Jesus."

"NO!" my cries were growing more violent; my fear was skyrocketing, and my heart was so frantic and out of sorts that it seemed to be dashing to and fro, thumping all over my body. "That is *NOT* the Injil—there is *one* Injil, and you Christians have *four*!"

"The four Gospels," he said, his tone and demeanor as calm as ever, "can be likened to biographies of Jesus, each composed by a different, first-hand biographer, who recorded Jesus' message. If, according to the Qur'an, Jesus spoke the Injil He was given, these accounts will demonstrate what was in that revelation from Allah."

"That book," I growled, "is no more than a novel—a work of fiction. And it's *dangerous*! The corruption it contains sends people to *hell*!"

"You have been told this book is corrupted."

"IT IS!"

"How did it come to be so?"

"Altered by the faithless, those in opposition to Allah—those who wished to follow their own way, take their own gods over the one true god! They bent the words of the most high to be what they wanted those words to be!"

"What about the Qur'an? Has it too been corrupted by liars and faithless men?"

"NOT AT ALL!" The fire from my enraged roar could have set ablaze a green forest in the midst of a monsoon. "Allah defends his words! He has guarded this revelation! It is today as it was when Muhammad received it! Perfectly preserved!"

"Allah defends his words, you say; and Allah gave to Moses the Torah, to David the Psalms, and to Jesus the Gospel. And he defends his words, you say?"

"Yes!"

"Look here." He turned to Qur'an 6:34. "'There is none that can alter the words and decrees of Allah.' Now, later in verse 116: 'None can change his words.' We see the same again in Qur'an 18:27. And in Qur'an 10:64, we read, 'No change can there be in the words of Allah.'"

Snapping together the covers of the book, he looked me dead in the eye.

"Qur'an 2:87 and 3:3 tell us how Allah sent down the law, the Torah, to Moses; Qur'an 4:163—David receives the Psalms; then, Qur'an 57:27: 'Allah sent after them Jesus the son of Mary, and bestowed on Him the Gospel.'"

"So, *what*?" I barked.

"Qur'an 5:48: 'To the people of the Gospel, Allah sent the Scripture of truth, confirming the Scripture that came before it, and guarding it in safety.' If Allah said he was guarding the Scripture—the Gospel he'd given to Jesus, which confirmed all that had come before it in the Torah and the Psalms—how could any man have corrupted it?"

My blood ran cold.

"Can Allah protect his words, or not?"

His speech was sharp and stern, and much like the careful removing of a deeply imbedded splinter.

"And," he continued, "if he can't, how do we know he can't also prevent the Qur'an from being corrupted?"

All the air in the room seemed to have dissipated into nothingness; my body slid slowly to the floor, petrified, enraged, perplexed, and bemused, grasping for something, anything—life was leaving me, it seemed; I was exposed, naked, trapped in the dark, cold and alone, my life's raft punctured and sinking beneath the waves.

Just then, a tender hand coiled about my arm, tightening ever so carefully; and, slowly, I began to rise from the sea of despondency and was guided back to my seat.

The tall man set aside the Qur'an.

Placing his palm atop his Bible, he said, "What we have in here are the words as confirmed by documents still in our possession that long predate Muhammad, the prophet in whose revelation is found affirmation that the word which came before him could *not* be corrupted." Leaning forward, he gently captured my gaze in his and said, "We've been talking about Isa, Jesus, the Word of God; let's test that which is said about Him."

Mere moments ago, as it had been all my life, even touching this book had been viewed as a certain impossibility; but this aching for truth, this need for reason and understanding, forbade me from covering my eyes to the vast and twisted field of contradiction and emptiness the Qur'an was revealing itself to be.

My eyes widened and my heartbeat hastened as he peeled the cover of his Bible and handed it to me, saying as he placed his finger at the top of the page, "Read the first verse, here."

Taking a deep breath, I slowly, carefully read my first words from the Bible, in a book called the "Gospel According to John."

"In the beginning was the Word, and the Word was with God, and the Word was God."

My gaze lifted slowly from the page and locked onto the tall man from beneath a deeply furrowed brow.

"This book speaks of the Word of God?"

How amazing! The Bible contained a truth from the Qur'an I had known since my youth! Maybe it did have something to teach me, after all.

"If God speaks," said the tall man, "His Word represents who He is—and who He is..."

"Isa?"

It made perfect sense—corruption may be deceitful, but at its core it is senseless.

"We've seen that the Qur'an speaks very highly of Jesus; this," he said, tapping the Bible; "this is a book *about* Jesus. It recounts His whole story, from the very first pages to the very last."

"But it says the Word *is* God! How can Isa be both Isa and God?"

"Just as the eyes are two organs but one vision," he explained, "so too can the Father and Son be seen as two persons in one being. And, through Jesus, the Word of God, which came down to us with the Good News, we can come to know God and have a personal relationship with Him!"

"A *personal* relationship?"

How strange a concept, for Allah was far above such things.

"Yes! He is our heavenly Father! And to those who receive Jesus and believe on His name, this beloved, heavenly Father gives us the right to be called His children!"

"A father?"

The Qur'an was clear that Allah was no father and has no children.

"Yes! And through Jesus, we come to learn of His great love and mercy and grace, sending His Son to die for sinners!"

"We can *know* God?"

"There are two ways that I can come to know you," he said: "by your words and by your deeds. Read on through verse 18."

Doing so, I came to verse 14: "And the Word became flesh and dwelt among us, and we have seen His glory, glory as of the only Son from the Father, full of grace and truth."

"Wow!" I exclaimed, taking in all I had read. "There it is!"

All at once, that heavy rain that had been pooling atop the rock began to sink, seeping into the cracks of the stone that had grown long and wide with every realization that the Qur'an might not have been so reliable a text, after all. And we read further and deeper, supping revelation after revelation, while I came to see the reality of Jesus and His mighty work to save us from our sins.

"For God so loved the world," I read with infant eyes, "that He gave His only Son, that whoever believes in Him should not perish, but have eternal life."

I had ever viewed that the Christian story of Jesus, being God and coming to earth, was so humiliating a thing to say about one's divine deity—and, as it turned out, I was right! God—yes, God Himself—in such a great contrast to the god I had ever served, humbled Himself, left His throne of glory, took on filthy flesh...all this out of love! This was not a distant judge to be appeased, who could cast me into hell no matter how my good deeds might outweigh my bad—this is a loving Father! A blessed friend sent to die in my place!

Deeper and deeper we dove, my heart growing hungrier and hungrier; for here were words of power, soul-touching passages that were spoken, it seemed, for me, and only for me—these words were cutting through me like a double-edged sword; nothing could stand against its power.

Then, we came to John 14:6.

"Jesus said to Thomas, 'I am the way, and the truth, and the life. No one comes to the Father except through me.'"

At that moment, the tall man looked at me and said, "Jesus came to you in a dream. He loves you, more than the mind could ever fathom. How rare it is for Him to appear like this to someone; but His words are clear: Come to Me and find the truth. *He* is the truth, and He's asking you to come to Him, right now. Will you repent and come to Jesus?"

And, so, all we had been studying came to a crescendo—the Qur'an had crumbled to dust beneath the weight of its own feeble structure and foundation, pulverized by more contradictions and incoherencies than this narrative can contain, razed by the truth that now captivated me.

Reflecting on the past week, I could feel the power of God's love surging through me, something Allah had never even offered, much less bestowed. His words, beckoning me to join Him, were as clear as a crystal pool, and all the more pure.

How could I resist Him any longer?

Jesus had walked with me in love and grace, from Saudi Arabia to New Zealand—here, to the very ends of the earth! He'd led me to this pastor, who had patiently explained the Good News to me, spending days and hour upon compounded hour, diligently and carefully building a foundation of trust, without which nothing our time had produced would have been able to stand.

This was no accident.

When a blind man receives his sight, sees at last the color of darkness, and knows, surer than the heart that beats within him, that he no longer dwells within that darkness.

There was nothing else to do, no other way to go.

Here was truth.

I could not reject it.

Not for another second.

Falling to me knees, I called out to the heavens, "Oh, Father! You are my Father, my God! By the name of Your Son, Jesus the Christ, I call to You! He is my mediator, my propitiation—I beg You, forgive me of my wretched sin! Jesus, You are Lord! I believe You are God, my Savior! Take me as Your servant forever! Bless Your holy name!"

I had never seen such rejoicing—even at the grandest Saudi wedding feast, attended by hundreds upon hundreds of revelers, even on the tragic day of 9/11, sung by thousands upon thousands of bullets fired into the sky; even these could not compare in jubilation or volume to the "HALLELUJAHS!" ringing from the souls of three people in a small house in New Zealand. There was not a fiber in my body that wanted the celebration to cease—I wished to go on screaming praises to God, my new Father, until the sun arose, then to cheer and dance as it climbed to its peak, then to stand on the rooftops and shout of the glorious work Christ had done in me, until the sun fell behind the horizon, and then to do it all over again! But sleep I did, eventually; and there, lying atop the bed, nuzzled comfortably beneath the covers, shades drawn, windows opened, and door unlocked and unblocked, I sighed a sigh of peace, while tears streamed down my face, and my soul embraced my Jesus, enraptured, in love, and in desperate, fervent gratitude.

While the journey had stretched me intellectually, had tested the vast recesses of my knowledge of Islam as engraved in me by my culture, my environment, my study, and my religion, my mind had not been changed or renewed by an intellectual process; rather, God had used this time to show me His great love through a humble, patient pastor, who'd fed this infant naught but milk: the simple, yet powerfully nourishing, truths of the Gospel. And using this did God reach down and lift the veil of darkness from my eyes—a supernatural, revelational experience, of which I could and can offer no explanation other than this: that I was lost, but am now found; I was blind, and now I see; I was fumbling about in the dark, peering at shadows I thought I knew well, until a light was suddenly turned on, and I saw clearly all that was before me. All things had been made new, and my life started afresh. Truly I am born again, and I say simply that I see now as absolutely true what I once knew beyond a shadow of a doubt to be false. In the gentle touch of Jesus, there can be no uncertainty. I am His, as He is mine, now and forevermore.

My last thought of the night was a marveling at how hard and blind I must have been for so simple a truth as the Gospel of Jesus Christ to have been so hard for me to see and accept. Dead was I, and as such was I unaware of my need for life. Now, overflowing with life abundant, I was completely and blissfully unaware of the cost my faith in Jesus would require.

***

Morning came all too soon, bringing with it a plane readying to depart for Saudi Arabia—but I was already flying high on the wings of Christ's salvation, being carried to a new destination, leaving the old world behind, while I soared safely in the arms of my beloved God, high above the desert of my past. There was not a molecule in my body that did not feel brand new, not a color painted into the fabric of this world that was not bursting with life, making all my memories appear to have been surrounded by dull, muted hues. The sound of the birds was an angelic chorus; the gentle breeze was a divine embrace. I set my face before the morning rays peeking over the distant hills and felt a heavenly kiss upon my cheek, and when I emerged into the unveiled world, there to sink my feet into the dew-sprinkled grass, there fell from the cloudless sky above a cleansing rain, washing over me like a mighty waterfall, ripping the last of darkness' scales from my eyes and casting into the dust every chain binding me to this temporary realm. I saw in every detail the works of the hands of the Most High, His precious creation; and for it all was blossomed in me a love I knew then as I know now will take an eternity to fully satisfy and quench my overabundant desire for it. How different were the sights, smells, and sounds of my world— every rock bore the signature of Jesus, every blade of grass, every wisp of wind, every rush of warmth, every mighty mountain and tiny anthill; and in every passerby I beheld the very likeness of God, whereupon also rested a downpour of His endless, unconditional love. Strange, thought I, as I watched these people pass, one after the other, going here and there, driven by whatever care the day had set within them; strange, thought I, how even to these strangers, whose names I may never know, whose voices I may never hear, whose hearts may to me be never opened—strange how I feel so desperate a love for them, for these handcrafted creatures like me, who, like me, are so beloved to have the one true God of all the earth, cosmos, and beyond step down from glory into the filthy flesh we have made our own, and here, in our place, suffer all that was ours to bear, and die that we might live! And how strange, thought I still, that anyone could have lived as I had done beneath that downpour of love from above: as one hiding under an umbrella.

It was then, amid my wide-eyed marveling, that a hand fell upon my shoulder.

"Are you ready, Ahmed?"

My teary eyes turned to see the tall man standing beside me. A single nod answered his question about going to the airport—a resounding and all-out triumphant "YES!" bellowed from within my new heart of flesh answered his question about everything else.

He and I drove to the airport, feeding off the joy radiating between the both of us; and when at last we had arrived, gathered my bags, and exchanged tearful goodbyes, the tall man reached into his pocket and extracted a parting gift. No bigger than the size of my hand, it was a little book with a beautiful, green leather jacket, upon which in gold had been written in Arabic, "The Book of Life."

"It's a pocket New Testament," he said, as I turned about the precious gift in my hands. Then, firmly grasping my arm, he looked me dead in the eye and said, "I will pray for you, brother; but this book," he added, tapping the gift, "this book will guide you."

"Oh, yes!" I cried aloud, throwing my arms around him. "This is God's Word! It will surely guide me! Thank you! Praise be to God! Thank you!"

I practically skipped through the airport to my gate; a review of the security footage might even contain a heel-click or two as I danced through the crowds. There was in me life at last! What had been a pile of dead bones had been remade, given new flesh—I was reborn! And in my hands was the Word of God, my Jesus' red letters, a book that was living and active, just as I had now become.

Presenting my ticket, the attendant uttered a robotic, "Enjoy your flight," to which I ebulliently replied in my yet broken English, "God is with me, and Jesus loves us both!"

Appearing as though my words had startled her from a deep sleep, the attendant, as well as those behind me, shot me a most perplexed look.

Mine was not a candle on a mantelpiece; it was a flamethrower on a skyscraper. And, bags in hand, I pranced along the bridge toward the plane.

The flight from New Zealand to Saudi Arabia, from takeoff to landing, took roughly ten seconds; I'm told it lasted nearly a whole day for everyone else. And in that relatively brief trip, all I could do was think about how wonderful it was going to be to pour over every single word in my New Testament. But I dared not pull it out just yet, as many Saudi nationals were also on the flight, and I was sure they would be, at the very least, displeased to see such a book. And, so, I contented myself with the anticipation of reading and re-reading and memorizing the magnificent words of life, and to reciting over and over the words I had already learned with the tall man.

However, though God had rescued my soul from the fire, and there was bursting in me life and hope and joy indescribable, I had absolutely no concept of just how powerful this Word really is, nor just how costly it would prove to be.

10

A Storm Before the Calm

WHEN at last my foot touched down again on Saudi Arabian soil, there was burning in me a fire so intense and glowing in me a light so brilliant, pure, and bright that it's a wonder the sun itself didn't take a day off. However, gazing down the long hallway to customs, my eyes perceived a great darkness. Home didn't look the same anymore. Light was in me, and I knew it would shine in this darkness and be not overcome—but this darkness would not go down without a fight.

Before leaving New Zealand, the tall man had pointed me toward the words of Jesus, as recounted in the Gospel according to Matthew.

"Ahmed," he said gravely. "I don't need to tell you about the position your native government takes on Christianity. By accepting the yoke of Jesus, you have a target now on your back. Your own people will hate you for this."

"Yes," I replied, pausing to consider—for the first time, surprisingly—the great sacrifice that would be required for the truth.

"Look here at what Jesus says; Matthew 10:37: 'Whoever loves father or mother more than me is not worthy of me.' I'm sure you know what this will mean to your family, especially to someone as revered and elevated as your father."

I said nothing while the words of Christ sank slowly beneath the surface.

"Your home is no longer a safe place, Ahmed," he continued. "Matthew 10:6: 'Behold, I am sending you out as sheep in the midst of wolves, so be wise as serpents and innocent as doves.'"

My every step echoed, "Be wise."

I had nearly reached customs.

As the tall man's warning danced about in my mind, *do-si-do-ing* with the knowledge that the discovery of a Bible could lead to arrest and severe punishment, even death, I carefully and discreetly slipped the pocket New Testament into the thick pages of one of my English books, then stacked my textbooks in such a way that they were tightly condensed together, virtually eliminating the evidence of the book within a book.

The customs agent and I exchanged greetings.

He then ordered me to hand over my bags.

Every ounce of my strength and mental ability was dedicated to making me appear as unassuming as possible: keep eye contact, but not too much or too little; relax the shoulders; don't breathe any faster than five seconds per breath; maintain steady hands and subtly dry your palms on your garment; try to distribute focus evenly between your bags and your surroundings; be careful not to let them see you watching them work, and don't let your eye betray the English book!

As the seconds ticked into minutes, I could feel beads of sweat forming along my back, and I carefully attempted to raise my chest and arch my spine, in as tactful a manner as I could manage, hoping the passing air would dry them before they congregated to form a physical manifestation of nervousness down the length of my garment.

One by one, he carefully and intently inspected every item, turning this and that over and over through his gloved hands, checking all sides, holding things up to the light, shaking for sounds, feeling textures, thumbing, scratching, picking, pulling, twisting, shuffling, sniffing—the customs agent I'd been assigned must have been part human, part bloodhound!

Then he got to the books.

All at once, my eyes became fixed on my bag, my shoulders tensed, my breathing hastened, my hands trembled and rained with sweat; and no matter how much I tried to help it, I could not look away from the English book.

His fingers tracked the compacted line of spines.

My eyes, wanting to squeeze themselves shut, widened all the more.

He pulled the first book away from the others and shined a tiny flashlight into the gap.

My cheeks felt like the surface of the sun, and I couldn't recall when I'd taken my last breath.

He peeled back another book and shined the flashlight.

My teeth nearly bit right through my bottom lip.

Just then, his hands grabbed the English book.

My heart screeched to a halt, and immediately I closed my eyes and prayed.

"My God!" I cried in my heart. "God of all truth! Come quickly to my aid! Turn away unfriendly eyes from my concealed condemnation!"

When I opened my eyes again, I saw the agent staring at me.

My eyes bored deeply into his.

"So," he said, his voice like the yawn of a lion.

This is it...here it comes.

"You're a medical student?"

I looked back at my bag; his hand was now on one of my medical textbooks.

"Yes!" I replied, heaving an exhale that surely left my lips at thirty miles per hour. "I'm in my first year!"

"Very interesting! What sort of things have you been learning?"

"Well," I said, gasping as if I'd just swam the length of the Pacific, "I've just had a thorough lesson on myocardial infarctions!"

"On *what*?"

"Heart attacks."

We exchanged farewell pleasantries, and I gathered my bags and went on my way, praising God for keeping my secret hidden, and asking Him to shower a blessing upon the agent and to save him.

***

Jesus was now my life, and the only life I wanted, and wanted more than anything. It's no surprise, therefore, that what had once been my routine was drastically altered. Day by day, nothing about my life in Mecca was the same. The upside down, shady, and dark version of Jesus that I had been fed when He was called Isa had been replaced with someone I could know and love, someone who'd first known and loved me! The words of the Qur'an had been revealed for what they are: a twisted lie, in stark contrast to the truth that had been revealed to me in the Bible. The book I'd once called noble and sacred would never be the same in my eyes, nor would it ever sink through my ears and meet anything but intense scrutiny, a fiery testing by the words of the Bible, from which it never emerged as anything but a pile of ashes.

To keep a low profile among the wolves, I outwardly participated in the daily life of a Muslim: I bowed at each call to prayer, but my words of praise and worship now went up to my heavenly Father; I attended the mosque, but I tested against the Word of God all the teachings of the Imam (an Islamic pastor, of sorts). Even my studies were affected, as studying the Bible took precedent over everything else. I was now back in medical school, toiling to memorize all the necessary terms and procedures, doing so in English; but there were words sweeter than honey that I craved daily to memorize! When I was supposed to be meditating on things of medicine, I was meditating on the things of Christ. His words drew me in, and in them I found joy, for I was like a dying man in the desert, desperately thirsty, who had just discovered a well overflowing with the most delicious, refreshing water!

With God's help, I managed to allot just enough focus and energy to keep up with my education, even as the work increased and the days became busier. Every morning I would rise early to study the New Testament, after which I would carefully hide the tiny book in my desk drawer, or under my pillow. After school, I would dig it out of its hiding spot and feed some more, tattooing verse after verse into my memory, for I wanted to be in God's Word even when I didn't have a physical book to read. And so went my daily routine for much of the semester, yielding abundant fruit and renewing me each and every day.

One afternoon, having returned home from a major exam, I climbed the stairs to my room to change clothes. Shutting the door behind me, I set my bag down upon the bed, glad the day was over and more than ready for my next serving of the Word. I had only just started to remove my lab coat when the door was suddenly blown off its hinges, and into the room charged several of my brothers. Before I could turn to see what had happened, something like a freight train had crashed into my spine, and I was thrown violently to the ground, as if I were an intruder in my own room. All the air had been expelled from my lungs, and every time I gasped to restore my breathing, a fist or a foot would come flying into my body to cast it out again. Vicious blows rained down upon me from all sides, slamming into ribs, thrashing over my face, and stomping until my flesh felt like one gigantic bruise.

My brothers said nothing as they beat me, refusing to answer my pleas for mercy, or tell me what I had done to offend them.

When at last their fists had ceased to fly, they dragged me from my room on the second floor of our beautiful home to a secure tent just outside; they made sure not to hurt their backs lugging my thrashing body down the stairs—I was forced to take the length of them all at once with a hurling start.

The tent that would serve as my prison was a modern Arabian tent, very much unlike those used for camping. It was like a guesthouse, with climate control, a bathroom, concrete walls, and a fireplace—not exactly the harshest of prisons, but it was an independent structure, and as such the best holding tank available at the moment.

Without a word, my brothers flung me inside and locked the door from without by a padlock contraption they'd installed before my return.

As the pain throbbed throughout my body, I sunk slowly into my thoughts, where I settled into a deep pool of anxiety and worry—I hadn't yet reached Philippians 4 of the New Testament, in which Paul instructs us not to worry.

I sat there for the remainder of the day, and well into the next, completely unaware of what could have led to all of this.

About midday, our Filipina housemaid entered to give me a hot meal.

"Please," I begged, hobbling my aching body near to her, "what have I done? Why has this happened?"

But she said nothing.

Her eyes to the ground, she set out my meal, then turned and walked away, locking the door before returning to the house.

Once a day she would come to give me a meal, and each time I would beseech her tell me what I had done.

Finally, when the hurt of her silence could be born no longer, I gently touched her arm as she turned to leave; and with my heart bleeding, said, "Do you no longer know me? Was it not you who brought me up from before I could speak, even before I could crawl?"

She remained turned away, her eyes to the floor.

"You used to cradle me in your arms when I was afraid; when I was hurt, you'd comfort me and tend to my wounds. Was it not your name I'd learned before all others'?" Tremors rippled through her arm, against my fingertips. "Am I now a stranger to you? Why will you not answer me?"

Slowly, she turned toward me, but she would not look up.

Following a silent deep breath, she parted her lips and spoke very cautiously with the voice of a mouse.

"Your mother's servant had been sent to clean your room—she found an odd book inside."

My heart fell through my chest to the floor.

"Thinking it looked interesting, she picked it up...but when she realized what she'd found, she rushed to give it to your mother."

I was in shock. The days leading up to my exam had been rather stressful and hectic, and on that day I had been in such a rush to get out the door that I must have neglected to hide my New Testament after my morning study.

"Your mother was in an uproar," she continued, her tone very grave. "The whole house was filled with her screams."

Amid my whirling mind, I could do nothing but pray, repeating over and over, "God, help me. God, help me."

"She called an emergency meeting with the servants, and we were questioned about the book. But we all denied knowledge of it; we know such books are forbidden."

"God, please," I begged, "let this not be happening!"

"When she realized the book belonged to you, she called your brothers together and ordered them to beat you and place you under house arrest."

Quietly clearing her throat, my beloved housemaid lifted her enormous, frightened eyes into mine.

"Your father is on his way," she whispered, then, looking as though she might burst into tears, she whipped around and disappeared through the door.

Given the details of her story, I could fully picture the scene she had described, and just how panicked and chaotic the family had to have been. But the real kicker was my father.

He had been out of town, his trip involving rather serious religious duties. Nothing but the worst circumstance imaginable could have snatched him away from such an errand—I wonder if even my death would have compelled him to make the long trip home. A Bible being found in the house of a well-known and immensely respected Islamic scholar is a very serious situation, one no collection of the harshest, most intense words can overstate.

My father would be arriving soon.

Fear coiled its mangled hand tightly around my body, as I sat staring at the door, the days passing like seconds.

Then, the nob began to turn.

***

Few things in life can compare to the sensation of having the barrel of a fully-loaded AK-47 rifle pressed violently against your forehead. For days, my body had bellowed tormented screams from the grisly bruises littering my beaten body; the hard ground in which I knelt gnawed mercilessly at the bones in my knees; and fear, like a shrieking, spectral choir, echoed its all-consuming poison through my veins and violently trembling frame. Yet, even with the chaotic cacophony of bruised body, gnawed knees, tumultuous terror, and a cold steel rod boring angrily into my skin, driving right between my eyes with so vicious a pursuit that it seemed only moments away from puncturing straight through to my skull—even with all these clanging together in what should have been a deafening death knell, I could hear only the rubbing of a rage-filled finger against a pristine, polished trigger, and the heavy snarls rumbling from the face behind that finger: my father's.

Many times had I trembled before this mighty Meccan Mufti, but the look on his face this day was one like I had never seen in all my life. Not even in those times as a boy when I had greatly offended him had I seen this wild, maniacal look of hatred—those times when he would loom over me, his voice booming like thunder, and repeatedly strike the palm of my hand with a round, wooden rod, pouring into my soul more terror than the arduous pain could overwhelm until the next day. I was, right now, in his eye, like a swine that has tracked filth through his house and gobbled up his sacred treasures. Whatever bond beyond blood that had tied me to this man had now been permanently severed. I was no longer his son; I was his despised and mortal enemy.

There was no turning back now. Even if I survived this moment, I knew my life would instantly become even more unfamiliar than I had already anticipated it would be. Call me crazy, but even though I knew full-well the cost, the reality of being forsaken by my own father and divorced from my own family—my mother, brothers, and all those whom I love dearly—seemed too extreme to come true, to actually happen to me. I had been called to forsake father and mother and this temporary family of mine, and take up a cross on a new road; only, they'd beaten me to the punch, casting me from their bosom and hurling me onto a road unknown with a burden I knew not if I could bear.

From this day forward, I would be a stranger in a strange land—if, that is, this Muslim son, now declared dead by his kin, would be found alive tomorrow.

His wide eyes gazing eagerly over the body of the rifle, my father parted his snarling lips.

"Do you think you can shame me in front of our family?" he growled with a bone-shaking voice. "Do you think you can shame me in front of our *tribe*?" His booming speech was gaining momentum, readying for an eruption. "You would shame me in front of the whole Muslim nation?" Then, after several rumbling, hastening breaths, sucked and spewed through his tightly clenched, gnashing jaws, he roared, "I WILL NOT ALLOW IT!"

As his words echoed about the space, he whipped out my pocket New Testament and hurled it onto the ground before me. I can still hear the *THUD* of that precious Book of Life hitting the floor and see the dust from the sand rising about it like a miniature explosion.

The fury he had expelled over me began to draw inward, where it churned and readied itself for a second outburst.

"If you do not recant," he growled in a sharp whisper, like the distant resonance of an approaching, violent storm, "and *BURN* this evil book," his heavy breathing suddenly stopped, his wild eyes glowed with the rage of a dark hatred, and he jammed the gun barrel even more viciously into my forehead, "I will unload this *entire* clip into your WRETCHED SKULL!"

While his words were yet ringing in my ears, I heard his finger rub against the trembling trigger; then came the all-too familiar *click* of the gun's safety being released.

Death lurked but a moment away; sweat rained off of me into large pools mixed with the blood from my forehead.

"DO YOU RECANT?" he screamed with a voice that sounded like the very foundations of the earth splitting in two.

Shaking like a leaf in a whirlwind, I knew he would kill me in the next instant; but I could not betray my God!

Faster than the bullet waiting to meet my brain could have flown, Matthew 10:16 popped into view; and all at once I blurted out, "I'M A MUSLIM!"

There could not have been a truer statement. The word Muslim means, "Submitted to God;" and, out of everyone in the room, I knew only I was submitted to the one true God.

It was as wise a phrasing of the truth as could have been spoken, but not of my conjuring.

After a brief hesitation, my father lowered his rifle. Then, turning a disgusted look toward the book, he spat upon it and barked, "*Burn* this abomination!"

Jesus said in Luke 21:33 that "Heaven and earth will pass away, but My words will not pass away." This book, though I loved it dearly—it was of earth, just paper and ink. The words contained within, they belonged to Jesus; and no fire of earth could touch them.

Without hesitation, I sprang to my feet and tossed the book into the fireplace and watched the flames slowly devour it.

Once my father was satisfied that it had been completely consumed, he and my brothers promptly left, locking the door on their way out.

***

The days crawled by, dragging with them Eid al-Adha, the Festival of Sacrifice. From my confinement, I could hear the shouts of celebration and revelry slipping through the walls of the tent. While everyone was praising Allah for his provision to Abraham, I was crouched in a corner viewing the story of the festival in a different way.

Eid al-Adha celebrates the merciful outcome of a tale told in Qur'an 37, wherein Allah commands Abraham to offer his son as a sacrifice to God; this tale is also told in the Bible in Genesis 22, with, however, some key differences, namely the son demanded. In the Qur'an, Allah requires Ishmael; in the Bible, God requires Isaac—a very important divergence separating Muslims and Jews, as it pertains to the lineage of God's chosen people.

Abraham's faith is greatly tested by God's command. Ultimately, he places his trust in the Lord and carries his son to the alter; but just as he is about to strike him dead, God calls from heaven, ordering him to stop, at which point God provides a ram to be sacrificed in the boy's place. Abraham showed he was willing even to give his own son to die, and God showed His mercy by providing the sacrifice of atonement He Himself had demanded.

This had ever been an inspiring story, one bidding reverence, devotion, and obedience to Allah. And though I had yet to scour the Old Testament version, the seed of the revelation of Christ had already been implanted in me, and by the words of John 3:16 was it watered: "For God so loved the world that He gave His only begotten Son."

No more was this festival a day to celebrate the provision of a ram, to slaughter an animal, and divide it three ways between ourselves, our family, and the poor; rather, this had now become a day to recognize how God had spared Abraham's son, but had not spared His own. God had given His own Son, Jesus Christ, as the sacrifice His holiness demands of us, because of our unholy sin. And when His hand was raised to deliver the deathblow, He did not hold back or provide a substitute; and Jesus took that blow willingly. And this is not a sacrifice just for ourselves, our family, and the needy— as Jesus said in Luke 22:19, "'This is my body, which is given for you,'" and in the very next verse, "'This cup that is poured out for you is the new covenant in my blood.'"

Christ is the lamb God provided, and His sacrifice is for all, freely given for the forgiveness of sins as a gift of mercy and grace for those who would believe.

What greater love than this can be found? That God would offer His Son for a wretched people, and that His Son would lay down His life willingly and take the blow that should be ours to take? There, in that tent, I wept for gratitude of so overwhelming a love; but I shed also bitter tears for the man I called father here on earth. Where my heavenly Father had given His Son to die to save me, my earthly father was presently contemplating giving me up to die to save himself, for to have a Christian son would mean for him to lose everything he held dear.

What favor I had sought to gain in the eyes of my father via my devotion to Islam, memorizing the Qur'an, and heart for jihad—all these things had come to nothing; winning his favor was now forever impossible. But I had gained an everlasting Father, one whose favor I had done nothing to win, but had now been granted by the blood of Christ, in whom I was now alive.

But the disentangling of one from this world is a painful process; I'd bound myself in ponderous chains saturated in super glue, which Jesus was now slowly peeling away from me. Though it was all for my good, the fear to which I yet clung blinded me all the more as the days progressed into weeks, and I became deathly starved for the Word of God, until I was teetering on the brink of hopelessness. And the lower I sank, the more I allowed fear and anxiety to poison my soul, and the darker my days became.

"Father!" I cried, as the void closed in around me. "Intervene! Rescue me! Oh, Father—hear me! I beg You, take away my fear! Rescue me!"

11

Outcast

SOMEWHERE above my head, I could hear two men engaged in a discussion. Their voices were not heated, nor where they somber; but the weight contained within them could not be denied, nor could the chill that rained over me, like sleet spilling over their lips, be ignored. My body throbbed, but it would not move; and it was only after a great deal of struggle that I was able to open my eyes. Upon doing so, I gazed up at the figure of my father, looming over me, his feet right beside my head. He was holding his AK-47 rifle in one hand and talking to someone on my other side. Turning my eyes that way, I saw a police officer, a man I found rather familiar, but could not place where exactly I'd seen him. They spoke gravely but casually, and often one of their hands would extend downward toward me.

I could not sit upright; a great spike seemed to impale me to the ground. And as I struggled, the words of the conversation became clearer, and I recognized the story of Noah's son, as told in Qur'an 11:41-47.

Different from the Bible's version, the Qur'an tells a story of an unnamed son who chooses not to enter the ark as the floodwaters rise around him.

"'O my son,'" my father quoted Noah, "'come aboard with us and be not with the disbelievers.'"

The police officer nodded and murmured knowingly.

"'There is no protector today from the decree of Allah!'" he thundered, his words landing over me like boulders tumbling from a fiery mountain.

Throwing my eyes downward, I discovered a mangled mass of something attached to my neck that I did not recognize. Great pools, like natural springs, vomited geysers of crimson; they spewed with my every pulse, saturating the horrifying scene before me, while a red mist sprinkled over me like the cloud at the base of a waterfall. And there beside my head, right next to my father's feet, was my little green Book of Life. It had been torn in two, with its pages buried in the grisly pool growing around me.

"But here lies my son," my father continued, motioning to me with his free hand, "who said, 'I will take refuge on a mountain to protect me from the water!' Just as the foolish son of Noah spoke, showing his rejection of Allah, so has my son rejected the one true god and all I have taught him since his youth!"

The officer pressed his lips together and shook his head.

"And, so, like that forsaken boy, this infidel has been swallowed by the waves, there to float among the drowned."

The talking above me suddenly stopped, and I looked up to see my father's frigid glare raining over me. Then, slowly placing the barrel of his rifle upon my forehead, I watched in terror as his finger slithered over the trigger and began to squeeze.

BANG

Shooting bolt upright from the floor, I watched as my father and the men of our family's tribe stormed into the tent.

Today, my fate would be decided.

As they spread out before me, with my father in the middle, I was overcome with a sense of certainty that this would be my last day on earth. Given what I had seen in my upbringing, I would either be dragged out into the street and shot, or handed over for beheading.

I was ordered to stand.

"You are not of this family," growled my father, speaking a paraphrased version of Allah's words regarding Noah's drowned son. "Your works are other than righteous, and I will not be counted among the ignorant to beg Allah for your life to be spared."

These words, which had once filled me with resolve against the unfaithful, now stuck icicles into my spine.

Wearing the face of one regarding a pile of human refuse, my father stepped forth and looked me dead in the eye.

His upper lip curled and quivered.

His teeth ground and scraped against one another.

A blazing inferno raged behind his eyes.

And with such resolve that there could be no doubt regarding the sincerity of his heart, he breathed this frigid fire: "You are not my son. You are a foul deed, a shame upon me and the whole tribe of Joktan; and so shall you be until the Day of Judgment."

"No, father," I begged.

Flames danced about his nostrils; he drew back slightly with a full breath.

Then, he spat in my face.

Before I could think, my brothers rushed forward, seized me by the arms; and as my broken heart bled, spilling such sorrow upon the ground that all the earth was made red, I was lifted into the air.

"Father, *please!*"

His eyes bore through the opposite wall, as I was marched through the door.

"*FATHER!*"

My scream still in my throat, I was thrown violently into the street.

"Go!" yelled one of my brothers. "Take your place among the dogs!"

When I crawled toward them, a fist struck me across the cheek.

"You're dead!" hollered another. "Go quickly to your grave!"

As my trembling body rose from the dirt, I caught sight of my mother standing nearby.

Her gaze passed right through me.

"Have you no love for me, mother?" I called from beneath my tears. "Has the place that was mine in your heart been forever destroyed?"

Her face was like stone, her eyes fixed; she would not have cried, even if she had wanted to, for all emotion, especially sorrow, is forbidden toward the apostate, even if it is one's own child.

Tearing at my heart, I wrenched myself away toward the road ahead, thereupon to wander, forsaken and disgraced, as one dead. The blood of my demise was to fall upon the earth through starvation or disease, or upon my own hands through crushing despair. And so I went, unable to look back, taking into the wide, desert unknown only the clothes I'd been wearing for weeks and the nothing in my pockets, utterly rejected and cast out by my entire family.

I never saw them again.

Cast in an instant from a life of inordinate wealth and into abject poverty, I roamed day after day between this abandoned shack and that one, taking up residence for the night in dark corners amid the snakes and scorpions, sharing the folds of my skin and the sweat-dampened ripples of my filthy, noisome clothes with the cockroaches that crawled all over me. Sleep was forbidden by the nibbling of a roach upon my belly, or the hissing of a snake slithering nearby, or the tickling sound of a scorpion scurrying under my legs.

I didn't care.

I just wanted to die.

From a young man of great honor, with a most prestigious Islamic family and impressive resume of achievements—how far I had fallen.

It may seem an easy thing for me to have feared that my suffering was directly related to Allah's disapproval with my decision to follow Christ; thus, turning me to believe I had been wrong about the deity of Jesus. But Allah, according to the fiction in which he exists, does not serve man; he would not stoop to acting on my behalf. If Allah had wanted to, as it were, give me what I deserve, that would not come until the Day of Judgment, and I should not expect a warning sign to turn me back to the truth, after I'd taken an idol to worship in his place. Such is unforgivable.

No, I never questioned my decision—how could I have done, when the words of Jesus, as recounted in Matthew 10, had just been proven true? "Do not think that I have come to bring peace to the earth," He said. "I have not come to bring peace, but a sword. For I have come to set a man against his father, and a daughter against her mother...And a person's own enemies will be those of his own household."

The choice to put my faith in and follow Jesus had been the sword that had divided my family; those I love, my own tribe and household, disavowed me as their enemy. And why? "If the world hates you," Jesus said in John 15:18, "know that it has hated me before it hated you."

These things I knew to be true; they were made manifest in my own life. But I was nonetheless shaken to my core, facing something I knew full well could happen, but could never quite have imagined happening to me. As one dead, my family had forever buried me into ignorance; yet, I mourned for those who had rejected me, as if I stood now at their graves.

As the days wore on, blending together night and day, the stupor of my shock and depression only grew; tangled thoughts twisted about my head; adrenaline pounded painfully through my heart, causing bouts of hyperventilation, most of which left me gasping on the floor, completely unable to breathe, while the shadows of the rotting coffins that were my shelters rippled and scurried, hissed and slithered: a dance of death, with me at its center. Often these bouts would leave me so numb and exhausted that I truly wondered if I had died.

But my flesh persisted, warring constantly with my will to be swallowed into the dirt through which I crawled. I fed off of refuse and madness, drank murky water and delirium, wondering if there was any hope at all to find aid in my homeland.

Then, with my physical desperation nearly at its peak, a light suddenly appeared, shining through the door on the other side of my coffin. Against my now vehement will to wait just a little longer for Death to arrive, my spirit screamed at my failing flesh to make it to that light, and I began to drag my decaying body across the roach-infested ground, lugging lifeless legs in my wake. Feeling as though I were towing a jumbo jet, I sunk my claws into the rotted earth, crushing roaches as I did so and scraping their carcasses along my belly. It may have taken hours, it may have taken days; I don't know—all I know is that I at last emerged into the sunlight, covered in my own filth, earth, and insect guts, where I collapsed to boil beneath the midday sun.

At that very moment, a car pulled off the road.

"Are you all right?" yelled a man, quickly rounding the front of his car.

A good look at me seemed to answer his question—even in the midst of this horrendous situation, I can be thankful for my decayed appearance and condition, for it spoke the words I had not the strength to lift.

Sprinting back to his car, the man soon returned with a shopping bag and a bottle of water. Hastily unscrewing the cap, he very carefully dribbled water into my mouth, before setting the bottle beside my head, stripping the filthy clothes from my body, and dressing me in the very clothes he was wearing. He then extracted from the bag some canned food and fed me a few bites.

"Keep the rest," he said, motioning to a whole bagful of canned food, as well as the water bottle. "Come," he continued, "let me give you a ride home. Where do you live?"

All at once I burst into tears.

"I have no home!" I cried.

And there I wept for quite some time, while the man remained by my side to comfort me.

When at last I had been composed, the man, wrapping me in a gaze of pity, extracted his wallet and gave me what money he had.

He said nothing more.

He simply climbed back into his car and drove away.

My strength slowly returning, I rose to my knees and watched as his car disappeared into the dust. Even now I don't wonder what one sees when one encounters an angel.

I eventually forced myself to my feet, at which time the garment the man had given me showed itself to be rather large; a tall man was he—it hung loosely, making me appear as a child in his father's robes. But I could not have cared less! God had refused my silent pleas for death and had sent a tenderhearted angel to help restore me! And all at once I was reminded of the love of God, and into my heart were placed words of the Old Testament, from Deuteronomy 31:6, which I'd not yet even read: "The Lord your God goes with you. He will not leave you or forsake you."

So humbled was I that I instantly fell on my face and worshiped Jesus for having delivered me from despair and given me hope, once again.

The thought, however, of what I was now to do suddenly entered my mind.

"Jesus," I prayed, "You have graciously spared my life, pulled me out of the darkness, and fed me with hope. Guide me now, I beg. If I am to live in poverty, homeless for the rest of my days, may I glorify You in my poverty. You say in Luke that 'Foxes have dens and birds have nests, but the Son of Man has no place to lay his head.' I ask only for my daily bread, and for Your hand to guide me."

When I had finished praying, I stood, taking up the water and bag of canned food, as well as the money I'd been given, which I paused to count that I might better plan for its use. As I did so, one of the banknotes worth 10 riyals slipped from my grasp; and when I had recovered it, my eyes fell upon the image printed on the back of the King Abdul Aziz Historical Center in Riyadh. All at once, the word "education" popped into my brain; and with a slap on my forehead, I suddenly remembered that I lived in the Kingdom of Oil, abundant in riches, which offered its citizens free room and board at public universities in the Gulf States, as well as a monthly stipend! Having come from wealth, there had never been a need to keep this fact top of mind, the very spot it now staked its banner in the light of a glorious sunrise.

Without a second thought, I took off toward the main road, hobbling like a penguin in my oversized clothing; there I hailed a taxi, which carried me to a university and my new home in a college dorm.

12

A New Beginning

JUST a few signatures later and I was no longer homeless! By God's abundant grace, I was able to move right into a dorm; the administration even allowed me to postpone a semester of medical school, no questions asked—another blessing, as I did not wish to explain the reason for my need of physical and emotional healing.

My new reality was difficult, to say the least; but God relentlessly picked up the pieces of my shattered life, starting with guiding me to a place in which I could read the entire Bible! That's right! Though Christian and Bible websites are blocked in Saudi Arabia, with a little digging I discovered VPN (Virtual Private Network), which allowed me to create a tunnel beneath the government's radar, hiding both my identity and location; and through this wonderful gateway and secure connection, I was able to uncover all 66 books of God's glorious Word and read it without fear of being discovered by the religious police! The entire cosmos had been opened up to me! I read of the beginning in Genesis; I drank in the whole history of the chosen people I had been trained to hate above all others; I supped on the stories and words of the great king David, his faith, failures, and fantastic poetry; I dove headlong into the wisdom of Proverbs, Ecclesiastes, and Job—oh, my goodness, Job! Here, in unparalleled, undeserved suffering, we learn of the fleeting perspective of our world and the infinite perspective and purposes of God! What a story! How vast is the wonder of God, thought I, as I devoured like rich honey every single letter of that book! Almost every waking moment of my semester off was spent studying the Bible from cover to cover, and back again, endeavoring to memorize it, as I had the Qur'an. And by the time classes resumed, that flamethrower atop a skyscraper had become a roaring volcano.

Among the truly amazing revelations that filled my heart and the beautiful passages I was blessed to memorize is one that had become (and still is) my own personal emergency hotline, a Christian 9-1-1, if you will: Psalm 91:1, which reads, "He who dwells in the shelter of the Most High will abide in the shadow of the Almighty."

God was training me in his Word—and it is a living Word! So unlike the dead and empty words of the Qur'an! Reflecting on the verses of Islam, I found not one applicable to my life; yet, here in the Bible, words penned thousands of years ago were shown to be present, relevant to my life and experiences—it's pure truth! And as the days progressed, my entire world became focused through the lens of God's Word. Of all the fruit that came of this semester, I count this among the greatest: that Christ gave me His heart for the lost and taught me to forgive. With new eyes, I saw my father for the man he truly is: a spiritually blind person, dead in his sins, and in desperate need of Jesus' salvation, the life found only in Him! Not one day has since gone by that I have not lain on my face and prayed to God for the salvation of my beloved father, mother, and brothers; for my entire family, my dear Filipina house-maid, my tribe, and Muslims everywhere—so long as I have life in my veins, I will never cease to pray for them.

Part of my immersion into the Bible and my newfound Christian life consisted of seeking out followers of Christ for fellowship, discipleship, and support. Through the internet, God connected me with a group of American missionaries working in Bahrain, a sovereign state in the Persian Gulf, just off the Eastern coast of Saudi Arabia.

"I want to be baptized!" I told them one day. "Jesus said in Matthew 28 that His followers should be baptized! Would you be willing to baptize me?"

"Of course!" cheered my missionary friend. "But we can't do it in Saudi. Can you come to Bahrain? It's a long drive—ten hours."

If I remember correctly, he'd not yet finished speaking by the time I'd arrived on his doorstep, bubbling with joy and ready to take my cleansing plunge.

"Wonderful to see you, brother!" he said, shaking my hand with a smile.

God is so good; here He had given me a new brother—ten, in fact!

After being introduced to the nine other missionaries who would accompany us and witness my baptism, my friend said, "All right; we go by cover of darkness to the Gulf. Let's go over the drill once more."

Saying this, he laid out all the precautions we were to take to avoid government detection; then, we all gathered in prayer and waited for the sun to disappear behind the horizon.

Once the world was dark, we all piled into our cars and made our way to the Gulf, where we walked silently through the hot sand. While eight kept watch on shore, two of my new American brothers waded with me into the warm water.

"Are you ready, Ahmed?"

My whole body was shivering with explosive excitement.

I nodded to avoid screaming an elated *YES!* into the night.

"Okay," he said, then took a deep breath. "Ahmed," he began, very sternly, but lovingly, "do you believe Jesus is the Christ, the Son of the living God?"

"I do."

"Have you put your faith in Him, and Him alone, for the forgiveness of your sins, to be covered by His blood, given for you as a propitiation, making you blameless before the Father?"

Through reddening eyes, I answered, "I do."

"Ahmed," he whispered, smiling as tears flowed freely down my face, "I now baptize you in the name of the Father, and of the Son, and of the Holy Spirit."

With that, I was lowered gently beneath the surface; and as the cleansing fire of the Holy Spirit descended upon me, a drop of water passed through my lips, spreading its saltiness over my tongue, recalling for me the words of Jesus from Matthew 5:13, when He spoke of His followers, saying, "You are the salt of the earth."

As had the water of Jesus' Word, I was engulfed in an all-consuming torrent, washing over me a downpour of the emotion contained within the spiritual rebirthing that was the very day this moment symbolically and publicly represented and proclaimed. My filthy, former self, heavy in the flood, sank dead into the darkest depths below; and I, raised in new-ness of life, was lifted from the water a new, clean creature.

Falling into the arms of my friends, we shared an eternal embrace of brotherhood.

***

"Freely you have received; freely give."

These words from the lips of Jesus, as recorded in Mat-thew 10:8—how deeply did God begin to engrave them upon my heart!

I supped day and night upon the Word of Life, basking and feasting in time outside of time. A filthy pauper was I, wretched and poor, lifted by the hand of the King from the slums my sin had built as my dismal dwelling, summoned by name to dine at His table, to be called His child and as such be robed in the glory of His Son. There at His table, I tasted the heavenly fruits, prepared just for me, even before the fash-ioning of my body. Wine so sweet and meat so satisfying—this is the Word of God! Yet, through it all—though so many de-lectable flavors did fill my heart with such delight and quell what I had ever known to be so unfulfillable a longing—these words from Matthew 10:8 were every day etched deeper and deeper and deeper into my soul.

Here I was, walking freely in the light of Christ, while my fellow Saudi citizens were crawling blindly in the darkness, bound to the chains of sin and death. God's Word, I knew, was not only to be read and enjoyed; it was also to be obeyed.

I could not sit still. The light of Jesus had been ignited in me—I would not, could not, bury it beneath the fear of man. I had been freely given the truth, that no ocean of good deeds could wash away the stain of even one sin. The Muslim religion compels its followers to buy the redemption of its god, to toil in the pursuit of making oneself worthy of reconciliation. But, like all mankind, a Muslim is helpless to do so, for there is but one way to be reconciled to God. "I am the way, the truth, and the life," said Jesus, in John 14:6; "no one can come to the Father except through me."

This is the free gift I had been given; this was the truth I had to share.

And so was born "Jesus for Saudi Arabia," a video chat room I created to spread the Gospel on the platform Paltalk. It was the first of its kind; never before in the history of Saudi Arabia had there been a homegrown haven for hearing from the Bible. Truly, no one could believe an actual Saudi Christian was the administrator—people were sure I must have been from Iraq, Iran, Jordan, or Egypt, for who had ever heard of a Saudi Christian? This doubt, unfortunately, led to some distrust and worry that I might be a spy, working to identify and trap Muslims considering converting to Christianity. I did my best to demonstrate my sincerity, but the fear instilled by the Saudi government is a foul odor of death, overpowering the senses.

In spite of this, I forged ahead, knowing it is God who changes hearts and minds, and unveils eyes. I left it to Him to fight this battle. And all went quite well for a while.

One day, while ministering to a delightfully diverse group, a young woman joined the chat room. She listened quietly at first, but soon became hostile.

"This is *shirk*!" she cried, rather out of nowhere—*shirk* meaning the unforgivable sin of idolatry or polytheism, of which Christians are accused of committing both in taking a god other than Allah and believing God is Father, Son, and Holy Spirit. Muslim scholars consider the Christian doctrine of the trinity to be polytheistic: a worship of multiple Gods; when, in reality, the doctrine speaks of a single, unified God, comprised of three distinct persons.

"Isa himself," she argued, "denied being a deity or equal with Allah!"

"Yes," I replied; "in Qur'an 5:116, Isa responds to Allah's question about whether He had told people to worship Himself and His mother Mary, who bore Him as a virgin, saying, 'It was not for me to say that to which I have no right. If I had said it, you would have known it.'"

"Exactly!" she declared. "So, how can you take the words of Isa—as told in your corrupted Bible—and use them to deny the words of the noble Qur'an?"

"What happened to Isa?" I asked.

Curious whether her Qur'anic knowledge was liturgical or academic, I endeavored to draw out what understanding she possessed and let her fit the pieces together for herself.

"Allah raised him to himself," she replied astutely.

"Exactly—Qur'an 4:158. A verse earlier, we learn a bit more about that day. Do you remember what it says?"

"Of course! The people sought to kill him, but Allah made it look like he'd died."

"Qur'an 4:157 tells us that those who sought to kill Isa, quote, 'did not kill him, nor did they crucify him; but someone else was made to resemble him to them.' Correct?"

"As I said!" she replied, emphatically. "You're kind of making my point! The Qur'an clearly shows the corruption of your Bible, which claims he *was* crucified! Corruption confirmed!"

"Maybe," I said, "but let's take it a step further—or, backward, actually, to Qur'an 3:55. Here, Allah tells Isa that he will raise and purify Him. However! What did Allah say of the disciples?"

Eyeing me carefully, she muttered, "That they'd be made superior to those who disbelieved until the Day of Resurrection."

"That he did!" I cheered. "Let's now compare this promise of Allah to what we know historically. How did the apostles die? Rather, *why* did they die?"

Her mouth opened, appearing ready to speak; then, all at once, she clammed up.

"Was it for a profession that Allah is the one true God?"

Her eyes wide and lips pursed tightly, she remained silent, while her face reddened.

"According to historical documentation, both in the Bible and independent of it, we know that they preached Isa, Jesus, as God; and for this they were willing and did go to their deaths—just as Jesus, according to the Bible, said they would. Now," I concluded, "if Allah had declared these men would be uppermost, how, then, could they have preached anyone other than Allah to be the one true God?"

That which had been a reddening instantly burned white hot, and there was a great and terrible explosion, followed by a rather abrupt departure.

Though I had tried to preach truth in love and not hurt her, I was saddened to think she might not return. And, before continuing with my evangelizing, I whispered a prayer for her.

Over the course of the next few weeks, she periodically popped in and out of the chat, only to curse and shame the rest of us; then, after a while, she disappeared completely.

Every day I prayed for her and hoped she would return, so that she might, even for just the one minute she'd probably spend cursing us, know the love of Christ we all truly felt for her.

Time passed, but she did not pass from our minds. And then, one day, right out of the blue, she joined the chat once again. This time, however, the animation in her body was not born of hatred and reviling; the words rushing out of her mouth were not aflame with malice or curses. The very minute I saw her face, that split second before she began singing to us her new song, I knew that this young woman was a new creature.

"I am born again!" she cried, bursting through every pore with glorious sunlight. "John 3:3—it happened to me! Jesus is Lord!"

"Slow down!" I said, laughing as tears of joy streamed over my face. "Tell us what happened!"

"I just did!" she cried again. "Jesus saved me! Oh, I am so sorry for all the horrible things I've said and done to you all!"

Before her lips could release a plea for our forgiveness, the entire chat room had given it to her gladly.

"Our talk about Qur'an 3:55 stuck with me," she continued, having bottled up her overflowing joy enough to speak without shouting. "I couldn't get it out of my mind! It just kept nagging me! And that's why I became so angry! I was trying to blame you for the torment that verse and all we'd talked about was causing!"

"What was it about the verse that caused this torment?" I asked.

"Those who commit *shirk* are not uppermost!" she replied. "I began to wonder, was Allah somehow wrong about them? Was he lying? Because, according to him, their path from that day was rooted in idolatry and polytheism! They preached Isa as the risen Lord, as God, because they saw Him die and rise from the dead, as stated in their creed—AND THAT'S THE OTHER THING!" she blurted, appearing as if a revelation past had hit her again as a re-revelation. "If Allah had deceived them into thinking they'd seen Isa die, only to have Him reappear alive because Allah had spared Him, and then watched Him ascend into heaven, Allah himself, through his deception, is responsible for Christianity! The very sin he says he won't forgive!"

As I sat and listened, I marveled at the work of Jesus, how He was lifting the veil from this young woman's eyes and, through His abundant grace, showing her the truth.

"I started to get the sinking feeling that the Qur'an might be corrupted, because this is quite a strange contradiction! So," she said, taking a deep breath and refusing to hide the gigantic smile growing on her face, "I started reading the Bible; and, slowly, everything started becoming clear. I could actually *see* Jesus!" she screamed like a child on Christmas morning. "He was leaping off the page! His words were for *me*! They cut right through to my soul and called to me! I've been saved!"

We all went on to have a most wonderful discussion about her conversion and the enlightening truths of the Bible, as well as the evidences of those truths, both in history and in our lives today. And, before we signed off for the evening, she asked us to pray for her, as she desperately desired to share her faith with her beloved uncle, a man deeply learned in the Qur'an and devoted to Islam. The entire chat room took turns praying over her, and she left that day looking a thousand times sunnier than she had when she'd entered.

The next day, however, that sun was hidden by a great raincloud.

"I've never heard such things come from his mouth," she wept. "He has always been so kind and loving to me; but, the second I showed him the Bible, he began to mock me mercilessly. I don't know if I'll ever be able to forget that horrible look of loathing he'd cast upon me, that gaze of contempt, completely devoid of the love I'd always known."

We spent the day in the Scriptures and in fervent prayer.

"Mark 9:23," someone read: "'All things are possible for one who believes.'"

"Psalm 43:5," read another: "'Why are you cast down, O my soul, and why are you in turmoil within me? Hope in God; for I shall again praise Him, my salvation and my God.'"

"Micah 7:7: 'But as for me, I will look to the Lord; I will wait for the God of my salvation; my God will hear me.'"

I encouraged her to keep praying for her uncle, to pray for him all through the night, as would I.

Thanking us, she went away.

And that would be the last we'd see of her for about a week, when, to my abounding joy, she returned to the chat room.

"Who's this?" I asked, pointing to the man seated beside her.

"MY UNCLE!" she erupted with a scream of glee, blowing the speakers of my computer. "He has something to tell everybody!"

He introduced himself, and we all huddled in to listen.

"All through the night, I tossed and turned," he told us, recounting his journey to the present day. "'What if she's right?' I kept saying to myself; I just couldn't get the thought out of my head!"

It was quite clear to everyone, including this man, why his night had been a sleepless one, for it had been the same night his niece, after praying with us, had indeed spent the entire night pleading with God to open his eyes.

And God had answered her prayer.

"This was not mere curiosity," he continued, speaking of his sudden compulsion to forfeit all attempts to sleep and examine the Bible. "It felt like something was pulling me from my bed, demanding that I see for myself what it is that had so changed my niece."

He explained that he had tracked down the Bible online via a VPN and began to read through the New Testament.

"The words of Jesus!" he explained. "Truly, no one had ever spoken like this man! These were words of power and love and truth that I simply could not deny! But my stubbornness was not willing to face down that truth and concede just yet. So, I whipped out my Qur'an."

Well into the morning, the man studied both books, comparing them side by side, testing each by the other, analyzing every word and phrase and meaning; and as he did so, the words of Jesus, and all that had been spoken about Him, sunk deeper and deeper into his soul, touching his heart in ways the Qur'an had never been able to do.

"It proved itself to be a collection of dead words!" he cried, speaking of the Qur'an. "It collapsed in upon itself, crushed by the weight of its own claims, unable to stand by its own merits—and no matter how I tried to tear the Bible to shreds, it withstood every flame and endured every sword, showing itself stronger with every increasingly vicious blow I dealt to it. And," he concluded, as tears filled his eyes, "after a rich study and thorough examination of these texts, conducted over the course of the past week, I had not a shred of stubbornness left, nor a leg on which to stand to deny the comfort and love and salvation found in Christ alone!"

The entire chat room erupted into a loud, long, and glorious *HALLELUJAH*! For here before us was a block of immovable stone made moldable clay by the love of Jesus!

"I BELIEVE!" he cried. "I believe, and I want to be baptized!"

He didn't need to say it twice; I was at his door in a matter of seconds—several thousand of them, but who's counting?

It was indeed a very long but not the least bit burdensome journey, as I seemed to soar over the dusty roads, carried swiftly on the wings of heaven's joy.

I arrived at his doorstep, and, greeting me with great excitement, he led me into his home.

As I stepped into the living room, I saw near the back door a stack of personal items, much of which appeared to be Islamic ornaments, trinkets, and keepsakes.

"No room for that stuff anymore," he said with a sigh, the kind one heaves upon dropping a boulder from his back.

Just as I turned to follow him into the kitchen, where he'd prepared tea, a flash of forest green and a glint of gold, caught in the sunlight streaming through the opened window, grabbed my eye. Turning back, I discovered, framed in wood, a piece of Islamic art. The canvas was like rich grass, in which had been sprinkled a golden dust; and in that dust, written in Arabic, was the name Ali, referring to Ali ibn Abi Talib, the successor to Muhammad claimed by the Shiites.

My eyes widened, their rims ran red; and I turned to see the man standing beside me, holding a cup of tea in each hand.

"I take it," he said, speaking in a low tone, bearing a look of grave understanding painted across his face, "you are a Sunni?"

Fourteen hundred years of war and divided doctrine, of bitter hatred and devastating destruction, hung heavily in the air between us; right here, in our midst, sat the great, gaping divide, into which our ancestors had been pouring their corrosive contempt and hostility for generations upon generations, willingly unable and wholly unwilling to bridge that gap, and having never accepted the power to do so, even if there had been but one shred of desire to grasp it.

The man set down the tea.

I set down the frame.

And then, as the towering, fortified wall set between us—built continually, relentlessly, for over a millennium, bearing bricks laid even by our own hands; as that wall suffered a shattering split from base to summit, to one another we reached forth the hand of fellowship; then, by the throwing of our arms firmly about one another, we were united wholly, eternally in brotherhood, there in the midst of the dust that had once been our irreconcilable division.

"For He Himself is our peace," says Ephesians 2:14 of Jesus, "who has made us both one and has broken down in His flesh the dividing wall of hostility."

***

"Immediately thereafter," I said, wiping a tear from my eye, "he was baptized—God gave to me the honor of baptizing this blessed brother, right there in his bathtub!"

"Praise God!" cried the tall man, who had been listening ever so eagerly as I spoke.

About a year had passed since I'd departed from New Zealand, and I had returned during a short break from school to spend time with the man who had pointed me to Jesus, to study the Word and tell all the wonderful news regarding God's working in my life. Though we kept quite busy with this two-pronged schedule, my ten-day stay would include some additional blessings, namely my being invited to speak publicly in churches across New Zealand, to give my testimony about Christ's salvation and my surrender to His lordship. Everywhere we went, the tall man and I, people were astounded by Jesus' miraculous work in one of the world's darkest places; and, together, we praised Him for his great mercy!

We had just returned from Marsden Cross, the very place in New Zealand where it is said the Gospel had been first preached when at last it had arrived.

"Jesus commanded the Gospel to be preached to the very ends of the earth," said the tall man, gazing with a distant look of reverence upon the spot I was to speak. "And here we are."

The hour was now late, and I was scheduled to leave for Saudi Arabia in the morning; and yet, even ten days had proved too short a time in which to cram all the amazing stories of Jesus' work in my life over the past year! Just as John says in the last sentence of his Gospel, that if all the miracles Jesus performed in His short life were to be written down, there would not be enough books to contain the record of them; so too did I find the sheer abundance of work He'd done in my life over the past year: I had not enough time to recount, nor enough breath to speak—nor, even now, do I have enough paper to pen—every glorious miracle!

"How amazing!" I cheered. "God took this man and me from opposite sides of the shattered foundation of Islam and set us upon the rock of Christ! Who would ever believe a Sunni and a Shiite could have become brothers?"

"All things are possible with God!" he cheered in reply. "The very God who loved us so much that He died for us willingly—us, His betrayers and murders! Tell me," he continued, "has there been any resolution with Paltalk?"

"I think it's officially permanent," I said, shaking my head. "Even with the support I've received, there doesn't seem to be any chance of my account being reinstated. And," I added with a shrug, "I can't exactly blame their being concerned about my background. The Saudi government has many nefarious ways of rounding up defectors from Islam."

"You, a Saudi spy!" he laughed. "I'm sorry, but I just don't see it. I guess your unassuming nature is what makes you such an effective government asset!"

"If only I had a meaner-looking face," I chuckled, "I might still have my chat room!"

"Better stick to the kind face—I'm sure even the best bedside manner could not outshine a bone-chilling countenance."

"I'll join you in that laugh when my English lessons get to the word 'countenance.'"

"Just a fancy word for 'face!'" We shared a laugh, and he continued. "But, tell me, how's medical school? Are you enjoying it?"

"Incredibly! Even with all the work and constant translating, it's simply fascinating! The study of medicine truly shows the intricate majesty of God!"

"Indeed, it does! And what a field of ministry, too! Why, God is getting you prepared to meet some true challenges, people facing the daunting shadow of mortality; in a valley in which fear, pain, and uncertainty abound, the light of Jesus shines brightest."

"Being a vessel for God's healing hand, both physical and spiritual, is an overwhelming honor. I feel like a spectator to His mighty work! Just seeing how He heals people, provides cures and advancements in technology—His mercies are new every day! That reminds me, I've just had some of my research published in the U.S. National Institute of Science."

"Really! Wow—that's wonderful! What's the topic?"

"A possible cure for an autoimmune disease. I was blessed to have been a part of a most accomplished team of doctors. Their list of credentials could fill a novel's worth of pages!"

"No kidding!"

"Yeah; I learned a lot from these guys. Anyway, our trials returned some amazing results on animals. The transference to human treatment looks promising."

"Wow!" he exclaimed, rubbing his forehead. "That's really awesome!"

"As you say, I am constantly in awe of God's love and mercy! He's been so good to me, better than I deserve. But," I continued with a sigh, "as much as I love medicine, my heart still bleeds for reaching Muslims, and that's been a bit of a bumpy road, with doors opening and closing so rapidly. It can sometimes get pretty discouraging. But God will open another door," I added after a pause. "Somehow, someway—I just *know* He has work yet for me to do. In a kingdom as massive as Revelation 21 describes His to be, there certainly is more than enough room for my Muslim kindred!"

"Have you felt Him calling you to that next opened door?"

"Yes, actually!" And, quickly flipping through his Bible (it was so wonderful to have a physical Bible in my hands again!), I pointed to Luke 9:2-6. "Right here," I said, tapping the page. "Jesus sends His disciples out to spread the news about the Kingdom of God. He says, 'Take nothing for your journey...Don't take a walking stick, a traveler's bag, food, money, or even a change of clothes.' *This*," I declared, tapping the page all the more, "this is what I feel I have to do."

"Go back to Saudi with nothing?" he asked, a tad surprised.

"Exactly! And that brings me to my next point." Slowly, I leaned in closer to him and asked in a low voice, "Do you think you and your wife would mind if I left my things here with you?"

"Of course you can!" he cried, letting out a hearty laugh and slapping me on the shoulder. "But, tell me," he continued, "what do you plan to do? Where will you go?"

"I will do just as I have been doing here: publicly preaching Christ. But first," I added, taking a deep breath, "I will again perform the Hajj; only, this time, I will do so in the name of Jesus, and so test the words of Allah—now, for the last time."

***

Surrounded by more than three million devout Muslims making their pilgrimage to the city that had been my home, I fell to my knees before the Kaaba: Mecca's grand sanctuary. There, bowed before the *bayt Allah* (or, house of god), the reputed center of the world, where Allah's holy realm is said to intersect with our own; there, bowed before the very spot to which I would daily face when performing *salat*, my daily prayers; there, set beneath this ostensible gateway to heaven, I laid to rest the demon that is the great lie of Islam by praying, ever so fervently and boldly, in the holy name of Jesus Christ.

Ardently, loudly, with all my heart, I beseeched the Living God to have mercy upon the innumerable lost souls praying around me, to soften their hearts, to lift the blinding veil of lies, and bring them to the Father through and in the name of His only begotten Son, the Savior and King of this world! And so I did for all around me to see and hear; I prayed earnestly, my every word bleeding from my heart, spilling hot onto the ground with agonized groans for the lost; but I also lifted my voice to expose the emptiness of the Qur'an, to disprove its teachings, and show Allah to be as the idols that had so ensnared the people of God for centuries. For here in this sacred place, Allah, as the Qur'an asserts, will never allow his name to be defiled, nor his sovereignty challenged, through the exaltation of any other name apart from his own.

Yet, I lifted the name of Jesus.

According to Qur'an 105, I should have been destroyed, just as Allah had done to a pagan army of old. They came with their mighty host, mounted on elephants, and Allah called forth a swarm of hell-born birds to cast down upon them stones and petrified clay, utterly obliterating those who would dare defy his holiness and threaten the Kaaba. Qur'an 22 also details Allah's intolerance for such actions as these; yet, I lifted high the name of Jesus and declared Allah to be a false and impuissant god of lies!

This was many years ago.

Even after a public defilement of Islam's holiest mosque in its holiest city, I live to tell the tale.

Allah made no sound.

He sent no fire from heaven to devour me.

Rather, the Holy Spirit burned over my head, as Jesus moved through me that day, and the Father was glorified.

"Father in heaven!" I cried. "Let Your mercy rain down upon this place like a mighty waterfall! Let the love of Your Son, Jesus Christ, in whose name I lift my prayer this day—let His holy love overflow within these lost souls! Grant them eternal life by the atonement made by our Savior when He was crucified! Let the scales fall from their eyes, Lord! Throw this idol into the dust, and let Your light shine through this deep darkness; for He who is in me is greater than he who is in the world!"

Allah was nowhere to be found, his retribution absent.

But Jesus was there. "For where two or three are gathered in My name," said He in Matthew 18:20, "there am I among them." And three of us there were: I, crying out for the salvation of all Muslims, and two American missionary friends, who live-streamed the whole thing on social media, praying the same prayer that was on my lips, as they documented my not getting pelted by an army of hellish birds or being instantly swallowed into the void of eternal punishment.

That night, I sat aloft from a distance, gazing down upon my former home. It had been the most amazing year of my life, but I knew the struggle had only just begun. Satan would attack; this was a certainty. "Our struggle," said Paul in his letter to the Ephesians, "is not against flesh and blood, but against the rulers, against the authorities, against the powers of this dark world and against the spiritual forces of evil in the heavenly realms."

For now, Satan, the prince of darkness, was the ruler of this dark world. Only when Christ returns to set up his eternal kingdom will the fallen one's power be forever vanquished— and I refused to wait until that day to bear witness to all I had seen, everything that had happened to me; for then it would be too late.

This, I knew, meant war.

The spiritual battle had just begun; I had stepped boldly onto one of the deepest, darkest, most treacherous battlefields, marching directly into the stronghold of a satanic powerhouse. I was not afraid to enter Satan's fist, there to proclaim the power of the true Isa. But my faith would be tested. Satan would not easily release his death grip on this people, not without a fight employing the full-strength of his malice. And, in the following days, hell itself would seem to have opened up, with the fallen son of the morning launching an all-out assault of fire and brimstone on my life and the lives of those who'd joined my quest.

13
Conversion Therapy

"**M**UHAMMAD loved his enemies! That's not exclusive to Jesus!"

I had met the man online through one of my evangelism channels. He was a Saudi citizen, and had been very interested in the Bible, asking many questions, primarily about its authenticity and the distinction of the Jesus of the Bible and the Isa of the Qur'an.

"Killing one's enemies is hardly a way to show them love," I replied, citing the numerous times in the Qur'an Muhammad condones and commands the slaughter of his adversaries. "Jesus said that we should love our enemies and pray for those who persecute us. He neither killed nor commanded anyone to kill—quite the contrary, actually! Dying for those who hated Him—it's the exact opposite of Muhammad's life!"

He and I had been reading the Bible together online. Then, one day, he asked if we could meet and discuss the Word face to face. As he still considered himself a Muslim, exploring the Bible with a critical mind, and given the fact that this was Saudi Arabia, showing my face in such a context would pose a major risk. So, rather than agreeing right away to a meeting, I prayed, both for him and for guidance. In doing so, the words of Jesus, commanding His disciples to "Go!" and spread the Good News, kept coming to mind.

"Yes, Lord," I replied, scrolling through the pages of my online Bible to Matthew, searching for chapter 28, in which these words were spoken. "I know You say to go, and I want to do Your will; but this is a dangerous place, and I cannot help but be afraid."

Passing Matthew 10 on my way to 28, my eyes were halted by the word "fear," typed in red letters.

"So have no fear of them," said Jesus in verse 26, "for nothing is covered that will not be revealed, or hidden that will not be known. What I tell you in the dark, say in the light, and what you hear whispered, proclaim on the housetops. And do not fear those who kill the body but cannot kill the soul. Rather fear Him who can destroy both soul and body in hell."

I read on, absorbing Christ's words that the Father is so attentive to us that He knows even the number of hairs on our head. This He promised: that I am of the utmost value to God, and if I acknowledge Jesus before men, Jesus would acknowledge me before His Father.

Praying amid three million people in the name of Jesus was one thing—the crowds are all basically screaming their prayers in a deafening commotion that I wonder if anyone around me paid any attention to my words, which had been for Jesus and in defiance of the Islamic lie. But in a one-on-one context in public, talking openly about Christ—this could draw some costly attention. However, to remain hidden in my room behind a computer screen for fear of man would be to deny the command of Jesus.

I contacted the man, and we set a time to meet in a local coffee shop.

"Not only did Jesus never kill anyone, as Muhammad had," I continued, "Jesus died for His enemies! And He did so to save them!"

"Well," he argued, "when Muhammad returned to Mecca, he didn't kill his own people."

"That's right," I said. "He did not kill the members of his *own* tribe. Yet," I reminded him, "Muhammad *did* kill many in Mecca who were *outside* of his tribe. He was glad to destroy anyone who had insulted him. Jesus, on the other hand, never killed anyone, but instead demonstrated His love to us, in that while we were yet sinners, He died for us. Moreover, He returned dead people to life in public resurrections! Remember 1 Corinthians?" I asked, wishing I had a physical Bible with me so we could read directly from the Scriptures. "In the first five or six verses, Paul mentions how many of the people who witnessed these things—Jesus' crucifixion and resurrection—were still alive at the time of his writing the letter. He's inviting the readers to go ask those people, and not just take his word for all he claims."

The man sat perfectly still the whole time I spoke, studying the movements of my lips.

"Paul encouraged the Corinthian believers to interview the eyewitnesses," I continued, "but Muhammad's acts had no witnesses. Qur'an 17:1 says Allah ascended Muhammad into heaven by night—no witnesses. Muhammad then returned and told his followers of his experience, providing no firsthand accounts or any evidence. On the other hand, Jesus' acts were almost always in front of witnesses. When He was baptized, before a great crowd, there appeared a visible manifestation of the Spirit."

"A dove, right," he mumbled thoughtfully.

"Yes!" I declared. "Matthew 3—we just read this, how the Spirit descended and the voice of God came down from heaven; all done before many witnesses. Now, God is holy," I continued, "and His justice cannot accept less than a full price for our sins. Our own attempts at righteousness cannot cleanse us from our unrighteousness; a payment greater than we can afford outside of a second, eternal death is required. The true Isa made that payment for us on the cross. *Jesus*," I stated, looking him dead in the eye: "He is the Word of God; He is the perfect representation of the Father. He is holy and perfect, and, therefore, was sufficient to satisfy the justice of God."

The man remained silent.

Then, after a long pause, he said, "I see. Jesus is the Way, the Truth, and the Life."

"Yes!" I cried. "No one comes to the Father except through Him!"

Falling silent again, the man bowed his head; and then, almost in a whisper, he asked, "Will you pray for me?"

Abundantly delighted, I laid my hand on his shoulder.

"God Almighty," I prayed, "I thank You for this man and for the time You've given us to dive together into Your Word. Please continue to reveal Yourself to him through Jesus, Your Son, in whose holy name I pray. Amen."

I had hardly spoken the word "Amen" when the man leapt violently to his feet, kicking his chair halfway across the café, and screamed at the top of his lungs, "YOU ARE AN ACCURSED INFIDEL!" His face boiled and great infernos blazed through his eyes. "You are a *PAGAN*! How *dare* you pray in the name of a *HUMAN BEING*! MAY ALLAH RAIN DOWN HIS WRATH UPON YOU!"

All eyes were upon us, as he continued to rage.

Unable to look away from the savage eruption exploding before me, I again lifted up the man in prayer, asking God to have mercy on him and to save his soul.

His anger would not be spent quickly, and he stormed out into the streets, still cursing and screaming.

I had a sinking feeling I knew exactly where he was going.

***

"JESUS!" blared a bloodcurdling scream in my head. "TAKE ME QUICKLY! PLEASE!"

The first blow had left me numb to the pain, but only for a moment; and all was silent, save for a high-pitched ringing in my ears, following the blasting of my door from its hinges by the charging of an army of bloodthirsty beasts. Almost the very second my hand had fallen from the doorknob upon my return to my dorm, it had been thrust open by a man overflowing with ire, who instantly grasped the back of my head, as one might a basketball, and threw me to the floor with the full weight of his strength, ejecting not a few teeth from my mouth.

All the world had gone silent at this very moment, my vision filled with a suffocating fog; and I seemed to be floating somewhere outside of myself, desperately trying to discover just what had happened to me. And I might have preferred to remain a little longer in this state, for as my senses returned, I was made aware of sweltering pain: a breathtaking, shocking, inhuman sensation, as if my every fiber were being ground beneath a mighty, jagged boulder.

Through the mist that filled my eyes, I could see in the blurs surrounding me, as I writhed and screamed, familiar colors in familiar places, all set atop humanlike figures. As the fire intensified and the various pains from various places compounded into an enveloping cloud of torment, my eyes broke through the mist, widening to see the room with greater clarity than they'd ever beheld anything; and I saw above me many bearded faces, all dripping with sadistic delight as they spat over me vile curses and rained upon my body vicious blows from bloodied fists and clubs painted a crude crimson. Eyes aflame with the insatiable hunger for murder, they tore at my flesh like fell, feral wolves, brutally beating, bruising, and breaking me into a bloody pulp; like blunt axes their clubs crashed against and crushed my bones; their claws tore like double-edged swords; their feet smote like the mace and chain; and their hands carried fistfuls of lightning.

"JESUS! PLEASE!" I begged, filling my head with my desperate echoes, beseeching Him on this day that would surely be my last to swiftly end my life and take me up to be with Him.

All at once, the beating stopped.

Two of the men hoisted my torso, taking my arms from either side, until I was held in a kneeling position.

There before me was a large, crimson pool, wide and deep, in which swam thirteen pulverized teeth.

A set of black boots then stepped forward, stopping along the opposite bank of the lake of carnage.

Lifting my weary, weeping eyes, I beheld an officer of the religious police, gazing down upon me with a sneer. He wore on his head a black beret with a golden emblem, set above a tight, jet black goatee and a uniform like wet sand, adorned with various badges and marks of lofty rank; around his waist was a thick belt of black, and in his claws of white, starkly contrasted against his sun-stained skin, he clutched a stack of papers and a journal, all of which contained notes from my study of the Bible: a very incriminating stack of evidence against a suspected Christian. With a scoff, he hurled these into the lake before him, and I watched as the precious words of my Lord Jesus were painted red.

At the flick of his finger, iron shackles were hastily fitted about my neck, wrists, and ankles; and I was thereafter dragged through the dormitory, paraded before my fellow students like a circus animal, all the way to a line of black cars waiting outside, ready to carry me away to the very palm of Satan.

"CRY TO YOUR DOG!"

The cord of fire screamed again across my back.

"Beg your demon, Jesus, to save you!"

A flash of white-hot fury exploded down my spine, blinding me and stealing the breath from my lungs.

"Call his name, *PIG*!"

Like a beam of ferocious lightning screeching forth from the deepest pit of hell, an all-consuming rage of searing agony pierced through my every pore.

"MAKE HIM STAY MY HAND!"

The tumultuous storm suddenly burst into a squall of fury; and with a surge of strength no human can by himself possess, the hand that lashed my back flew into a wild rampage, raining down flesh-splitting blows from the leather strips clutched in its bloodied talons, each craterous impact landing before the crack from the previous lash could reach the ears.

All my muscles seized; my fingers and toes, as if desperately trying to detach themselves from this body of torment, stretched and spread to full length in every direction; my eyes, so wide they nearly fell from their sockets, could not escape the full awareness of the scene; the iron tang of blood rained over my tongue, and my head was filled with the noisome stench of mangled flesh strewn upon the cold floor, and with the roaring, mocking laughter echoing about my dark and filthy confines.

I couldn't breathe.

I could hardly think.

Life was made a plague, and existence a curse; Death itself seemed to mock me at the sides of my tormentors, his black hands bound by only his will and hidden behind his back.

There was no day, no night, no time at all; there was but the potent, present now, with every second an eternity of unrelenting agony, and I was made intimate with every one of them.

The lash suddenly fell silent; only a heavy, chuckle-laced panting could be heard.

My eyes fell heavily to the floor, as the swelling and throbbing intensified; and from that perspective I watched as a familiar set of black boots stepped forth. As before, they walked only to the bank of my blood, pooled there beneath my toes, from which it sluggishly dripped, while I hung suspended from the ceiling by my arms.

He whose authority filled those boots must have given some silent order, for my body was hastily dropped from the hook on which my shackles had been draped; and I collapsed, without any ability to break my fall, onto the frigid, stone earth that was my cell.

The black boots remained but a little longer, as the silence amplified.

Just then, another set of feet entered, scurrying to my side.

At my face was set a pail.

Whomever had entered knelt beside the pail, and I could hear a hand dig into its contents; the sound was like a foot plunging into a mound of sand.

The kneeler rose, and I watched as a fine, granular dust, as white as snow, rained over his fist and sprinkled into the blood in which swam my face.

I knew not how many days I had been in this place of torment; I knew only the routine—whipping, scurrying feet, pail of white dust—and that there had been no getting used to its final step, this climax of pain, no preparing for what I had throughout the merciless lashing been dreading.

My heart pounded so wildly that I could see the crimson pool in which I lay growing, sense its warming. And then, about the time I had lost nearly all my breath in maddening anticipation, I heard a voice looming over me let out a derisive snigger, and exclaim, "He is a Christian! And didn't their prophet John say that *pig Jesus* would baptize them with fire?"

A roar of knowing laugher filled the room, as I mixed tears with my pooled blood.

"Then!" the voice shouted. "Let him be so baptized!"

The blaring approval shook the very foundation of the cell; the pool of blood rippled as if the footsteps of a giant were close at hand.

"I baptize you!" screamed the voice amid the chaos. "I baptize you in the name of your swine, *JESUS!*"

Their cacophony was immediately swallowed whole by my face-splitting squeal, as a torrential downpour of acid rain fell upon my shredded flesh—the more I would screech, the deeper the acid would sink, further and further, seeping slowly through every nerve, scorching them from within, sending pulses of desperation through my every limb, making all that was attached to me writhe to free itself from its place upon the heap of anguish I had become.

Higher and higher rose their laughter; my screams drowned them all. The hand bearing the salt from the pail dug meticulously through the canyons carved in my back, squeezing mangled mounds of flesh and clawing at exposed sinews. Only by the hand of Jesus was I stayed from barreling over the threshold of irreversible insanity.

When at last the hand had ceased to grind at my flesh, the feet that had brought in the pail walked back to my face. A handful of my hair was clasped, and my head was wrenched upward, there to behold the image of the man who had so many times punctuated my torture.

His appearance was unremarkable, normal; it fit without note or consequence into the world I'd always known.

At this, my blood was made like ice.

Regarding his free hand, he heaved a laugh at the caked balls of reddened salt saturating his palm and lining his fingers, before locking eyes with me and viciously smearing the salt over my face.

"See you soon, *salt* of the earth," he giggled, then took up his pale and disappeared.

Even before the cell door had slammed shut, the loud speakers set in the four corners of the cell, which blasted night and day into my confines, were turned on again, bombarding me with an endless chanting of the Qur'an, screaming verses telling me that Allah is the only god, and whoever believes in Jesus over him is an infidel. In their minds—perched beside indiscriminate, sadistic urges that saw them lap at my suffering like starved, voracious beasts—there sat a firm belief that no son of a Mufti (as they had come to learn I was) could ever have been persuaded to follow Jesus. Surely, knowing my father, as they did, they must have assumed my life had been the Qur'an, its teachings and its practices; and it had. For them, there could be no explanation for this radical transformation, other than to assert that I was possessed by a demon, which could be expelled only through daily and nightly assaults by the words of the Qur'an, as well as extensive, unspeakable torture, which they were happy and hungry to provide.

The salt still burned in my back, as I crawled to my designated corner—it was the cleanest of the four, and that's not saying much; it was away from my designated area for defecating, and the spot which looked like a few pieces of another infidel that had been left behind long ago.

I did not get there in a hurry; my feet had been thoroughly lashed earlier in the day, leaving them looking like shredded meat laid over a pair of balloons; my body trembled violently, and my arms were so weak from a lack of nourishment, being given only enough food and water daily to keep me alive and feeling, that I exhausted a marathon's worth of exertion to move even one inch.

Hiding in my dark, dingy corner, I sought for sanity beyond the noise rushing into my cell from all sides. But above the blaring Qur'an were only the screams of others like me, likewise condemned, for crimes I knew not, whose torment raged without end.

There would be no rest this night; there had been no rest since my arrival. But on this darkest of my daily, dark eternities, a new voice split the earth with such screams and cries that the chanting voice berating me in the hopes of exorcizing the demon from my soul was swiftly drowned in a sea of arduous suffering and maddening terror, like nothing I'd ever heard in all my life and can never forget. These spine-twisting shrieks imbedded themselves deeply into my bones, shaking them with such tremendous force that I felt as though my entire skeletal frame was being pulverized to dust.

It was the terrified, desolate screams of a woman.

Such screams come not from lashings, nor the cutting of flesh.

She exhausted every plea for mercy, petitioning with every breath for deliverance; the frantic clawing of her fingers against her cell wall was like nails on a chalkboard, projected in stereo; her weeping, carried on the black wings of throat-searing screams, ground the very foundations of the world. And through those wails I could hear the loud chanting of her assailant, offering up prayers to Allah, as he savagely defiled her. For as the Islamic cleric advised, one should "perform a ceremonial washing first and say prayers while raping a prisoner."

Words such as his broke upon me, as she cried for hours upon hours, words with which I used to nod in agreement—such barbaric, sadistic lies, that to rape a female prisoner, condemned to die or not, would bring the rapist a spiritual reward up to that of a pilgrimage to Mecca, stating plainly that she could be defiled by whatever means the rapist so chose. All this is permissible under the law I once claimed to revere and obey—this place, my cell, my torture, and the unspeakable torment of those suffering around me; *this* is the bedrock and the foundation of the Islamic religion: a pure, unbridled evil that seeks to shred and defile all that God has created, to turn it backward, to mar light with darkness, and soil the bread of life with the fecal poison of death.

And my shattered heart gazed into the heavens and screamed with the voice of a little child lost in the darkness, calling for his father, "GOD IN HEAVEN! WHY?" All through the night I cried thusly, and all through my next bout of torture—as I lay stretched long upon the cold ground, while tiny drops of liquid salt, falling from the teeth of mouths bellowing sadistic laughter above me, were slowly dripped along my freshly lashed back, split wide to the ribs; as I lay helplessly like a trapped animal, hurled alive into the fire, I screamed to Him who had fashioned the very flesh being now ripped apart, "WHY, GOD? I have turned from my sin! I follow You! Why do You ignore my suffering? SEND YOUR WRATH TO CONSUME THESE WIELDERS OF EVIL!"

"Your Jesus is a dog!" laughed a voice that had become as familiar as was the dawn before my banishment into darkness—he dragged my limp and lifeless body across the floor, pulling me by the shackles that I had come to regard as my own writs, giggling wildly and yelling once more, "Your Jesus is a *dog*!" Hoisting me from the ground with the aid of several others, and laying my shackles over the hook suspended from the ceiling, he clasped my face with his claw and spewed loudly, "A *dog*! *SAY* IT! Say Jesus is a dog!"

My body shivered uncontrollably; I was so terribly cold from loss of blood and malnourishment.

"He's a pig!" he shouted, spitting in my face and squeezing my jaw even harder; my mouth felt as though it had been caught in a vice; hairline cracks branched through my jaw. "SAY IT!"

"Why, God?" I begged in my heart. "Why will You not deliver me? Why will You not kill this man?"

"I SAID SAY IT!"

The ear-splitting *crack* of the lash joined the echo of his voice, as it bounded about the walls.

"He's a donkey!" he screamed, crushing my face, his claws ripping out clumps of my beard. "SAY IT!"

Tears streamed freely down my face; and, as my heart sank, slipping further toward the black pool of despair, I sucked my lips into my mouth and shook my head.

He snarled like a rabid lion, and another lash scorched my spine.

"Jesus is a pig!" he bellowed through gritted teeth.

Again, I shook my head.

Again came the lash.

"JESUS IS A PIG!"

My head shook.

The lash snapped.

"JESUS IS A DONKEY! SAY IT!"

What teeth remained bit slowly through my lips, as I again defied his order and again begged God, "Why?"

And again the lash fell, ripping so hard this time that my back was split wide open; I could feel a warm and sluggish waterfall running down my legs.

Lifting my fading eyes, I saw the maniacal glare of the man still holding my face; his cheek had been caught by the tip of the whip, and a weeping of red had begun to trickle over and stain his face.

My wounds thoroughly salted, I was left alone again.

"God...my God...why?"

On the brink of despair, but a breath away from plunging into the depths of Death's pitch darkness, never to return, I turned my eyes again to heaven, and spoke aloud in a hoarse whisper, pushing forth all I had left, "Father! Oh, God, my Father! You see all things! Why, then, do You watch as I suffer, and do nothing? Why did You not stay the hand that bore the lash? Why did You not consume with fire those who so wickedly defiled that woman? Why do You not step forth and rid this world of the evil that pollutes it?" By this time, I was sobbing with my whole body, spilling over the burnt stone what few tears I had left. "Why do You not kill them all? WHY? Oh, God, ANSWER ME! AND LET ME DIE!"

In silence, I waited, listening for the oars of Death's ferry that would soon arrive.

Only faint whimpers broke the stillness that surrounded me, until I could hear naught but the labored breathing in my chest.

Ever persistent was the silence, as I waited for God to answer.

And that's when I realized...

That's when I remembered...

He had already given His answer.

Lying there on the cell floor, my demand of God tumbled about in my head, like an echo reluctant to dissipate. And I realized, someone else had similarly demanded an answer for his suffering, many years before the present time.

Job labored chapter after chapter to discern why he, an innocent man, had been made to suffer—his children had all been killed, his servants put to death, all his property and wealth stolen, and his health replaced with agonizing sickness. And yet, God Himself had called him "a blameless and upright man, who fears God and turns away from evil."

In the entirety of the book that bears his name, Job never learns why he suffered; though, the reader is shown that he had been selected as one to be tested and so disprove the accusation of Satan against God, that man serves God only for gain; and in so doing demonstrate to the countless billions who would come after him and read his story a glimpse at infinite and eternal wisdom.

I lay there for quite some time pondering the story of Job, turning about in my head all I had memorized, reading in my mind the verses, line by line. Job never became aware that his undeserved suffering was being used for something far grander than what he could see on his finite plane of existence; but he did learn all he needed to know: that man is indeed of small account when compared to God, that his own wisdom does not even begin to stack up next to the never-ending scope of understanding that is God's; for if man could fully grasp God, then God would not be God.

Still I puzzled. Surely, I could not sit here and assume I was so distinguished as to have been declared to Satan himself as blameless and upright—I know exactly from what I was saved, and there is nothing blameless about it. Was I simply supposed to sit here and suffer, content with the fact that I have no infinite understanding by which to grasp the bigger picture in which my story is presently being played?

My mouth opened to pose this very question to Jesus.

Jesus.

Jesus!

My mouth stopped.

A cloud in my head cleared.

This was not a revelation that I, in my present state of torment, was in any way comparable to Jesus—on the contrary! While there is no doubt my torture was unjust, in the court of God I was and am deserving of far greater than this for all the sins I have committed! And there was Jesus: a wholly blameless man, having never once sinned, made to suffer far greater than I, even unto death, whereupon the cross He willingly accepted the full punishment for every single sin of mankind! He was mocked, laughed at, hated, beaten, mauled, ripped to shreds, stripped naked, shamed, and barbarically murdered upon a cross; and yet, He did so willingly, because He so loved His creation—the Creator Himself died to save His creatures, who'd spat in His face and killed Him!

And so passed another cloud from my eyes, and through it broke forth a sort of re-realization that Jesus died for *everyone*! Not only did He die for me and for that poor woman, He'd died also for the men torturing, raping, and killing! Christ was willing to give His life to save even those showering merciless evil upon us and others—by such people was He crucified, only to beg His Father to forgive them, as He hung dying. God loved even those who beat the skin off His own Son with splintered whips, pressed a crown of thorns into His head, mocked Him with robes of royalty, drove nails through His hands and feet, and hung Him to die, naked and disgraced, before a horde of His own creations, cheering His death. With the same love by which I had been saved did Jesus die to offer salvation, even to my tormentors.

"The Lord is not slow to fulfill His promise as some count slowness," I recalled from 2 Peter 3:9, "but is patient toward you, not wishing that any should perish, but that all should reach repentance."

I slowly came to realize that God wants the men who tortured me to turn from evil; He wants the ones who raped that woman to accept the love and salvation of Jesus Christ. He loves them with the same love with which He loves me and loves the woman. God did not reach down and save His Son from the hand of evil; He allowed Jesus' suffering.

And then, suddenly, as these thoughts began to whirl faster and faster in my mind, the book of Isaiah, chapter 53, leapt out of my memory and stood before my eyes; and it did so not as words scrawled upon the ceiling into which my gaze had become cemented, but rather as a crystal-clear image of the very scene about which the prophet spoke, when he said regarding Jesus, the coming Messiah, "He was despised and rejected by men, a man of sorrows and acquainted with grief...He was oppressed, and He was afflicted, yet He opened not His mouth...By oppression and judgment He was taken away."

And as I watched these things unfold, as I felt the lash beating against the back of this rejected man of sorrows—afflicted, oppressed; yet, with no protest or curse, nor a call to God to kill his tormentors; as I watched this Jesus, feeling but a taste of His anguish in my own flesh, I saw Him nailed to the tree; and from above, while He yet remained silent, I watched the wrath of God fall with the weight of all creation, both here on earth and into the vast recesses of the universe, illuminated in this next verse: "Yet it was the will of the Lord to crush Him."

I was at last coming to learn the very heart of God—though I knew, believed, and rejoiced in the giving of His Son to cover my sins, my perspective lifted from myself and took up residence beside the Father, who surely did not revel in the suffering to which He'd given over His only begotten, but who'd willed it, so that the lost might be saved, their sins forgiven. As Paul asserts in his letter to the Colossians, "For in [Jesus] all the fullness of God was pleased to dwell, and through Him to reconcile to Himself all things...making peace by the blood of His cross."

"But my suffering will not save anyone from their sins!" I cried. "Jesus, You are God! What good does my suffering? Of what good is this injustice? Am I to be like Job, never to learn the reason behind this affliction?"

A final cloud passed from before my eyes. In the scene playing before me, beside Jesus, who had just breathed His last, stood a Roman centurion, his gaze turned upward at the man he'd helped to kill; and he declared without any reservation or doubt, with such conviction that he expelled his breath as if it had been punched out of him, "Truly this man was the Son of God!"

Though my body was more pain than flesh, I shot bolt upright in my cell and threw my eyes to the door, where behind I could hear the men discussing my next bout of torture.

"JESUS!" I cried. "MAY YOU BE PRAISED! Father in heaven—bless Your holy name!"

Joy like I'd never know it, even more abundant than when I'd first received the Spirit of God, suddenly began to rocket through every inch of my body, springing as from a mighty fountain from within! At last I understood what it had truly meant when the apostles rejoiced at being counted worthy to suffer!

"JESUS!" I cried aloud again. "Oh, my Savior! You have counted me blessed, for You have appointed me to a great task! You have chosen me for Your work! I will not die in this place—indeed, You have allowed this evil that good might come of it! For these scars will endure until the day You call me home! And by them will You proclaim Your holy name to the world! By them will You rip down the veil blinding and deceiving all to believe Islam is a religion of peace! You will tell my story to the nations! These scars, this suffering—You have allowed it that Your name might be glorified, that evil will be exposed, and people everywhere will, like the centurion, gaze into heaven and declare You are truly the Son of God! Lead me where You will, and I will go!"

And as these words fell from my lips, my mind was suddenly filled with the words of Job 19—they came to me as an answer to everything with which I had so long been wrestling: "Oh that my words were written! Oh that they were inscribed in a book! Oh that with an iron pen and lead they were engraved in the rock forever!"

"YES!" I shouted with all my might. "Let this story be told, Father! Show the world my scars! Proclaim the suffering of the woman nearby. I will never cease to tell her story! I will carry these scars with rejoicing!"

The Word of God, spoken through Job, continued to flow through me, rushing about my body like a raging river overflowing its banks: "For I know that my Redeemer lives, and at the last He will stand upon the earth! And after my skin has been thus destroyed, yet in my flesh I shall see God!"

My entire body shot forth in every direction, as if an explosion had just gone off within me; and I hollered at the top of my lungs, "PRAISE BE TO THE CHRIST!"

And then, as the room fell silent again, I heard passing through my ears something like a whisper.

"Blessed are those who are persecuted for righteousness' sake, for theirs is the kingdom of heaven."

I fell on my face and wept.

"Blessed are you when others revile you and persecute you and utter all kinds of evil against you falsely on My account."

"Christ," I sobbed, "I am so unworthy."

"Rejoice and be glad, for your reward is great in heaven."

"What am I, Jesus," I begged, "that You would choose me for so grand an honor? What love is this that You would not only die to save me, but also choose me to suffer for Your name, and share in this promise? Who am I, Father?"

As if summoned by a siren, several of my captors burst through my prison door.

"What *is* this demon?" asked one in awe. "Have we not yet done enough?"

"The dog has been beaten into madness," mumbled another.

A man stepped hastily forward, dragging a lash at his side.

Glaring down at me over a snarl, I perceived the slash on his cheek. And as he drew up to raise his hand and strike, I lunged forward, falling over his arms, holding onto them with

201

all my might, and crying, "Father, forgive this man! I know not by what evil he moves to destroy me; but he is in darkness! Give him Your holy light!"

Seeming stunned by my actions, he staggered for a moment; to my surprise, he held me upright the entire time.

"Forgive me!" I pleaded. "For I wished this man to die! I called to You, demanding they all be destroyed! You have called me to love my enemies, and so I shall! Jesus, show this man the love by which You've saved me!"

All the world seemed to have stopped to listen. Even though I had prayed to Jesus, right there before them, they moved not against me. They were like statues, frozen into place; and through my body I could feel the tremors of the man's mighty frame, trembling as he held me.

I repented loudly and with all my heart, forsaking the hatred I had harbored for these men. In truth, as contrary to the situation as even I would have previously declared possible, I did love them; I still love them. I wept over them, there in that dark, dingy cell, as one weeps over a lost brother; I cried desperately for their souls to be rescued from this darkness, and still I do.

His breathing quivered; his snarl receded into a stunned gape; and, ever so slowly, he lowered me to the ground, before turning away quickly and hastening out of the room. The others followed soon after, their eyes fixed curiously upon me.

The next span of indeterminate time was spent in prayer, laying the words of my grieving heart before the Father, beseeching with my every breath for Him to cut through the night that consumed their lives and lead them to a new day.

I knew not what was to follow, but I knew the battle against this darkness would only intensify until the day of Jesus' return; so, I prayed for God to fill me with His strength.

Again, the whisper filled my head: "Be strong in the Lord and in the strength of His might," says Ephesians 6. "Put on the whole armor of God, that you may be able to stand against the schemes of the devil."

No sooner had these words passed through my brain did my door open, and in walked a familiar set of black boots. Behind them stepped several others; one carried a chair, the other a lamp; two more arrived with a table.

I was placed in the chair with my hands kept shackeled behind my back, then pushed up to the table, while the blinding lamp was shined directly into my eyes, making all before me black silhouettes.

This routine had taken place a few times prior. The first time had entailed a thorough explanation of my demonic possession: Yeshua was the demon's name, they said, and he was to be exorcized that I might be set free to again worship Allah. How kind and sympathetic their words had sounded; their "exorcizing" lashes, however, spoke much louder and seemed to be the more honest speech. Other times, I was made to know how my family was suffering because of my disobedience. They spoke as if they knew my mother personally, as if she had dictated to them a full transcript of her heartbreak.

"Your mother is calling for you, crying bitterly," they said; "she wants her boy to turn from his wayward path. She longs to hold you again and see you reconciled to Allah, free of this deep deception."

"Do you not know the Western man hates the Muslim?" they said at another time. "How better to exercise his malice than by turning a devout servant of Allah away from the one true god to follow the idol of the West?"

"A false god has dazzled your mind with his lies—but Allah is merciful. He will accept your repentance and set you back on the right path."

"Isa himself will return; and when he does, he will destroy all crosses, all churches built on the lie that he is god; he will slaughter the idolaters found therein. You know this. Your family pleads with you to not be counted among the condemned."

Their words became increasingly sly and cunning, even terribly convincing; but the lash always demonstrated their true nature; and not once could they convince me even to blaspheme or forsake the name of Christ.

But this marked the first time he who possessed the black boots conducted the interrogation.

His presence and authority pressed against me like a mighty wrecking ball.

Closing my eyes, I let my soul strap on its armor: Helmet of Salvation: "Jesus Himself is my Salvation;" Breastplate of Righteousness: "By Christ's blood, I am counted righteous before the Father;" Shield of Faith: "No weapon forged against me shall penetrate the defense that is my faith in the Almighty God;" Belt of Truth: "Jesus is the truth that holds me together, and naught but Him will I claim;" Shoes of Peace: "I struggle not against flesh and blood, and I will strive to live at peace with all men;" and the Sword of the Spirit: "Spirit of the one true God, fight for me today and give me the words to speak at this appointed time."

"You are to be taken today to the courts; there, you will face judgment."

My eyes still closed, I asked God for His strength.

"Your father will not speak for you," said the man. "He has said he knows of no son by the name Ahmed."

As a tear fell from my eye, I whispered in my head to God, "You, O Lord—*you* are my father, now."

Just then, the blinding light turned downward, and I opened my eyes to see the man, holding the light to the table, and staring coldly back at me.

"You need only renounce this apostasy," he said. "Renounce this false god, and you may yet find the mercy of Allah."

My heart pounding, I remained silent for a moment to sketch into my memory the image of this man's face.

Then, wetting my lips, I took a deep, steadying breath.

"I have seen Jesus," I replied, "and I long to see nothing else but Him, my God and Savior."

Expelling a slow, frigid exhale through his nostrils, the man muttered a grave, "So be it," then rose and disappeared, while the others hoisted me from the chair and dragged me through the prison to a car waiting outside.

As we sped along the waking streets, my eyes fluttered with amazement at the sight of sunlight, of which I had for a time unknown been deprived. Its rays were like the gold paving the streets of heaven, I thought—perhaps, today I will lay my feet upon those streets, there to walk forever with Jesus.

Stepping before the religious judge, my case was read aloud.

I heard not one word of what was recited, for in my mind were the words of Paul, as written in his second letter to Timothy: "The time of my departure has come."

"Step forward!" called the judge, after hearing all there was to hear about my crimes against Allah.

I did so, and he, looking over his high position, examined me closely.

For a long while, he said nothing. He just stared at me in silence.

In his hand was the power to apply the law of apostasy. One word from him, and I'd be shipped off to my former home in Mecca, there to kneel in the streets I once walked and wash them with my blood.

But I was not afraid. The thought of taking my testimony across the world had been nice; but if Jesus had purposed for my suffering and loyalty to be shown only to my captors, that was a kingdom in itself.

The judge cleared his throat.

"You are so young," he said at length.

His tone carried something of disappointment.

My execution lay in his next breath.

"You have been deceived."

So unexpected and so definitive were the words of this declaration that I could not help but regard him with cue ball-sized eyes.

Such a statement stripped my record of intent—I was deemed a victim!

"Therefore," he concluded, "the law of apostasy will not be applied."

As my jaw settled into its new home atop the tile floor, the judge read the verdict of my case: I was not to be given any formal sentence; rather, I was to be committed to an Islamic mind renewal institute (a fancy term for brainwashing center), not to be released until I had been successfully rehabilitated.

Just like that, my hearing ended and I was handed over to have my mind "fixed" by the reforming hands of Islam's foremost pioneers in intellectual treatment and religious reconstruction, to be wrung through the wringer of conversion therapy.

It may seem, on its face, that this was yet another terrible hurdle placed before me; and, while I can't say the next three months of captivity in brainwashing school were particularly fun, I knew the moment I had been sentenced that Jesus had not only ended my physical torture, but had also opened the door to my freedom from captivity. And, so, I rejoiced all the way to the clinic; for in this rehab institute, I was placed under constant bombardment with Islam, with the marks of my reformation being my ability to demonstrate my knowledge and comprehension of what I was being fed—if I could answer their questions correctly, I was to be labeled reformed! Well, I was the son of a Mufti, who'd grown up surrounded by Islam, its texts, and their interpretations; more than that, I had memorized the entire Qur'an in Arabic, without a single error! How could I *not* answer these questions with expert ability? Truly, I can attribute this most incredible scenario—that a man known by the state to be the son of an Islamic scholar, and officially recognized as one who has memorized the Qur'an; I can say only that this was of God's doing, for these prodigious intellectuals of Islam actually declared me rehabilitated, convinced that my knowledge of the Qur'an and

Islam was proof that I was once again a devout follower of Allah.

Still, a constant shelling of lies upon one's soul is not a little taxing; but Christ guarded me through it all. As I answered questions from the knowledge of my head, my heart recited the Bible verses I'd been memorizing.

"My sheep hear My voice, and I know them, and they follow Me," said Jesus in John chapter 10. "I give them eternal life, and they will never perish, and no one will snatch them from My hand. My Father, who has given them to Me, is greater than all, and no one is able to snatch them out of the Father's hand. I and the Father are one."

I am in the pierced hand of Jesus; as such, I am in the Father's hand; and no amount of torment or brainwashing was going to change that.

God had made what these men called the most comprehensive, intellectual examination and reform an exercise in folly; and eventually, with Jesus at my side, my hand in His, I walked from that place a free man and alive— but, most of all, uncompromised.

Time slowly came back into focus; the world again settled in about me. What should have been my final semester of medical school had been swallowed up by the abyss of captivity. My hopes of becoming a doctor had, by all accounts, ended, with all that work I'd done laid to waste; for such an across-the-board failure to meet the standards, as an absence such as mine will produce, automatically disqualifies one from the pursuit.

I could conjure no recourse other than to pray.

"Okay, Lord," I said with a calming sigh, as I walked the streets of freedom, back to the university to see what fate awaited me, "if You want me to be a doctor, I'll do it. If not…"

I paused to let the love of my labor and stock in my ambitions pass away, and did not speak again until my eyes could see the glory of God through the passing haze.

"If not," I whispered, as a joyful smile was painted with a broad brush across my face, "I have faith that You will always provide for me and never abandon me. May Your will be done."

Playfully kicking a few stones as I walked, I read through the pages of the Bible I'd packed away in my head and my heart, in a place no man could touch. And I was there led by the hand of God to Paul's first letter to the Corinthians, where, in the fourth chapter, he explained the path of the apostle; and from these words, God fed me strength to face all that was yet to come: "When reviled, we bless; when persecuted, we endure; when slandered, we entreat. We have become, and are still, like the scum of the world, the refuse of all things."

The world had made plain to me its feelings regarding my following Christ; I had become no more beloved to it than refuse. For I had been born again—the identity of Jesus had been imprinted onto me. Of me and my brothers and sisters in Christ, Jesus said in John 17, "They are not of the world, just as I am not of the world."

And, so, as a stranger in a hostile land, I walked, knowing I could no longer blend in among the mire of this temporal plane, for I had been given the light of Christ, and He had appointed me to expose just how dark is the evil warring against His good creation, masquerading as light and peace— by the fang marks of the ravenous wolves prowling for light to devour, marks that were like a wicked creed carved in stone etched permanently into my skin, God would show Himself more beautiful than the darkness the blind desperately love, and so add to His glorious kingdom a host of new rooms, prepared for the heavenly homecoming of the saints.

14

Thirteen Hours to Church

"**A**ND just where have you been all this time?"
Though the dean of the college had conceded that it was not at all like me to have missed even a minute of class, much less an entire semester, he was a man of zero tolerance for those who would let their studies fall by the wayside and discard so great an opportunity as the university offered. Medicine, he asserted, is serious business; and those who take it lightly, even neglect it, are not fit to bear the honor the coat of white demands.

"A great personal matter insisted upon my absence, sir," I replied, knowing I could not share with him the exact details of that matter. My dramatic exodus the day of my arrest had not reached the administration's ears—given that the dorms were far from the university and not managed by it, but were rather under the authority of the Ministry of Higher Education, as well as the fact that I had not been given a formal sentence, the religious police, per their manner of conducting affairs, had not contacted the school or announced the cause of my absence. Only those given a sentence have their schools or places of work notified that the condemned will not be returning, having been barred by bars or beheading. As it was, no

211

rumors or stories had seemingly circulated or gained traction after my grand exit, at least none that had reached the administration's ears; and those details were not about to breach my lips. "It was most unexpected," I added, "and I sincerely apologize that I was, as a result, unable to fulfill my responsibilities."

My speech was slow and careful, very deliberate—partially due to the delicacy of the situation, but in no small part as a result of my having lost so many teeth and suffered such oral damage during my imprisonment that I had been struggling to regain my speech ever since my release, practicing basic word-formation mechanics and training my tongue to articulate in its seemingly foreign, more vacant environment.

"You should have notified us immediately," he answered sternly. "Maybe then we could have been able to help you work around this, as you say, 'personal matter.'"

"I ask only for your mercy, sir," I said, my back upright and eyes locked into his, while my words lay prostrate before him. "Whatever you would require of me, however mountainous the task, if you would give me another chance, I can say unequivocally that nothing will be able to hinder me from meeting and exceeding your standard."

Thusly I spoke with the utmost confidence, for I knew that if I were given a second chance, it would be a door opened by God—the kind no one else can open, and no one can close. Without God to open the door to my being a doctor, my medical career was already over.

"We'll see," he replied with a smirk. "Unfortunately, it's not up to me alone. This will have to go before the board of directors. In the meantime," he added, seeing me to the door, "act as if you've already received the thing you seek—a head start wouldn't hurt, if indeed they vote in your favor."

I watched with mouth gaping as the door closed before me, and stood there for some time in stunned silence.

"I'm going to be a doctor," I mumbled to myself, unable even to move my lips, for God had just spoken through this man the words of Jesus.

"Whatever you ask in prayer," He said in Mark 11:24, "believe that you have received it, and it will be yours."

Jesus was not done teaching me faith. Though I had learned much during my imprisonment, I realized in this moment that faith would never be something I could just attain and have—I would have to work at it daily; and here was God, speaking through a Muslim the words of Christ, teaching me faith.

What more did I need? I raced back to my dorm, fell on my knees and prayed, petitioning the will of God to make me a doctor and to use my position to reach the lost; then, I sprang to my feet and hit the books, studying as if every test I'd missed were being administered that night.

Amid the firestorm of translating and cramming into my skull more medical terminology, facts, figures, and procedures than any host of men could shake a stick at, my gaze—which had been racing left to right and back again, up and down the pages, as if my eyes were trapped in a game of Pong—broke through the confines of the page and landed in the midst of my room, where lay a throw rug I had recently purchased and, as the name suggests, thrown there upon the floor.

All at once, my frantic studying came to a halt, and I rose slowly from my chair and stepped carefully, as one approaching a sleeping lion, toward the spot.

The rug had been procured to produce silence, but it could not even muffle the screams over which it lay.

Kneeling, I gently took a corner of the rug and peeled it back, revealing thereunder rows of timber painted red.

A slow, trembling breath passed through my lungs, as I placed my hand in the midst of the crimson stain, tracing the long scratches etched into the wood by these very hands.

Closing my eyes, I let the recent past fill my gaze, permitted the chill of my cell to wrap me in its mangled claws, dipped my tongue again into the stale haze of death and pool of blood, and opened the doors of my ears to the raging ocean of tormented, terrified screams—but every time my present day seemed moments away from crumbling into the night that was the past, the words of God, as spoken through Paul in his second letter to the Corinthians, swooped in to preserve the new day and forbid my descent: "For we were so utterly burdened beyond our strength that we despaired of life itself. Indeed, we felt that we had received the sentence of death. But that was to make us rely not on ourselves but on God who raises the dead. He delivered us from such a deadly peril, and He will deliver us."

"On You, Christ," I whispered, finishing the verse, "I have set my hope that You will deliver me again."

Placing both hands gently into the midst of the dried pool of my blood, I prayed, borrowing the words written in that same letter: "Father, I was afflicted in every way, but I was not crushed. I was perplexed, but not driven to despair. I was persecuted, but not forsaken; struck down, but not destroyed. I carry now in the body the death of Jesus, so that His life may be manifested in me. More stains like this one may yet be painted upon this earth," I continued on my own; "yet, though worse things than this may still lie before me, let man hate me, beat me, break my bones, kill me—my life is forfeit to You, and my soul secure in Your hand. What, now, can man do to me?"

Rising again, I returned to my studies, leaving the rug rolled off to the side.

"Thank you for coming, Ahmed," said the dean. "We have discussed your case at length and have reached a decision."

The room had taken this moment, shortly after my entering it, to put on display its cartwheeling ability, selecting me as its exclusive audience. Standing before the board of medical directors, I did my best to exercise subtlety as I leaned into the spin; each passing second felt as though it could be my last in the upright position before I was sent sliding on a mountainous incline into the wall below. Indeed, I was at peace about the decision—it was the excitement of watching in real time as the hand of God descended to set me upon His chosen path that set my head in a whirl. I just hoped I would maintain consciousness long enough to see it happen.

"You've been an excellent student," he continued. "Your marks are truly impressive; your professors have vouched for your hard work and dedication. And, as you know, your published research is moving now to human trials. Your superior efforts have resulted in worldwide distribution of your team's discoveries and have become a mark of pride for this university."

Here it comes, I thought—the magnificent payoff, or the rug-pulling "but."

"Therefore, we have decided to give you another chance."

"THANK YOU!" I shouted, unable to check the volume of my bellow before it left my lungs.

"But!" he added—I wondered if he'd not yet given up the idea of pulling the rug out from under me. "*But*, you will be granted no leniency, whatsoever. You have one month to study for all your exams, and that's it."

Wishing not to betray my awed reaction to the truly steep task set before me, I nodded to demonstrate my understanding; but I wonder if I came off looking a tad crazed, as I know my eyes were as wide as baseballs.

"I suggest you get started," he said at length, eyeing me curiously.

Clearing my throat, I stepped forward and, very professionally, thanked each board member for the opportunity, after which I inched toward the door, dropping *Thank You*s all the way until I had exited the office and shut the door behind me.

The moment the latch clicked, a long streak of light flashed through the hallway with a great gust of wind, as I took off in a mad sprint for my dorm.

Seventeen hours a day I studied, devoting the remaining seven hours to Bible study and the singing of joyful prayers, born of the overabundant thanksgiving that was bursting through the very seams of my body—at some point in that month, I'm sure I ate and slept and saw at least a ray of daylight; but as for when and how long I cannot say. And when at last the time had come for my exams, I plopped myself down, uncorked the brain, and funneled through my pencil every drop of information I'd crammed into the cranium, until the tests were awash with the medical knowledge I'd acquired and I was back in my dorm, ardently counting the sheep I'd let graze about unnumbered over the past four weeks.

I arose the next morning and immediately turned on my VPN to start my day in the Word of God. My recent study had been in the letters of Paul and the apostles in the latter portion of the New Testament; and as I picked up from where I'd left off in Hebrews, reading in chapter 10 about the importance of Christian fellowship for the building up and encouraging of believers, I was drawn back to a prayer for spiritual strength found at the end of chapter 3 of Ephesians, in which Paul wrote, "Now to Him who is able to do far more abundantly than all that we ask or think, according to the power at work in us, to Him be the glory in the church and in Christ Jesus throughout all generations, forever and ever. Amen."

Just then my computer let out a faint chime, and into my inbox dropped an email from the administration, its subject line referring to my exams.

Closing my eyes, I prayed, "Jesus, You have taken me this far. A month ago I was a prisoner; today, I am whatever You wish me to be."

I finished my Bible study, and then opened my email.

***

"That was very fine work you did, Ahmed," said the dean, having finally managed to squeeze a word into the fray that was my bombardment of gratitude.

Hardly able to contain myself, I'd darted from my dorm to his office to tell him what he already knew: that I had passed and was now a bona fide doctor! Had I have been any more outside of my control, I might have taken him into my arms and begun dancing all about the room—but as it would not have been wise to terminate my doctoral career mere minutes after it had begun, I allowed my words to do the embracing via a vehement outpouring of appreciation.

"But now the real work begins," he added, eyeing me from under raised brow and tilted head, "and you're not exactly off to a running start."

"Sir?"

"The fact is," he stated emphatically, "you've missed the boat. All of your peers have already secured their junior doctor internships."

"I'll apply to every single internship I can find—today! I'll go right now!"

"THAT!" he shouted, as I turned to dash through the door. "That is easy enough to say, Ahmed—and, with your resume and the marks you put up on your exams, you could have discovered securing an internship as easy as finding sand in the Rub' a Khali. But you're late. The grains have been picked to the bedrock."

"Are you saying it's impossible?"

"Honestly," he sighed with a shrug, "it may be. It's not just that any remaining positions will be few and far between; you'll also face hostility regarding your tardiness in applying. You won't come off as an attractive candidate."

Pausing a moment to digest his words, I turned my gaze to his and asked, "What must I do?"

"Apply!" he declared, rising from his chair. "Apply, apply, apply—and hope that whatever sustained you through the last month can lift you over this obstacle, as well. You literally can't afford to fail this time," he added opening his door to see me out. "As a graduate, you will lose your government stipend—you need a job."

"My dorm contract is about to expire, as well," I mumbled, lost in the processing of all this information.

"All the more reason not to fail. Without this, you'll be a doctor by degree only. And of what use is such a man?"

Back in my dorm, I began researching and making a list of all the hospitals I could find that offered junior doctor internships. But the more my list grew, the more my mind became distracted by the verse I'd read earlier in Hebrews 10: "And let us consider how to stir up one another to love and good works, not neglecting to meet together."

I had indeed been longing for Christian fellowship— something more than what I could get over the internet: face to face, interpersonal relationships based on Christ.

"Father," I prayed, "I know fellowship is important, but so is finding work. You made me a doctor; now I actually have to *be* one!"

Something about how a man's got to eat seemed poised to fall next from my lips; but God had destroyed that argument, both in His Word and in His work in my life.

"Therefore I tell you," Jesus said in Matthew chapter 6, "do not be anxious about your life, what you will eat or what you will drink, nor about your body, what you will put on. Is not life more than food, and the body more than clothing? Look at the birds of the air: they neither sow nor reap nor gather into barns, and yet your heavenly father feeds them. Are you not of more value than they?"

If that weren't enough, God had already given me food when I'd had none, taken me off the streets, delivered me from suffering.

About this time, as all these things were reminded to me, there came an intense gurgling—not from my stomach, but rather from deep within my soul, sounding off with the moaning of spiritual starvation.

"All right, God," I said, laying down my pencil, "What must I do?"

Even as the words formed in my mouth, the answer was made plain, and I quickly diverted my internet search from hospitals to churches.

Now, locating a Christian church in and around Saudi Arabia is about as easy as finding an apple on a fig tree. Christians are outlaws in my country; therefore, they weren't exactly broadcasting their identity and location. This was truly a search for a diamond in the rough—I was chipping away at the stone of the Saudi world for the prize that lay beneath, buried somewhere deep within the virulent bedrock that is the heart of Islam, following whatever leads or trails I could find.

My efforts eventually produced a list of underground churches, scattered all over the nation; they were each comprised of foreigners living and working in Saudi: Filipinos, Americans, Africans, and many others. Groups arranged secret meeting times and places; these I committed to memory, so as to not risk exposing and condemning them by writing down locations on a piece of paper I could potentially misplace.

List made and carved into the brain, I finished off the night submitting internship applications, feeling rather confident that at least one of them would return a favorable response.

The next morning, I ventured off to find the first church on my list. I practically skipped the whole way, so sure that I would soon be basking in the joy fellowship with a new family in Christ—so sure was I that I nearly crumpled up my mental list.

I arrived at the designated meeting place: an apartment unit in Saudi; and, having checked first the surrounding hallways, corners, and crevices, I walked to the door, shot another glance in either direction, and gently knocked.

After a solid minute of silence, the door slowly creaked open, latched still by the door chain.

Very little could be seen of the apartment, save for layers upon layers of thick carpet lining the walls—doubtlessly as a soundproofing measure.

Suddenly, into the shadow filling the crack emerged the face of a Filipino man.

His eyes widened considerably upon seeing me.

I readied myself for whatever security question he might ask—maybe a Bible verse, or a fact about Jesus?

"Where do you come from?" he asked in a sharp whisper.

Rather surprised by this question, my brain immediately switched course; and, thinking the improbable reality of a Saudi Christian might fill the man with great joy, I donned a smile from ear to ear and happily declared, "From here! I'm a Saudi!"

The latter statement had just begun to breach my lips when there was thrust through my nose a magnificent blow, followed by a gust of wind slapping me across the face, while down the empty hallway danced a silence-inducing *SLAM*.

"What did I say?" I wondered, backing away from the door and rubbing my bruised nose; there seemed, however, no means of rubbing away the shattering of my hopes, nor finding any answer as to why a Christian would so adamantly reject a brother in Christ.

I puzzled over this all the way back to my dorm, where, shortly after plopping myself down on the bed to puzzle some more, my phone began to buzz.

"The deadline was weeks ago!" shouted the rather indignant voice on the other end. "Why would you even apply? Have you nothing better to do than waste my time, just because *you* wasted *yours*?"

I don't remember speaking at all during the irate lecture; I may not even have had the opportunity to say "Hello." The angry voice—probably pushed over the edge of a bad day by my late application crammed in their inbox—acted upon me like the swishing wind that had slapped me hours earlier, with the dial tone acting as the slamming door. My mind had already been towing an elephant after my first unfruitful endeavor; the last thing I needed was a second beast to further burden the brain. And so weighty was this rejection, compounded by the perplexity plaguing my mind and running like poison syrup over the giant bowl of ice cream that had been my excitement for Christian fellowship, that I slunk low to the floor and there remained until the sun had fallen behind the dunes, cemented in place by the ponderous weight of my thoughts, lost in a daze.

Christians aren't supposed to be hopeless; we're not supposed to give up when pain and confusion reign. Yet, we so often do just this. Jesus Himself rebuked His own disciples for being of such little faith. So, I prayed—through the night and into the next morning, I asked God for His strength, for the will to press on toward the goal. After all, it had been only one day, one fellowship, one hospital, and one rejection each. I had a whole list of Christian groups and hospitals yet without a vote on my case!

Setting out early, I found the next door and gave it a knock.

As if the Filipino man had coached him, an Anglo American opened the door but a crack, with the chain still latched, and asked, "Where are you from?"

A twinge of pain swirled about the tip of my nose; I stepped slightly backward and said with a wince, "I'm Saudi Arabian."

He didn't stick around for the "Arabian" part.

SLAM

I walked to the next meeting place.

"Where are you from?"

"I'm a Christian Saudi Ara—"

SLAM

"Where are you from?"

"I come with Jesus from Saudi A—"

SLAM

"Where are you from?"

"From Christ's direction...out of Saudi—"

SLAM

"Where are you from?"

"Saudi."

SLAM

It had been a long day of door slamming, and before the journey was through, I was announcing my origin and then slamming the door for them.

Hoping for a ray of sunlight to part the massing clouds, I returned to my dorm and checked my voicemail and inbox.

"This is extremely unprofessional! You should have applied before the deadline!"

"You think you can just stroll in whenever you please and be handed a position? Do you really expect us to offer an internship to someone who couldn't even be bothered to adhere to our rules?"

"This shows a great lack of responsibility! If you conduct your affairs thusly in applying for an internship position, what can I expect from you as a doctor?"

"You've failed the first and easiest test of reliability! How could we possibly trust you to care for our patients, to entrust their lives to you?"

"To accept you would serve only to downgrade our respectable establishment!"

SLAM

SLAM

SLAM

SLAM

SLAM

WHUMP (the sound of my falling face-first onto the bed)

This dual-rejection, one-sided boxing match went on for several days, with no end in sight to the pattern of crushing right hooks in the morning and pounding lefts in the evening.

Then, rather abruptly, a change of pace: some people from a church called the Latter Day Saints welcomed me. All seemed to be going well, with some signs indicating that I may have reached the end of my rejection...that is, until we discussed Jesus.

"He is my Savior!" I declared, reciting to them my testimony and confession of faith. "Jesus, the one true God, the only Son of the Father—that blessed holy trinity!"

Coming down from cloud seventy-nine, I found a room of hunched shoulders balancing precariously atop them gigantic beets, in which were carved the most menacing scowls.

Needless to say, given their response and what I came to learn of the twisted theology this group preaches, the slamming of that door was mutual.

"GOD!" rang my muffled cry, when again my face had *whumped* into the bed. "What are You doing?"

Terrible thoughts began to swirl about my head. I could see myself turned out of my dorm, jobless and penniless, toothless and wretched, begging for crumbs at stoplights, only to see my brothers drive up in their spotless Porsche—they would fall into a fit of uproarious laughter, spit at me and throw garbage, saying, "Look where your impotent Christ has taken you! Can't you see this is Allah's punishment for going astray to worship idols?"

Their words rang louder and louder between my ears, and before me a great void of emptiness felt as though it were opening between my Jesus and me.

I threw my eyes open wide to banish the vision, only to find myself lost in a long corridor, bleached white, and lined with doors on both sides—those on the left set beneath a giant caduceus; those on the right set beneath a towering cross. Darting from side to side, I jiggled the handles of each door, one by one; none opened. I darted some more, jiggled more handles—all locked. I flew to the next door and began to pound against the wood, then to the next, which I kicked repeatedly with all my might; then again to another, throwing my body against it, over and over; like a tornado of boulders, I cast blow after blow upon door after door, harder and harder, faster and faster, again and again; not one so much as trembled at my fury.

"Why are You doing this, God?" I screamed, falling bloodied and bruised to my knees. "Am I not following along the path You have paved for me? Do I not seek?" Tears began to rain over my cheeks. "Why, then, do I not find? Have I not knocked? Why, then, has the door not been opened unto me? Why not *this* door, God?" I cried, pointing with a lifeless finger to the one before me.

Like a feather falling through a warm, gentle breeze, a soft whisper from pages memorized fell over me.

"I know your works. Behold!"

As these syllables rained over me, my head was compelled to turn; and there in the distance I saw a doorway, falling into place at the end of the hall, not on either the left or the right side of the corridor.

It was opening.

"I have set before you an open door, which no one is able to shut."

Through that doorway streamed a great light—it felt upon my skin like a pool of warm water, engulfing me on all sides. And then, a mighty power filled my legs, and I stood in the midst of the corridor, facing the glory before me.

"I know that you have but little power," said Jesus, as from this third chapter of Revelation, "and yet you have kept My Word and have not denied My name."

All at once, the corridor and all its doors sped away into the distance, and I was driven upward through the void at breakneck speed, feeling like a fish caught on a divine line, until I was thrust bolt upright in bed.

"You've opened a door!" I shouted to the heavens. "Somewhere! But how will I find it?"

Naught but the silence of my room lifted its voice in reply.

I waited.

Still, only silence.

I heaved a sigh and ran my fingers slowly through my hair.

A door had been opened—but, where? Was I supposed to keep wading through rejection until I found it? While rejection from the hospitals was dejecting and frustrating, it was nothing compared to my being cast away from the fellowship of believers, with no more known about me than my origin.

That gave me an idea! I sprang to my computer and began scouring the Bible for any verse that stated explicitly or implicitly that believers should be sure to slam the door in the face of Christians of certain nationalities. And, so, I learned how God works even in spite of our foolishness; for the aim of this pursuit had sprung to life from hurt, and was doomed to fail in a pit of animus: my search turned up no such verse. But God has a way of working out His own plans in spite of our own, and for our good. Indeed, I found no such verse; however, my search—which took place mostly in Acts, as that book depicts the origins of the Christian church—uncovered the story of Saul of Tarsus: a vehement persecutor of early Christians, who, according to Acts 8 and 9, ravaged the church, going house to house and dragging off men and women to be committed to prison; a man who breathed threats and murder against the disciples of the Lord, until one day he encountered the risen Jesus, renounced and repented of his ways, and became the apostle Paul. Though he had put his faith in Christ and given up his life to follow Him, the former identity he had shed still loomed. "And when he had come to Jerusalem," it says of Paul in Acts 9:26, "he attempted to join the disciples. And they were all afraid of him, for they did not believe that he was a disciple."

SLAM

Like Paul, I had been a persecutor of the Church of Christ. Though the Christians who'd rejected me needed no more than my nationality to deem me a threat, had they known my past, the fear that slammed the door might have compelled them to leap from windows and dart through the streets to safer territory; for I had sworn a bloody allegiance to Allah; I had trained to be the soldier of a false god, to spill the blood of the infidel, especially the Christian; it had been my heart's deepest desire to murder those I wished now to embrace in fellowship.

I was humbled.

My hurt had led me to ignore the perspective of those Christians, who live in constant danger in this hostile land. They had every reason to suspect I was just as hostile as the sand beneath my feet. How, then, could I convince people that my faith is genuine?

Acts had the answer.

Speaking for himself, Paul would have been hard-pressed to persuade anyone that he was sincere. But God sent Barnabas, who took Paul to the apostles and declared to them Paul's proof as displayed in action: preaching Christ, behaving in stark contrast to the character of the Saul who had been persecuting them, enduring sufferings no liar or agent of evil would bother to endure, and casting into the dirt the respect and dignity Saul had enjoyed among the Pharisees and leaders of the ancient world.

Barnabas vouched for the act of Jesus in Paul's life.

I needed a Barnabas.

Kneeling beside my bed, I prayed, "Lord, You open doors that none can shut, and shut doors no one can open. Well," I said with a slight chuckle, "I've encountered a lot of shut doors. Lead me to the one door no one can shut; send me a Barnabas, someone who will hold fast to faith in You and test my claim; someone who will give me a chance. And please," I begged fervently, picturing those frightened believers I'd encountered, "comfort those who have rejected me. Lord, they have acted according to the fear of man. Show them that You are more powerful than the evil that surrounds them."

It may seem, per this literary arrangement of the timeline, that the very next thing to be detailed would be my finding of the opened door. And, it is. But this was not as immediate a happening as moving from one paragraph to the next. Another heap of rejection had first to be waded through, taking me down to the wire with my dorm contract. And the fulfillment of God's goodness in the two arenas of my life presently detailed did not happen all at once; rather, one became the "vehicle," if you will, taking me to the other.

"You are a lazy doctor!"

This wasn't off to a good start—or, a good finish; as it was, I had reached the last hospital I could find wherein one could work as a junior doctor. I had gone in to speak face to face with the director, a Filipina woman, and offer my application for consideration. If this one failed, I would be out on the streets in a matter of days.

"I truly am baffled! You come in here *now*? Why did you not apply months ago, before the deadline?"

She berated me for quite a while—I don't know exactly how long, nor can I recount the full breadth of her grievances regarding my fitness as a doctor; for I was lost in a battle for my soul, praying that God would forbid me from despair, and that He would give me the strength to trust Him, no matter where I ended up in the next hour.

Suddenly, her tone shifted and her speaking ceased; her inflection, I judged, meant she had said all she wished to say; her face suggested I was no longer welcome.

Rising slowly from my chair, I nodded, unable to utter a parting salutation, and turned to leave. But I never made it fully around, for so great was the war within that I was instantly overcome by a tidal wave of emotion, which robbed me of all my strength and sent me stumbling backward. I crashed with a *WHUMP* onto a sofa, set along the back wall; and there, face buried in my hands, while tears gushed freely from my eyes, I sputtered a silent prayer.

"Jesus! You promised not to leave us as orphans! Where are You?" I sobbed. "Everyone has left me...but I have faith. My God, You will never leave me!"

No matter how hard I tried, I could not stop crying; and when at last I had summoned enough control to lift my head, the entire room was a watercolor blur.

Knowing my welcome was long overdue for at least the next century, I wiped my eyes and rose to my feet. But as I did so, there came into focus a piece of paper taped to the wall above the director's head.

It was plain—something made unprofessionally on a word processor and printed on an office printer. The paper was white; in it was a rectangular border, containing a frame made up of a string of multi-colored diamonds. And in that frame were these words, typed in no special font and with no attribution: "For I know the plans I have for you, plans to prosper you and not to harm you, plans to give you hope and a future."

My despair vanished, and I leapt for joy, nearly sailing through the ceiling.

"THAT'S JEREMIAH 29:11!" I shouted, pointing like a child seeing fireworks burst suddenly into the sky.

The red that had painted the director's scowl melted into stunned white.

She darted past me for her door, which she hastily opened before peering into the hall.

Whipping her head back into the room, she slammed the door behind her and locked it.

"Who are you?" she snapped breathlessly. "Where are you from? How did you get here? What do you want? Who's with you? Are you from the religious police?"

As with her angry lecture from earlier, there was no edge in her speech to interject any speech of my own. Her machinegun questioning quickly turned into frightened shouting, a never-ending bombardment of barking.

Given my long beard and Saudi clothing, I can only assume she thought herself like an animal caught in a trap, and that I had come to interrogate her.

"Are you with the religious police?" she asked again, panting as a bead of sweat traced the curve of her nose.

She paused this time, allowing me a moment to reply, which I promptly seized.

"No! No!" I whispered, hoping a lower tone might help to calm her. "Truly, I have come only to inquire after an internship at this very respectable hospital."

Breathing heavily, she eyed me crossly and carefully from beneath a furrowed brow.

"Do..." she began, her voice crawling along the floor to my ears. "Do you...read the Bible?"

"Yes!" I cried softly. "I've memorized most of it—that's how I know the verse. Only," I added, "you've left out, 'Thus says the Lord.'"

Stepping forth, mere inches from my face, she gazed up at me and plunged into my eyes a dagger glare.

"Are you a Christian?" she asked, a hiss in her voice and a quiver under her eye.

How swiftly she'd turned the tables—appearing afeared that I had come to interrogate her, it was now she instilling that cold sense of dread in me. The traps laid by the Saudi government for apostates are cunning and often unassuming. Could this have been one such elaborate trap?

I stood before her, silence passing through my gaping jaw, while flashes of my imprisonment poured through my mind like a ball of fire through a dense, dry forest. Teetering atop the head of a pin, rising high above a pit of destruction: that was the feeling; and so shaken was I that I became extremely self-conscious, to the point where I could stand beside myself as an observer, watching this poor, tearstained man mumble from his mangled, toothless mouth indiscernible sounds—indeed, all the progress I'd made in regaining my speech went right out the window; I was like an infant, helpless to articulate a coherent reply.

"Lord," I prayed, employing the crisp and clear speech of the mind, "what do I say? If she's a Muslim, she may very well hand me over to the religious police—I'll be imprisoned again, lose the rest of my teeth! I'll probably be killed this time! But I cannot deny You! I cannot say 'no!' I will not lie! What must I say?"

"Be wise," came the whisper of the Word.

Then, all of a sudden, my mind's eye flipped through the pages stashed away in my memory to Luke 10:6, which refers to a follower of God as a Son, or Person, of Peace.

"I am a Person of Peace!"

Her glaring daggers did not immediately withdraw from my eyes.

Backing away slowly, her tense shoulders deflating like a pin-pricked balloon, she asked in a voice as deep as the bowing of her brow, "And what is a Person of Peace?"

Nodding carefully toward the verse taped to her wall, I timidly replied, "Read your Bible."

For a solid day and a half, she and I remained locked in a silent stare, with even our breaths tip-toeing cautiously over our lips, so as to not disturb the tension.

Then, in a whisper that sounded like a bomb had just gone off in her office, she said, "Give me your application."

Over the course of the next few days, I ceaselessly prayed the verse hung upon the director's wall: "Father, please, give me a future and a hope." In between syllables, my imagination would flash over my eyes like a blinking spotlight scenes it had invented, featuring the director as the main character in its quick but terribly detailed one-acts; she would play out various nefarious scenarios, of which the aim was always to arrange for me a permanent meeting with my Savior.

The more these wild images played, the more I prayed, until one day my prayers were interrupted by the buzzing of my phone.

"Hello?"

"Mr. Joktan?"

It was the director.

"This is he," I replied, doing my best to sound as doctorial as possible, not having any idea how that is done.

"Mr. Joktan, the hospital has reviewed your qualifications."

Here it comes—I braced for the *SLAM*.

"We would be pleased to welcome you to our team as a junior doctor."

WHUMP

***

It was true; it had happened: I was now officially a doctor, having regained consciousness quick enough to accept the offer before she hung up the line.

With my new situation, I rented a very nice apartment in the city and even purchased a car—that SUV and I went everywhere together, scouring as many Christian communities as I could find scattered all over Saudi Arabia, even venturing into other countries, searching in places to which I had been unable to travel on foot.

The door at the end of the corridor had been opened, and I saw better the plan of God that had been woven into all the door slamming. Rejection after rejection had narrowed my search for a job to a place in which the Word of God was hung high on the wall of a Saudi hospital director, and so abundant were my wages that I was able to acquire a means of finding fellowship beyond the hostile borders of my native land.

"That's so wonderful!" declared a friend of mine, to whom I had relayed my recent blessings, as he and I shared a meal.

I called him Chris; though his full name is Christopher, or Christoffel, in his native Dutch. He and I had long conversed online, until the day he traveled to Saudi to meet me face to face and so ensure that I was a real person.

"And have you found a church?" he asked, taking a bite of his food.

"Not yet," I sighed, "but God has been faithful, as ever He will be. I'll find my family of believers in His good time."

"You know," he said, "I have a connection to a local church; a group of solid believers, they are—rock solid Christians. Why don't I reach out to them?"

"Would they accept me? Practically everyone I've encountered is afraid of me—that is, except for the Latter Day Saints people. But they could use a few tips from 1 Corinthians 13."

"I can't imagine this church would turn you away," he replied, his speech laced with a few residual chuckles. "I'll shoot them an email—what do you say, huh? Worth a try, no?"

"Couldn't hurt. Where is it?"

"Outside Saudi."

"I thought you'd said it was local."

"More or less. About twelve or thirteen—"

"Miles?"

"Hours."

"THIRTEEN *HOURS!*"

"Give or take."

"That's some significant giving and taking, wouldn't you say?"

"Well, sure—but, hey, it's not like anyone around here is letting you into their group, now are they? Besides, it's like *nine* hours of driving, tops; add in stops for food, bathroom breaks, and gas—not to mention about two hours of border inspection—and you've got yourself a solid twelve to thirteen."

"That's more than an entire day there and back! And that's only if I turn around right upon getting there!"

"Uh huh—so," he added, taking another mouthful, "want me to reach out to them?"

I was blown away by how cavalier he seemed to be toward the matter! He was right about one thing, though: no other group was willing to take me.

"Where exactly is it?" I asked.

"Dubai. I'll email them tonight, if you'd like."

Shaking my head, I idly scratched my beard, while a zillion points of consideration flooded my head.

"God," I prayed silently, "is this the place you've picked for me? *Thirteen hours* away? How will I manage my hectic schedule at the hospital with such a place?"

I looked at my friend, who had taken another bite of food and become distracted with something outside the window. Looking that way myself, I saw a tiny bird flutter past the glass.

Breathing deeply, I closed my eyes and prayed, "Where there's *Your* will, there's *Your* way. God, You provide even for such creatures as that little bird. You've given me a car, a means to travel a great distance in but a trivial amount of time. If this is where You want me to go, I'll go. And if by this there will be any strengthening of my faith, I know it will be in no small part rooted in this: that I know nothing about cars or how to select them for extended driving; so, I'll have to trust You to keep it intact, so long as Your will sends me to this distant place."

Turning back to my friend, I took another deep breath and expelled it with an, "All right—let's see what they say. And, by the way, if they agree, I'm going to start calling you Barnabas."

"Why?" he asked, pushing the word past a packed cheek-full of food.

Chewing a mouthful of my own, I smiled back at him.

Barnabas was true to his word: he emailed the church that night. And he was true in his suppositions: first, that they would accept me; second, that I had a thirteen-hour trip ahead of me.

Having made myself comfortable with the church's confession of faith, their theology, and found peace in prayer, I packed my things for the long haul; then, at five PM, following a twelve-hour shift, I jumped into my SUV and hit the dark, dusty, and deserted roads for my destination.

The first hour sailed by in a mere moment; though immensely tired, I was beyond thrilled to have been welcomed by a body of believers! Hour two also kept a peppy pace, but its enthusiasm was markedly less intense than the first. Hour three featured a change in stride with a bathroom break and some leg stretching. Another hour ticked away, the increasingly sluggish second hand scraping along the face of Time, smearing the minutes and moments, hours and blinks into an indiscernible mesh of numbers and winks of daylight, in which the zombie version of myself pumped gas, swallowed untasted food, waded through border inspection, and inflicted periodic blows to my cheeks whenever my drowsy head hadn't been jarred awake by a face-planting into the steering wheel.

At last, as my SUV and I broke through the veil of morning light, I beheld the church, set neatly beneath the sunrise.

I pulled into the driveway—or, what I thought was the driveway.

A man walked briskly out of the building and began motioning at me to move the car closer to where he stood, in the paved portion of the church, rather than my selected spot on the front lawn.

Having done so, I stumbled out of the car and into an outstretched hand attached to a pleasantly chuckling smile.

"You must be Ahmed! My name is Rashid. It's a pleasure to meet you!"

As if a pair of anvils had been attached to them, I labored to lift my eyelids until I saw the man's beaming face. I rallied the muscles in mine to form a salutation.

"C—coffee?"

The lips spoke the mind; and, still smiling, the man took me by the arm and led me to a freshly brewed pot in the vestibule. I must confess, after my long shift and all that driving, I felt a twinge of annoyance that he handed me a mug, rather than forking over the entire pot for me to guzzle in a single gulp.

"How was the drive?" he asked.

He struck me as more of an auditory learner, rather than a visual one, for there was a whole novel's worth of an answer to that question etched all over my appearance.

"Long," I replied, once the coffee had adequately reanimated all my vital systems. I made a point as I sipped to praise God for what was surely a top ten good gift of His: the glorious brown bean brew! And what a gift it was, for this man and I had much to discuss. I questioned him up and down, testing the theology of the church against the Bible; and he, likewise, tended to the responsibility that was the flock, of which he was an appointed leader, casting fire upon my testimony to see if it was truly founded on Christ, upheld by the Spirit.

"Well," he said after quite a lot of challenging chatting and a few pots of coffee, "I think I've heard all I need to hear; the rest I leave to God. I'm honored to invite you to join our congregation."

"I'd love to!" I exclaimed, not a wink of drowsiness left in me.

"Great! Now, we meet Sunday mornings at ten, but we also hold an evening service at seven, if that works better with your commute."

"I'll arrange my shifts accordingly!"

"Sounds good—as for church membership, we require those interested to partake in a series of membership classes. The church elders will conduct these sessions, after which prospective members are to meet with an elder one-on-one to discuss testimony and faith, much like we've done here today, but far more in depth."

"Sounds wonderful! May I start now?"

Chuckling, he handed me a brochure explaining membership and listing the dates and times for meetings.

"We can work around your schedule, if need be. Call me if there will be any conflict with these dates," he added, handing me a business card, "and we'll see if we can find a way to work around it."

Our conversation lasted a little while longer, until Rashid was called away.

"I'll be back in a just a minute," he said. "Feel free to look around."

Drumming my fingers atop the arms of the chair, I did just that; only, I dared not leave my seat—it was imperative that I made a good impression, and I did not want to frustrate the man by forcing him to go searching for the wandering newcomer. So, the extent of my looking around was conducted in imitation of an owl.

Just then I heard the sound of footsteps approaching from behind. I turned to my left but found no one; the footsteps had also ceased.

Leaning further out of my chair, I ardently surveyed the entirety of the world behind me.

Nothing.

I could have sworn I'd heard something.

Heaving a *Hmm* and a sigh, I turned back around and was instantly bulldozed by a smiling face sitting opposite me.

"Hello!" said that very American-looking and sounding face, its cheeks shining like noonday suns and its mouth so wide I could count each shimmering tooth beaming back at me.

As I tried to recover my breath and steady my heart to a pace more akin to the trotting of a show pony, rather than the sprinting of a mustang, the face announced itself by the name Andrew.

"Ah-Ahmed," I replied in the same way some people say "A-choo."

"It's wonderful to meet you!" this Andrew exclaimed. "What brings you here?"

"I'm looking for a body of believers, followers of Jesus," I answered, my nerves calming.

"Well, you've found one!" he cried. "We are a body that loves Jesus! Do you know Jesus is the Word of God?"

"Yes!" I said, smiling. "Even the Qur'an says so!"

"Indeed, but He was no mere prophet. Jesus came to show us the way, yes; but did you know He preached that *He* is the way? He is the truth and life, and He took the punishment we deserve for our sin, so that we would be saved."

"Because He is the Son of God!" I declared, almost leaping to my feet.

Andrew was thrown back into his seat, looking absolutely stunned.

"You believe Jesus is the Son of God? Are you *not* a Muslim?"

"I will always be devoted to God, but Islam and its false god I have left in the dust of my wake!"

"Really? You're a follower of Jesus, too?" he exclaimed, his voice laced with childlike glee.

"I am!" I blurted joyfully, completely unaware that he and I were now standing face to face.

"Well, HALLELUJAH!" Andrew cried, and immediately threw his mighty arms around me and squeezed all the air out of my lungs.

Mere moments before one of my eyes popped out of my skull, Andrew released me and gave me a firm and affectionate pat over both shoulders.

"Boy!" he shouted, "I sure thought you were a Muslim, what with your beard and outfit! It seemed so much a divine opportunity to have a Muslim wander into this place that I thought you were maybe a man of Islam interested in knowing the true Jesus."

"And I am!" I said giddily. "I'm wholly submitted God, but I have forsaken Islam. Jesus Himself came to me in a dream while I was away in New Zealand—there, a kind man led me to Christ!"

"Wow! You saw Jesus in a dream? That's amazing! Tell me all about it!"

Taking our seats again, I recounted to him the steps of my journey up to that day.

"Incredible!" he cried, throwing his head back and slapping the arms of his chair. "God is so mightily at work in this area of the world! I'll tell you, I used to be wary of people who spoke of dreams and visions; but my path has taken me all over, and I've witnessed countless Muslims with similar testimonies of God stepping in and supernaturally interrupting their life."

"Are you a missionary?" I asked.

"I'm a retired Navy SEAL. And I'm a long way from the ol' stompin' grounds of Louisiana," he added with a chuckle.

I listened intently as he told me more about himself and his walk with God, while a gentle needle and thread weaved its way between our hearts. Here was a complete stranger, who, upon seeing what he thought was a lost person, veered off of whatever path he'd been on this day and sped to my side to preach the Gospel. His genuine, unconditional love and concern for my soul cut deeply through my heart and reminded me of the tall man. Though the impact he left on me this day might not have been the one he'd envisioned upon approaching me, it is nonetheless an everlasting one, bearing the eternal mark of Christ.

And so began a marvelous new chapter of life. Every week from that day forward, I'd saddle up in my SUV and blaze the thirteen-hour trail. Andrew was always sure to have a fresh pot of coffee waiting for me when I arrived; he'd rush out to meet me in the parking lot with a steaming mug and let me lean on him as we hobbled into the building to get a pre-worship refill.

He never missed a day.

Not once.

God had given me a forever friend.

There was nothing remotely easy about this new situation: working all day then driving all through the next. But this was true, Christian fellowship; I was being fed mighty handfuls of the Word of God, experiencing the Bible and my Savior in ways that had been impossible on my own! And I was on the cusp of being officially embraced as a member, as someone more than just a part of the worldwide body of Christ—this was to be an intimate bond, something I would take into eternity; this was to be a forever family, a blessing to fill the void left when my own blood tore themselves from me.

I attended every membership class—never missed one, nor was I so much as a minute late. This was far too important to neglect or let my hectic schedule get in the way. Knowing Andrew would be there motivated me all the more.

"Thank you, Father," I prayed during the seventh hour of another commute; thirteen hours is a bountiful time to spend in prayer, and it was my eager habit. "You've led me through the opened door—and now I'm being considered for church membership! It has been quite a journey," I sighed, tightening my grip on the wheel. "Where now does Your path turn? Where now will it go?"

His answer was already in motion.

15

Opportunity

WORKING in Saudi as a Christian junior doctor meant I was both an administrator of physical healing and a representative of the Great Physician Himself, the Healer and Redeemer of souls. My hospital was my mission field. During rounds, I would silently pray over patients and utter petitions for healing and salvation as I passed by room after room; but my greatest joy came in sharing the Bible to those in my care.

"But I feel fine!" cried a patient, wiping his leaky faucet of a nose on his sleeve for the umpteenth time and heaving a pair of hairy hacks. "Really! I don't need to be here."

"As a wise man once said," I answered, grinning, and scribbling on my clipboard, "'Those who are well have no need of a physician, but those who are sick.' And you, sir, are sick."

"Take these twice daily," I told another. "If your symptoms don't begin to improve in a week, give us a call. But be sure to also get plenty of fresh air and sunshine; actively seek out positivity. As the old saying goes, 'A joyful heart is good medicine.'"

"I'll get him for this," grumbled a young patient, who had been injured by a friend.

"You know," I said, gently placing my hand upon his shoulder, "I once read of a great teacher who spoke to this very situation: 'Whatever you wish that others do to you,' he said, 'do also to them.'"

And when a patient confided in me that she was afraid of an upcoming operation, I took her hand, looked her in the eye, and said, "Many years ago, my best friend offered me this hope: 'Fear not, for I am with you;' and I promise to be with *you* every step of the way. Be strong and courageous," I added with a smile.

"Fascinating; just fascinating!" said one of my new church friends upon hearing of this means of evangelism. "Let the power of the Word do its work!"

All the way to church, I had been bursting at the seams to tell everyone how, even in the anti-Christian land of Saudi Arabia, God's holy Word could still be spread.

"Yes!" I declared to the smiling faces seated all around me. "Jesus commands us to be as wise as serpents and as innocent as doves—how wonderful it is to follow Christ and reach the lost for His kingdom!"

"I wonder," said one of the elders, scratching his moustache, "if you do well not to attribute properly these verses."

"God put him in that hospital," said Andrew, quite sternly. "Not unlike the command to the exiles in Babylon, he is working for the benefit of the institution, submitting to its rules, but not forfeiting his service to God!"

"We shouldn't fear," he replied, looking directly at me. "Let God protect those who speak His Word boldly, and not give the dying a Christ-less Christianity."

Before I could answer, another man spoke in my defense.

"Or, let us trust that the Word of God is living and active, as the Bible says—sharper than the sword, able to penetrate anything."

"Exactly!" said another. "He's planting the seed—God will water it."

"I think that's enough for today," said the elder. "Let us close in prayer."

Heads bowed, eyes closed; yet, the weight of a host of stares was palpable, pressing me from every side like a collection of blunt rods.

With a final "Amen," the elder disappeared down the hall.

As the group dispersed, I caught Rashid by the arm and pulled him aside.

"Any news about the status of my membership?"

Thirteen hours riding in a cloud of dust following a long shift had not left me foggy to the things that really mattered.

His gaze remained distant for a moment, before slowly turning toward me.

"Right, right," he said. "About that...um, you've done all the classes, right?"

"You know I have! Weeks ago!"

"That's right, that's right...um..."

His speech trailed off, burrowing itself beneath the clamor of the fellowship going on around us.

Once again, his eyes became distant.

"Rashid," I said sharply. "I've been trying to schedule my final meeting with the elders, but no one has gotten back to me. Given today's tense discussion, I'd like to have that meeting sooner, rather than later."

"Look, Ahmed," he whispered after a pause, his eyes dancing chaotically about my face, "this isn't the best time for me to talk. I...I'll see what I can do."

"But—"

Just like that, he was gone, leaving me just as perplexed by the matter as I had been the last time I'd inquired...and the time before that...and the three times before that...and those other handful of times sprinkled in between.

What was this delay?

And why was there no one who could spare a moment to explain it?

A fiery tornado of confusion and frustration whirling over my head, I slunk slowly to my car, where, dropping my head to the wheel, I prayed for guidance—I prayed for patience, that my frustration would not turn into bitterness, that I would not assume motive; I prayed that God would show me the way. Truly, I thought, I had not been led down this thirteen-hour path for nothing.

It may seem a quick turnaround, a hasty response; but I can assure you that the commute set between these events carried with it a protracted perspective of time, making the minutes into hours and the hours into days.

Upon returning to my apartment, I face-planted into bed to dream away the time before my next shift, basking, albeit briefly, in the paradise of a forever family awaiting me, there, at the feet of Jesus.

A most unnatural noise quickly ended this glimpse of paradise, imbedding its blare into my bones, and reverberating long after I had chucked my phone across the room.

Sitting bolt upright, I wiped away the sleep glazed over my eyes and blinked the room into focus, at which time I was able to locate my phone and see that I had less than thirty minutes to get to the hospital for my shift.

In a single bound, I had leapt from my bed and into new clothes, scraped away the plaque and the mouth's morning perfume with a brushing that surely destroyed what enamel my few teeth had left, then rushed to gather my things—at which point my frantically flying hand bumped the mouse of my computer; the screen burst into life, and I saw a notification that I had in my inbox an email from my church.

"Dr. Ahmed," it began, "Thank you for your interest in church membership. Having completed the required membership courses, we would like to invite you to meet with our elders—"

That was all I read.

Leaving an Ahmed-shaped hole in my apartment door, I sprinted down the hall to my car, screaming praises to God!

"And that brings us to today," I concluded, expelling what seemed like the only breath I'd drawn the whole time I spent relaying my testimony. "Jesus is my life, now—the old has passed; the new has come. I am a new creation in Him, and I have no other joy than to share His Word, and no greater desire than to know Him more!"

"HALLELUJAH!" cried the elder to my right, arms raised to the heavens, as tears streamed down his face.

"*Hmph*," grunted the other, seated to my left, arms crossed, face dry and cracked like a barren desert, and moustache bent like a layer of sod draped over a high mound.

A pair of opposites sat before me. On one side, there emanated warmth and empathy; on the other sat a pillar of ice.

One side could not keep silent; the other seemed to lurk behind the hush. One side had eyes cast beyond this realm; the other perceived but flesh and earth. Light burst forth from a chest opened and singing; a haze surrounded a statue sealed tightly. And where one could not sit still, could not keep from stretching forth his arms, as if he could see Jesus Himself reaching out to him, the other was cemented to his chair, his arms hugging his body, and his eyes boring through me, peeling away the form fixed in his gaze, revealing something toward which he seemed disinclined to conceal his hostility.

"How mighty a God we serve!" cried the man on my right. "He has walked with you through the fiery furnace!"

"You say Jesus came to you in a *dream*?"

Having uttered the word "dream" in the same way some people kick the legs out from under a chair, the man on my left tilted his head forward and cocked his eyebrow, assuming a posture that felt to me like he was daring me to reply.

But without a doubt to even cause a single quake in my knees, I answered plainly.

"Yes. He did. Most miraculously and graciously."

The moustache rippled like a shredded flag in a tornadic wind as he expelled a great breath and sent his eyes to examine the underside of his skull.

It was all very plain to me what was troubling him—a dream had by another is not an easy thing to accept, as one has naught but the word of the dreamer to confirm its authenticity. A great deal of faith is required on the part of another to believe what I needed no faith to know. What proof could I give other than the testimony of my life, where it had been and where it was heading?

"What's the matter?" asked the elder on my right, snapping at the other. "Do you not believe what he's said?"

"It's quite a story," he answered with a sigh; "but I wonder if it's...well..."

"Wonder if it's *what*? Are you going to get hung up on the inception of this transformation and ignore the fruits that have come from it? This man endured *torture* on account of Christ—he was a jihadist, for goodness' sake!"

"Very convincing, very convincing," he replied, sighing again as he widened his eyes to better view his feet; then, looking up at me, he wrenched a smile onto his face and said, "Thank you for coming, Ahmed. We'll let you know how the voting goes."

"When will I know?" I asked hastily as the man stood and kicked his feet toward the door.

"Soon," he called over his shoulder.

As the door slammed behind him, my bemused eyes turned to the other elder, who sat shaking his head.

"I'm terribly sorry, Ahmed," he said at length. "Sometimes a pit of darkness is so deep, it looks to some like a mere stain on the sidewalk; thus, it can be hard to believe there is anyone living in that pit, much less anyone coming out of it."

"Sir?"

"Don't dwell on his response—rejoice always in God, and on Him fix your gaze. Let Him take care of the rest."

With that, he passed a gentle smile and slowly slipped from the room, after which Andrew darted in with an excited, "How did it go?"

"I don't know," I replied, feeling a tad beaten. "I don't think the one liked the part about my dream—he seemed suspicious of my faith's authenticity."

Andrew's face fell.

A host of words sat eagerly upon my tongue, poised to press the matter further; but none seemed inclined to join with another into a coherent question or remark that would demonstrate the frustration and hurt this process had brought, without carrying also something I would regret imbedding into the heart of a friend.

Thankfully, Andrew took up the mantle of speech.

"This isn't right," he said, heaving a chest-deflating sigh. "All this delaying, this run-around; it's childish. I sense that most of the elders are troubled," he continued, a pungent sadness falling over his lips. "Whispers and fears have been permitted to pervade and infect good intentions with the poison of doubt—doubt in God."

"What do you mean?"

Shaking his head, he said, "It's got to be your nationality, I think, your background—the fact that you're a Gulf State national makes them uneasy. One of them warned me today that you're not a believer at all, that you're actually a spy of the religious police."

My heart split in two—its bleeding flushed through my face, pressed hard behind my eyes, and clotted into a lump in my throat.

I could not utter a sound.

Feeling around behind me, I found a chair and sat down, while the room proceeded to topple end over end.

"I believe you, Ahmed." Andrew knelt before me and snatched my eyes into his direct, grave stare. "And so do many others. We are all weak, made of sinful flesh; and in the pursuit to guard the souls entrusted to them, some seem to have turned to their own understanding, rather than trusting in

God. No matter what happens," he added, taking my wrist and squeezing it tightly, "the authenticity of your conversion and the genuine nature of your faith do not depend any earthly membership. Christ has welcomed you into the eternal church, His bride. No power of hell or scheme of man can change that."

If it seems that I'm zipping through a vast timeline of my history, it's because I am—the events related in this chapter took place over a great long while, during which time these selected highlights played the biggest role in Christ's continuing work in me, producing patience, perseverance, trust, and a heart that could forgive in the face of injustice and be continually refined and reminded to seek God for the power to do so. Sanctification, it seemed, was not a one time thing; it would take me through this life and to the end, to the place of purification, where I would be finally and fully washed clean in the holiness of Jesus, transferred to me not by the touching of the end of His garment as I crawled behind Him, but rather in His embrace, held as a friend, close to His chest forever.

The moment arrived but a few days later when the names of those on whose case for membership would soon be voted were posted on the church bulletin. And though I had been somewhat braced, I was nonetheless shocked to see my name absent from the list, while a host of other names were present, some belonging to people who had been in attendance for a mere five minutes compared to my record.

Immediately, I went in search for one of the elders.

I had been rejected in writing; I wanted to hear it from someone's lips.

It wasn't long before I'd found the moustache for which I'd sought.

"Do you just not take Gulf State nationals?" I asked him, doing all I could to not let my hurt do any talking.

This was a wholly honest question; an affirmative would have at least been understandable—not a good answer, but one not outside of a traceable line of logic.

"We'll be voting on people whose commitment to this church has been demonstrated."

"Mine hasn't?" Astonishment struck me as does the burst of light when emerging from a dark room. "I drive thirteen hours each week to get here!"

"Members are committed more than one day every week," he said, lengthening his neck. "Church membership requires more involvement than merely attending a single worship service."

"That's not—" I checked my tone, swallowed the rest of the remark, and proceeded. "As much as I am able, I participate. My communion and fellowship with the believers of this body spans the entire week; we meet and read the Word over the internet. My present work and living situation do not permit frequent trips out this way."

"Well, it's more than that," he continued.

"What else? What more can I do to show you that I am committed to this body?"

"Your confession does not align with that of this church."

My eyebrows furrowed tightly.

"Which part? The Apostle's Creed? It is my own! I have confessed with my mouth that Jesus is my Lord—*Jesus* is my Lord; and I believe in my heart that God raised Him from the dead; that is certain. And now Jesus sits at the right hand of the Power—whoever trusts in Him will not be put to shame; whoever confesses Him before man, Jesus will confess before the Father. What have I not done? What have I not yet given? Where am I lacking?"

Casting over me a draped stare, he loosed a mighty arrow from the bow of his lips.

"I have serious doubts about your faith's sincerity," he said coldly. "And my responsibility is to this body—not to *you*. The decision of the elder council is final."

Leaving his arrow imbedded in my heart, he passed along on my side and disappeared.

As my body swayed in the breeze, a mere whiff from tumbling like a tree chopped at the base, a familiar voice rose up from behind me, carrying words that snatched me from the edge and held me upright.

"But with me it is a very small thing that I should be judged by you or by any human court," whispered Andrew's voice, reading the words penned by Paul in 1 Corinthians 4. "It is the Lord who judges me."

Stepping in front of me, Andrew took me by the arms, looked me dead in the eye, and recited 1 Corinthians 15:10.

"By the grace of God," he said, his voice booming deeply and with authority, "I am what I am, and His grace toward me was not in vain."

As I battled like a fissured dam against the welling of emotion pressing against the backs of my eyes, Andrew carved into his cheek a smile.

"This is an opportunity," he whispered. "Remember what you believe: that God is in control. Seek Him now, and don't stop—not until you see His face. Keep looking," he said sharply, giving my arms a firm shake, and so dislodging a tee-tering tear to fall over my cheek. "And keep going. Your brothers and sisters are with you forever."

Saying this, he handed me a business card; then, with a smile, he patted me on the shoulder and turned away.

When he had nearly vanished around the corner, I looked down at the card.

"Capitol Hill Baptist Church, Washington D.C.; *Biblically Building Faith Churches in America.*"

Just then I heard Andrew's voice echoing loudly down the hall.

"C'mon!"

"Where are we going?" I asked, scurrying to his side.

"America!" he said, beaming.

"*AMERICA*?"

America: the mighty land of the West, the land of the in-fidels, as ever I'd know it. The only time I had ever entertained the thought of going there was in fantasies of my carrying out the work of my childhood heroes and kinsmen, as on 9/11.

"Yup!" he replied, walking tall through the doors and into the night. "Someone there would like to meet you."

***

Having secured a two-week vacation from work, I boarded a plane bound for the United States. Being my first trip to the foreign world, I was eager to see what American Christians were like. It was well known and widely proclaimed to its detriment and discredit that America is a Christian nation; and this gave a great deal of fuel to the Muslim argument that

Christianity was a false, hedonistic religion, rooted in corruption.

"See how their women dress!" some would say. "They walk around naked; shameless women!"

"Such wealth spent on fornication and idolatry!"

"They don't even believe the things they claim! And they have no devotion to their god—none whatsoever! They pray only on Sundays—we pray five times a day!"

The perversities of American culture screamed to my Islamic kindred of what happens when a people depart from Allah to worship the prophet Isa. And while I no longer maintained the same thinking on which I'd once staked my life, I was curious to learn why a "Nation under God" displayed and exported so much in contrast to the person of Christ.

Andrew had gone on ahead of me to the States, while I squared away with work.

Taking off from Riyadh, the capitol of Saudi, I settled in for a thirteen-hour trip over sand and sea—it seemed my lot in life to attend only those churches thirteen hours away from home.

As the plane sped against the path of the sun, taking me from morning to morning, I turned about in my hand the business card Andrew had given me.

Mark E. Dever, Senior Pastor.

Andrew had spoken often of this man, and I had been greatly blessed by what teachings of his I had been privileged to hear. It was my sincere intent to make the most of this trip by thoroughly complaining to Pastor Dever about my experience in the Gulf States—someone had to get the word out to Muslim converts, so that they could avoid similar mistreatment. Having grown to love and respect Pastor Dever over the years for his powerful, God-anointed ministry, and for the abundance of spiritual food he'd offered through his sermons, I felt confident he would listen to me.

Landing in JFK Airport in New York, I hopped on a bus bound for Washington D.C.

Five hours later, I was being greeted by Andrew at the corner of a mighty, red brick building, from which stood a medieval-looking sign, proclaiming in golden letters the words, "Capitol Hill Baptist Church."

"What do you think?" said Andrew, upon releasing me from a bear hug. "Nice, isn't it?"

Reclaiming my breath, I managed to mutter a word of affirmation.

"How was the flight?"

Chuckling, I gave his shoulder a shove and said, "You didn't bring me my coffee!"

Donning a most theatrical display of offence and indignation, he declared, "My representatives were on every corner! It's called Starbucks!"

Sharing a few more laughs, we climbed the steps to the large, wooden doors.

The church was magnificent! It reminded me a great deal of the house of white pillars!

"Here," came Andrew's voice, breaking through my tranced gaping at the building's historical features—the arches over stained glass, the artful millwork, the beautiful craftsmanship.

Looking back at him, I saw an outstretched arm holding a giant cup, on which was printed the logo of his corner-stationed representatives.

"Thought you might need this," he said with a wink; and, together, both of us sipping some life into our limbs, we walked through the church to a long staircase.

Having ascended, we entered slowly through a door at the top; and there, reclining at his desk and singing a hymn, was Pastor Mark Dever.

"You must be our brother from Saudi!" he exclaimed, springing from his seat and marching toward me with an outstretched hand.

"I am!" I replied excitedly; it was a most fascinating experience seeing a person I had known only from a small phone screen come to life before me as a real person.

"Andrew, here, tells me you've been having some trouble," he said as we all sat down.

I wasted no time; my complaining proceeded forth.

But, as it passed, I liked less and less the taste it smeared along my tongue.

My speech began to slow.

Then, it stopped.

Heaving a sigh, I said, "I just don't understand. I am a believer! I have given my life to Jesus! What more can I do to prove it to others professing the same? How can Christians treat other Christians this way?"

He didn't muse or rub his chin, or cast his eyes to the ceiling to admire the streaks in the timber while he formed a thought. Rather, he looked me dead in the eye, and said, "Suffering is part of the Christian life. What you've witnessed and experienced is the work of fear, causing Christians to forget the words of Jesus. What you've gone through, what you're going through, and what I expect you will continue to go through—this is testing and proving your faith."

A comfort I did not expect fell over me.

He spoke not as one scolding, nor was this the Christian version of, "Man up!" Rather, he was like a father speaking wisdom and understanding to a beloved child; he was like someone who has endured a trial his brother must now face, who brings himself back to the place his brother now stands, to comfort him, encourage him, and demonstrate to him that what lies ahead, while it must be faced, has been faced, and that Jesus has promised to be at his side through anything and everything.

I expected we would continue discussing the matter, possibly even work out a game plan for my moving forward through this trial. But, instead, he immediately shifted gears and hit me with, "Would you be willing to share your story with the pastors gather here today?"

"YES!"

My instantaneous reply surprised even myself.

"Wonderful! I expect a great turnout for a conference we're holding today. There will be roughly 150 of us."

"*How* many?"

The very next second, I found myself standing before the confirmation of Pastor Dever's "rough" count: 150 pastors, with Andrew perched front and center among them.

My knees quaked all the way to the pulpit.

A cold sweat ran over my wide-eyed face as I surveyed the mass of strangers, all bearing heads filled with more Bible knowledge than I might ever be able to attain.

Public speaking had never been my forte. It had been hard enough praying in the mosque as a young man, standing there before my family and neighbors—how much more nerve-wracking was it to stand before a host of unknown faces!

"God," I whispered, "please help me. Give me the words."

Wetting my lips, I took a deep breath through my nostrils, and breathed forth the tale.

A critic writing about the first act of my speech would no doubt have noted the sluggish and stuttering pace my tongue maintained; however, if this same critic were to resist the temptation to hang up the pen and pad after this slow opening, he would certainly have marked a shift from babble to bellow, as with every breath I breathed in the power of an eagle's beating wings, until I was practically soaring over the crowd, shouting my story with boldness and clarity not my own.

"And how can the lost come to believe in Christ unless they hear the Word of God?" I posed, as my impromptu speech came to a close. "Jesus said, 'He who has an ear, let him hear!' Well, I've seen many an ear in Saudi Arabia—even there, most people have two of them! How will the lost come to believe unless they *hear*?" I posed again, throwing as much emphasis on the point as my broken speech would allow. "And how will they hear if no one is willing to go and preach? Jesus said the field is ripe for the harvest—He commands us to GO! Who among you is willing to come with me and take the Gospel to Saudi Arabia?"

***

Pastor Dever thanked me profusely for sharing my testimony and invited me to the next day's worship service. I accepted gratefully and shared in a most blessed fellowship with some truly Christ-loving, American Christians, who, though the world around them was lost in a manic pursuit of self-indulgence, led lives in accordance to the Word of God and demonstrated great fruit of the Spirit.

Following the service, Pastor Dever and I returned to his office, where he prayed over me and offered his final goodbye.

"Whether on this shore or the next," he said, taking my hand firmly in his, "God be with you until we meet again."

I left his office and met up with Andrew in the lobby, at which time a young man approached me.

"Excuse me," he said, very respectfully. "I heard about your testimony, and I just wanted to say I think it's incredible how God has worked in your life."

"It is, indeed!" I cheered, taking his hand in friendship and giving it a hearty shaking. "All praise and glory to Christ! For I surely didn't complete this work in me!"

"The whole thing," he continued, a distant look of awe and longing in his eyes, "—you can see the power of God in it all. You don't see power like that here."

"Don't you?" I said, rather surprised. "Did you not feel the Spirit moving here today? Hundreds of people turned out to sing praises to Jesus!"

"I'm talking about radical transformations. Most Christians here have had a Bible all their lives; it's almost a given, the facts of the Bible—they don't impact or inspire like I think they should."

"Do you expect great winds and earthquakes and fire?"

"Yes! Something like that!"

"Remember in 1 Kings 19 when Elijah was discouraged by the faith of Israel? God told him to go on the mountain; and there came that great wind, followed by an earthquake, and then fire—but God was not in any of it. God came, rather, in a whisper."

"But it's not *that*!" he said. "It's a sort of apathy, I think; like, casual Christianity, or something. People say they love God, but I don't think anyone has ever really experienced His power. Maybe if the things that happened to you happened to more people here in the States; maybe then there'd be something more tangible to believe."

"Jesus told a parable in Luke 16, wherein a rich man dies and goes to hell; from there, he pleads with heaven that a poor man—who had also died, but went to heaven—would be sent to his brothers, so that they could be warned and so escape his hellish fate. But he was answered in this way: that if his brothers had ignored all the warnings they'd already been given—this, in our case, would be the Bible and the generations of people who have testified to it; if the rich man's brothers had not believed after encountering so great a cloud of witnesses as they'd had, they would never believe, even if that poor man rose from the dead to testify. God works wonders all over the globe," I continued. "Here, from what little I've seen, one has plenty with which to distract him or herself on the way to the grave. Maybe that's why the great winds and earthquakes and fires erupting all around you can be perceived only as whispers, and these whispers fall only on deaf ears."

A look of great sadness came over the young man's face.

"Come," I said, laying a hand on his shoulder. "Come with me to Saudi; help me preach the Word there, share the love of Jesus with those trapped in darkness. I promise you'll see more of the power of God in a place where you can naught but live by faith."

"What!" he exclaimed, his eyes nearly jettisoning from his head. "Go to *Saudi Arabia*?"

"Sure! I'll buy you a ticket—we can leave today!"

"You're crazy!" he shouted.

"Guilty as charged!"

"And why not?" said Andrew, tossing in his two cents. "I've been there! The need is great and the power of God so stark and present that you would never again harbor any doubt!"

"You *must* be crazy!" he declared, rather as if this was an assured revelation.

"If we are 'out of our minds,'" I said, quoting Paul from 2 Corinthians 5:13, "it is for God!"

Shortly thereafter, I boarded a plane, alone, bound for Saudi and the mountain of kingdom-building work yet before me.

As I soared above the clouds, I pondered what was the purpose and ultimate outcome of this quick detour to the States. My curiosity about American Christians had been fed; but I had interacted only with people who professed and lived the Bible—I hadn't engaged any of those types at whom I used to point as proof of Christianity's folly and falseness. I had intended to complain my way to finding an answer from a pastor I respected deeply, only to be stopped in my tracks and handed a speaking opportunity. And I did speak, having nothing prepared; I exposed to 150 pastors the horrific realities of the world from which I come, and put forth a challenge for them to go further, go deeper, and spread the Word in the darkest of places.

I chuckled to myself as I thought about the fact that it had taken nearly 7,000 miles and a whole lot of hours to remind me that I should not expect anything but trouble from this world. So long as Satan is the prince of this temporal place, he will surely harass followers of Christ by any means at his disposal. How mighty a weapon is fear, especially in my native land; and Christians there are ever at risk of meeting its blade. So, I prayed to the One who has already won the battle that those who had been rejecting me would be freed of the bondage of fear, and never again withhold from anyone the love of Christ.

Still, could that have been it, I wondered? 7,000 miles, just for that lesson? While not at all trivial, was I so beyond reason and understanding that I needed to fly to the United States for a quick lecture? Sure, speaking to the pastors had been a most rewarding experience; and while I hoped they would take to heart all I had relayed, there was no denying the fact that I was flying back to Saudi alone.

Nuzzling my head into my seat, I continued to wonder as I wandered through the night sky. What had been the grander significance of this errand? Had there been one? What was God's purpose in bringing me out all this way? And how would He use it for what was still to come?

16
Collision

L IFE began to change rather rapidly. For starters, my internship had been a great success, and I was offered a position as a full-fledged senior doctor. I was given my own office, secretary—the works! And, right away, I collided headlong into a world of far greater responsibility and a much steeper workload. But through it all, I refused to lose sight of the most important work of all: fishing for souls.

"Not everyone who says to me, 'Lord, Lord,' will enter the kingdom of heaven," said Jesus in Matthew 7:21, "only the one who does the will of my Father who is in heaven."

This was my mission.

As soon as a shift at the hospital ended, a shift in the mission field began.

And though my online ministry was yielding tremendous results, a burning hunger began to churn deep within my soul, a hunger to go into the vast recesses of the world and proclaim the Gospel to all people. How I longed to travel every which way and sing of Christ's love and the Good News to everyone I met!

But, how?

Where?

And when?

I tackled first the last of these; and, taking a four-month, unpaid leave of absence, I sprang right into action to work out an answer to the first, scouring the internet for opportunities through which I could study the Word and train to be an evangelist. I tried enrolling for seminary classes in the U.S., but every institution I contacted required recommendations from a pastor and for me to prove my membership in a church. As every church I'd tried had denied me membership, I had no way of meeting these requirements, and they could offer no exceptions.

Disappointed though I was, when one walks with God, there is always a way.

I shifted my gaze from seminary to evangelistic ministry organizations. Unfortunately, my emails kept returning with discouraging rejections, almost all of which disbelieved the veracity of my testimony and faith, with some outright denying the possibility that anyone from Saudi Arabia could have converted to Christianity, much less have a desire to be an evangelist.

But then, just when it seemed I had run out of organizations to try, I was put in contact with a man named Douglas, the leader of a Pennsylvania group called Youth With a Mission (YWAM); and, just like that, I was on my way.

Head-on I collided with the world of evangelism, taking off without delay and diving right in; though, I didn't dive first into the deep end—some wading was required. My career as an evangelist started, as most do, with baby steps; and, in my case, there was a rather literal bend to this fact, as my first assignment was to teach the Bible to children at a Vacation Bible School in Pennsylvania. This I did on Saturdays; the rest of my week was spent spreading the Word in parks, schools, universities, on street corners—you name it! And what a wild and exciting new reality this was, to be able to waltz out in the open and proclaim Christ, without having to look over your shoulder for someone rushing to take off your head. All across the country we went: Maryland, Virginia, Indiana, Kentucky, Arizona, Montana, and so many other new and astonishing places, just dripping with the need for Jesus!

One day, very early in my time with YWAM, we broke off into pairs and started going door to door. Being that I had had before this point but one experience sharing my faith before a large audience, my nerves had not yet acclimated to the intensity of public speaking. Thinking Americans would be more receptive to a fellow American, rather than a sweating, stuttering foreigner, I hung back and let my partner, Vince, knock on the first door.

"Hello, ma'am! I'm—"

"Not interested," came a gruff growl, followed by an earthquaking *SLAM* that sent me leaping two feet into the air.

To my astonishment, however, my partner turned to me and, with a disappointed but perfectly unfazed and unsurprised face, shrugged his shoulders and motioned for us to go to the next house.

After about the fiftieth *SLAM*, I began to find the door-slamming of the home churches back in Saudi to have been a great deal more polite.

Sitting on a curb eating our packed lunch, Vince, who had had no luck that day sharing the Gospel, sighed and said, "I wonder if I've got this all wrong." Taking a bite of his sandwich, he mused for a moment and then spoke through a packed cheek. "Maybe I'd have more luck in Canada, you know? Jesus Himself testified that a prophet has no honor in his hometown."

I took his meaning.

The day really had been rather unfruitful.

What would we do now, I wondered?

Then, as I pondered his words, a great surge of courage suddenly rushed through me; and, dropping my sandwich, I marched across the street to the first house I saw.

I knocked before I realized what I was doing.

Footsteps could be heard shuffling toward the door.

What on *earth* am I doing?

The *click* of the deadbolt sparked against my nerves.

What do I say?

Slowly, the door opened.

A tall, American-built man stood before me; he looked like he ate the fruited plains for breakfast with a side of shining seas to wash it all down.

I gazed up at him with mouth gaping and eyes teetering on the edge of their sockets.

"Well?" he said, his voice impressing me like thunder clapping from a storm cloud directly overhead.

"I am here to share the love of Jesus Christ with you," I muttered, my speech trapped in a note as flat as a piece of paper and saturated with my Saudi accent.

The man drew back slightly; his eyebrows furrowed into one, and his mouth seemed to be warring with itself over whether it should fashion a scowl or a smile.

"You're not from around here, are you?"

A blast of air shot through his nostrils—his face offered no clarification as to whether this was a chuckle or a dragon's huff.

"I'm from Saudi Arabia," I replied.

"Really?" he exclaimed. "The country of oil! Don't think I've ever met someone from—wait, did you say *Jesus*?"

I nodded.

"But, you're from Saudi Arabia. Aren't you all Muslims?"

"Most of us are, but I have renounced Islam." That same surge of boldness I'd experienced when standing before the pastors flooded suddenly through me. "I am a follower of Jesus Christ! God has sent me all the way from Mecca to tell you about the love of His Son!"

"Well, c'mon in!" he cried, a most jolly look washing over his face. "Sit down! I'll get you a drink, and we'll talk!"

The man was very eager to hear my story. Laying it before him, I testified about the love and grace of Christ, offered to all sinners, by which He warns them to repent now and not turn away from the free gift.

"I'll tell ya," said the man with a slap on the knee, "it sure isn't every day a story like *that* lands on your doorstep. You've given me a whole lot to think about, that's for sure."

Vince and I left the man with a Bible, then thanked him for his most generous hospitality and went on our way.

"That was AMAZING!" Vince cried as we walked down the road. "Go on! You take the next house!"

And so I did—house after house, no one slammed the door; and Vince and I covered mile after mile proclaiming the love of Jesus to a multitude of opened ears.

God instilled in me a persistent boldness and courage, banishing all fear and nervousness, leaving my hand free to knock on any and every door without the slightest hesitation. And when at last my final mission came, there was not a nerve in me even remotely reluctant to accept.

"We've got business in California," Douglas announced during a morning meeting. "Our Cali coalition has got quite an ambitious goal, but I think we can do it. Seven weeks—22,000 doors. Who's in?"

Mine and Vince's hands shot up instantly.

"You'll be working with our California leader, Thomas," he said to us volunteers. "I'll be holding down the fort out here while you're all away. Warm up those knuckles, folks," he added with a smile. "We've got souls to feed."

Sunny California—beautiful, captivating, a burst of brilliant colors, wrapped in the finest climate a man could desire, and all of it rushing forth from its source of life, breaking upon the body like the waves crashing over those golden beaches; but the work of the Lord pours into my soul so abundant an over-flowing of life and a concrete, steel-fortified assurance that I am fulfilling the purpose to which I was called, that I could stand in the midst of Siberia in the dead of winter, wearing nothing more than pair of shorts, and be just as warm and alive as I felt in my days on the West Coast.

Our mission was seeing more fruit than was falling from the California trees. People opened their doors, welcomed us, listened, and many came to faith in Christ. We even held a baptism, during which forty people stepped forward to pub-licly confess their faith and take the plunge.

By all accounts, things could not have been going better.

But the enemy of this world does not sleep.

As Peter said in the fifth chapter of his first letter, "Be watchful. Your adversary the devil prowls around like a roaring lion, seeking someone to devour."

"Hey, Ahmed!" called Vince after one of our morning meetings, just as I was packing up to go blissfully bruise my knuckles again. "Thomas wants to see you."

Thomas and I had not yet had the opportunity to talk a great deal, and while I was eager to take to the streets, I jumped at the chance to get to know him a little better.

"Thanks for coming," he said, motioning for me to take a seat.

Thomas looked every bit like the Californians I had heard about while in Saudi: sandy blond hair, sun-kissed skin, swim trunks, flip flops, pale pink- and blue-striped tank top, and rainbow-tinted sunglasses.

"I don't wish to hold you up," he continued, "but I wanted to meet before long so I could hear your testimony."

Abundantly glad to do so, I recounted my story.

"I wasn't looking for God," I said. "How could I have been? Bibles and churches are outlawed in Saudi. But Jesus was seeking after this lost sheep. That's when," I continued, excited to reveal the pivotal moment, "Jesus came to me in a dream. That night, He—"

Before I could say another word, Thomas shot up from his seat, as if he'd been propelled by a spring set therein, and hastened out of the room.

What just happened?

I sat there, alone and in silence, replaying the instantaneous performance I'd just witnessed, doing all I could to piece together a play-by-play of something that took only seconds to transpire. Over and over I searched for a recollection of the face he had been wearing in the moments leading up to his sudden ejection.

Had I offended him?

My English had greatly improved by this time; however, I was still not fluent in American customs and etiquette. Having done so much door-to-door work and interacted with countless thousands of unique individuals, my education had not been sparse. Still, my default was to be as polite as I knew how to be, and to smile—when you're a foreigner, you never know how facial features, hand movements, tones, phrases, ticks, and twitches might be translated from culture to culture.

Maybe it had been my Saudi accent.

Perhaps I'd mispronounced something, which sounded to him like an offensive word or comment.

This couldn't have been about the dream, though—could it?

Surely, here, among evangelists, people who have dedicated their lives to spreading the Gospel, many of whom have traveled the world and risked their lives to do so—surely here the mighty power of God had been witnessed in a multitude of ways that nothing could be surprising; surely these people knew better than most that with God all things are possible, even dreams.

Surely, this had to be some sort of cultural or lingual misunderstanding.

So, I waited.

Maybe this wasn't even any of the above—he may have just been struck by a sudden urge to use the restroom.

Maybe Americans just obeyed the beckoning of the bladder without announcement.

I could see that.

Could be viewed, culturally, as impolite to announce the call of nature; better, rather, to just spring up and leave, saying nothing to anyone.

Could be that.

I waited some more.

And then some more.

"Ahmed! What are you doing?"

Vince rushed in and started pulling me from my chair.

"C'mon! Most everyone has already left!"

Saying nothing of the conversation, I followed Vince to the car that would be driving us to our designated neighborhood. My eyes darted about for Thomas as we scurried out; he was nowhere to be found.

It was unusually hot that day; the heat hovered like a menacing presence, its eyes boring into the back of my neck. But I had been well trained throughout my childhood for such days, and I scampered eagerly to every door I could find, telling anyone and everyone who would spare a moment about the love of Jesus.

Vince and I returned long after the sun had fallen. It had been such a glorious and fruitful day of service to God that I had completely forgotten about the events of that morning.

Then, I got a phone call.

"Hello, Douglas!" I cried. "My, my—California is a wonderful place! So much has happened!"

"What have you done, Ahmed?"

"What *haven't* we done!" I exclaimed. "All over the state, meeting all kinds of people, serving so many needs with the

Good News of Jesus Christ! I tell you, 22,000 is not enough! There are so many more doors out here than just 22,000, and I intend to—"

"AHMED!" His tone was like a bullet, speeding through the balloon of my joy. "Listen to me for a minute. I just got a call from Thomas. What did you do?"

The morning came rushing back to me.

I didn't know what to say.

"He's just grilled me about your testimony. He asked me if you're a legit believer in Christ."

The phone dropped from my hand.

Slamming my back helplessly against the wall, I slid all the way down to the ground, there to gape numbly at the opposite end of the room as it shrunk further and further, ever so slowly, into the infinite distance.

Heart broken, I felt around for my phone.

I mumbled something to Douglas and hung up.

Dropping my phone again to the floor, I watched the infinite space before me slowly twirl about, while the bright white room was pressed from either end by a set of mighty black walls, carrying with them a void of darkness.

"What more can I do?" I murmured, tears streaming over my face. "What more do these Christians want? Dear God," I prayed, "those who did not know You, the people I met in the streets—*they* believed me. Why can't Christians? God, I lost my family; a life of inordinate wealth and comfort was ripped from me; I've left my job to walk mile after mile after mile under the blistering sun, earning no money while I am away; my shoulders are raw from the straps of my Bible-loaded backpack; my knuckles are bruised, my feet swollen; my body is tired and my spirit stretched thin—and, yet, I would do more than this, for these toils do not compare to the cross You carried! Why, then, are these people so blind? Is there no way my fruit can convince them? Will I forever be haunted by the shadow of my heritage?"

Just then, Vince burst into the room, his Bible tucked under his arm and a piece of paper waving about in the other.

"There is neither Jew nor Greek!" he declared, quoting Galatians 3:28. "Neither will there be American or Indian—we're going to the festival to gather more souls into the body of Christ!"

Speaking thusly, he jiggled before me the piece of paper in his hands, advertising the Indian National Independence Day festival, taking place the next day.

A millisecond later, he blinked, and his face fell.

"Hey," he said, quickly sitting beside me, "what's the matter?"

Taking the flyer from him, I marveled at the beautiful designs and colors used to promote the event. So vibrant a culture is the Indian's, I thought. How much more would it shine if illumed by the light of Christ!

"Vince," I said with a sniffle, wiping my nose on my sleeve, "do you believe me?"

"Do I *believe* you?"

"Do you believe I am what I say I am? A Christian?"

Vince let out a loud bellow of a laugh.

"Well," he chuckled, "if you're not, you're sure not being a good whatever you are! More than that, if you're not a Christian, I'd have to wonder what God is doing taking up residence in the heart of someone not His own!"

"Then," I said with a smile, as more tears rained down to meet the others, "let us say, too, that there is neither Jew nor

Greek, nor American, nor Indian, nor Saudi—for we are all one in Christ."

Springing to his feet, Vince let down a hand.

I took it gladly and rose from the floor.

"Now, my friend," he said, throwing an arm over my shoulder and pulling me tightly to his side, "let's go about God's work, eh?"

***

Our group walked among a great parade and exuberant celebration of singing, dancing, and fantastic, lively music, moving it all with great compulsion from within swirling streams of pristine white, graced with ribbons of orange and green. Against the tide of this joyous commotion, our group collided with the current of the culture; and, before the day had ended, many had traded the pride of orange and green for the crimson donned by those found in Christ as a robe of graceful justification before a holy God, turning against the tide for the life of the Son, upstream of this world.

We had come among a group of Hindu priests handing out copies of their holy books. Drawn to them as if by a great magnet, I offered each man a Bible in exchange for their handouts and began to share the Good News. My team and I walked them through the Gospels—how incredible to see these men reading the holy Word of God, most for the first time!

As we spoke, my eye caught sight of a large, very distinguished, and dignified-looking man wading through the crowd, his head gazing over the top of the revelers, appearing very stern and set in his purpose and direction, his eyes veiled behind a fat set of dark sunglasses; on his t-shirt, he wore the calligraphic artistry of Arabic script.

Hastening to the man, I stepped in his path and gazed into the atmosphere, from which his stare fell over me with the might of a great landslide.

"Excuse me, sir," I said—or, screamed, rather, as the parade was rather loud and his ears were set among the clouds. "Your shirt—it's says 'Peace;' but this is Arabic script. Why Arabic and not Hindi?"

Raising his tree trunk of an arm, he peeled away his sunglasses to drop over my head like a boulder a look of annoyance.

Speaking crossly and with a sharp, stern edge, he let out a sound like the churning of the deepest waters.

"And who are you?"

Shouting to him my name, I said, "I am a medical doctor from Saudi Arabia, and I am here sharing the love of Jesus Christ with everyone I meet!"

Before I could ask his name in return, he glowered fiercely down at me and spat a bolt of lightning from his lips: "You're a liar."

As he pushed past me, I sighed and uttered for him a prayer.

"How'd it go?" said Vince, approaching me from behind.

He'd apparently seen the entire conversation; thus, his words were more commiserating than hopeful.

"That's Arabic script on his shirt," I replied. "Thinking he might have some connection to that world, I told him I'm a Saudi Christian."

"And he didn't believe you."

"Really, at this point," I shrugged, "I can't blame him. He called me a liar. How odd," I added, scratching my head; "he knows me for no more than thirty seconds, and already he's so sure I'd approached him only to offer him a lie."

"Don't let it get you down," said Vince, patting me on the back. "We can't force people to hear us; God must open their ears. Jesus commands us to go, and that's what you did: you went, and," he said scrunching his lips, "evidently, so did he."

"It's just so strange," I said, still puzzling. "A man wearing Arabic script at an Indian festival? And I, the only one among us who could read it—I run into that one man, here, among such a multitude, only to see a whole lot of nothing come from it?"

"If it's any consolation," he replied, "I know for a *fact* it wasn't nothing."

"How so?"

"Well, I'm sure when he came here today, his world was about as normal as ever it had been."

"Okay?"

"You no doubt gave him an impossibility to ponder—what *he* considers an impossibility, anyway," he chuckled. "I'll bet he'd never thought he'd hear the words 'Christian' and 'Saudi' paired as one! You've introduced an abnormality into his normal! God can do a whole lot more with a whole lot less, eh?"

And, so, we went gladly about the Lord's work, setting before the masses the off-ramp onto the straight and narrow path from the raging highway emptying out into an eternal darkness; and a great many were given the grace to perceive the warning sign and made a sure and deliberate one-eighty off the broad way.

As we gathered ourselves together at the end of the day, a man approached me from behind, tapping me on the shoulder.

"Who are you?" he asked hastily, even before I had fully turned around. "Where do you come from?"

My heart drew back.

Swallowing my reluctance to mention the repellant word of my origin, I answered, "My name is Ahmed. I am from Mecca, Saudi Arabia."

"Come speak at my church tomorrow," said the man, talking so quickly it seemed he had taken not a moment to process my reply.

"Pardon?"

"Please," he persisted. "Will you come?"

"I know my accent is rather thick and my English poor," I replied. "I said I'm from *Saudi Arabia*."

"Yes!" he laughed. "That's exactly what Aarav said!"

"Who?"

"He said he spoke with you today."

"I spoke with many people today."

"A tall man—you'd approached him because of his t-shirt."

"*Him?*"

I was flabbergasted!

How could any report from *that* man have resulted in an invitation to speak at a church? He'd called me a liar! Who hears tell of a liar and says, "Boy, I'd love to have *that* guy talk to my congregation!"

"Yes!" he said, laughing all the more. "Why, he spent the whole rest of the day watching you—how gracious that God set his head upon a crow's nest! High over the crowds, his gaze followed you; for hours he watched you sharing the Gospel! To see a Saudi national speaking so boldly about that which would cost him his head in his hometown—please tell me you'll come!"

A host of butterflies burst to life in my stomach and began to flutter frantically about my entire body.

"I'll be there!" I shouted with a wholehearted belting that probably split a few eardrums; and I took off in a sprint to tell my friends what had happened—part way through that sprint, however, I stopped and sprinted back to thank the man profusely for the offer and to ask for directions to the church.

Nuzzling into my cramped corner in the back room of a church building, which had been my home for the past few weeks, I quivered and quaked with explosive excitement, eagerly awaiting the morning. And when it arrived, I scurried to the shower—a hose behind the church—and gave myself a thorough icicle bath. But the chill could not bite me this day! No, sir! For my body and spirit were already at the address I'd been repeating to myself throughout the night.

Dressed, hair and beard combed, running shoes laced, and a handful of mints in my pocket, I set out to make a dash to the church, only to find the man who'd invited me sitting out front in his car, waiting to give me a ride. Another blessing! And very good sense on his part, for he surely recognized my story might be better received if my words were not also accompanied by the stale stench of sweat from a several-mile run.

We arrived and took a seat in the front row; and then, as the musicians gathered together to start the service, there stepped before us a large, very distinguished and dignified-looking man, his head gazing over the top of the worshipers, appearing very tender and peaceful in his purpose and position, his brilliant brown eyes glowing with a heavenly light as he led the congregation in song.

It had been a mistake to have popped a mint so early upon arrival; it dropped right out of my mouth the second I saw him.

When the singing had finished, I was given and introduction and invited to the pulpit, where I stood before a host of eager faces and proclaimed my testimony of Christ's salvation.

"To be an ambassador for Christ in this rebellious world is folly to those comfortable in the security used by the principalities and powers of this evil age to pacify us," I said, nearing the end of my speech, "to keep Christians living only on the milk of Scripture, never growing to consume the real meat, causing atrophy in our spiritual muscles—we were fearfully and wonderfully made for greater work than proclamations through bumper stickers, t-shirts, and bracelets with Jesus' name on them! We are called to more than church on Sundays! There is a great need in my home country!" God was fortifying my nerves, my boldness speaking before others becoming a characteristic increasingly foreign to the man I had been. "Who will join me? Who will go to Saudi Arabia to reach the lost? Who will stand by my side and preach the Gospel of Christ without fear?"

Even before I had finished laying out my series of questions, bodies began bursting out of seats.

"I will go!" cried one.

"Me too!" screamed another.

"Let me go, as well!"

"Yes! Yes!"

"I'm in!"

"Let's do it!"

"For Christ and His kingdom! Revival for Saudi Arabia!"

Never had I seen such enthusiasm! The response was loud, explosive; it was alive and busting at the seams! And it churned through the place like a mighty wind, surging through the bodies of the brave and bold in Christ, breaking with such force that I could not help but stagger as it crashed against me.

"What must we do?" asked one among the crowd.

"Yes! How do we get there?"

"First," I replied, wiping from my face an involuntary outpouring of tears, "you must apply for a visa to Mecca—not easy by any means, but we serve a mighty God! Nothing is impossible with Him! You will be like Paul," I continued. "As a Roman citizen, he was granted privileges in his time and place, afforded not to others; the same is true for Americans going to Saudi. The hurdles are many. But, when God carries you over them, the government will grant you a five-year visa; most other travelers get only two years, maximum."

"And how do we go about sharing our faith?" asked another.

"Will you plug us into underground Christian movements?"

"What about Sharia? How do we preach Christ when Christianity is outlawed?"

"Under Sharia law," I explained, "it is proper for one to ask of a foreigner, 'What is your faith?' Likewise, it is perfectly appropriate to answer in an honest manner that shares the love of Jesus—this is surprisingly not a violation. A sincere question can be met with an honest answer without breaking the law; this is a crack in the fabric of that law, and a door wide open for the Christian."

When the service had concluded, these eager volunteers approached me, and I expounded on the process and opportunities. Afterward, we prayed for God's blessing to be upon the group that had answered the call; and then, as one unit bound by faith and determination to spread the Word, they ran from the building to start their applications.

I elected to walk back to the church where I was staying; the Holy Spirit had so filled the church that day and revived my hope that I wanted to be alone to talk with God.

But before I could make it to the door, I was tapped on the shoulder by what felt like a boxer's heavy bag.

Turning, I came face to face with the bottom of a long, blue tie. Slowly, my eyes traced it upward; and there at the summit I beheld the face of the man I'd seen wearing the "Peace" t-shirt and leading worship that day.

His eyes were red and heavy.

"Please forgive me," he wept. "I called you a liar. I doubted your faith. I'm so ashamed. Will you ever forgive me?"

Throwing my arms around his tree trunk of a body, I let out a joyful sound of eager gladness.

"Of course! Christ has made us brothers, and I love you!"

"I could never have imagined a Saudi intellectual would come to know Jesus," he said, once disentangled from my embrace. "I'm a doctor, myself," he added. "Stanford University College of Medicine—I'm a research professor there. And I have met so many Saudis like yourself—doctors, intellectuals. They're so hard to the truth, so resistant. Surely," he said, heaving a breath of chuckling awe, "you couldn't have been any different, I thought. Either a liar, or proof of the impossible."

Taking his hand in friendship, I smiled and quoted Jesus from Luke 18:27.

"The things which are impossible with men," I said, "are possible with God."

***

The Son had shown brightly in California, as in the multitude of places all over the world my path would lead, funded by a substantial salary and generous time off permissions. Over the many years of my doctoral career, I would visit cities well-known and remote, some with abundant wealth, some destitute; in shimmering cities, in the middle of nowhere; across the Arabian world, in caves and deserts, among the ignorant and the hungry, the affluent and the persecuted, the needy and the proud; among terrorists and peacemakers; in Africa and the Philippines, and all over China, learning the cultures and customs of the people dwelling there, in places known and places forgotten, sharing the love of Christ, and through the Gospel message pointing them away from violence and idolatry, spiritualism and other entangling evils, to the Savior of mankind. And every time I landed back in Saudi, the cold wind of darkness would, without fail, hasten toward me and collide like a javelin with my spirit; but I was ever so filled with the warmth of my Savior's hand, which had moved so mightily in my travels, and from which no force of hell could snatch me, nor bar me from the power, love, and joy of Christ found therein.

This, however, was not for a lack of trying.

My friends from California were gearing up for their trip to the hostile sands, their visas finally approved, and I simply could not wait to share the news with my brothers and sisters in Christ living in the Gulf States—since my rejection at the first church, I'd visited many other fellowships in the area in and around Dubai, making a host of forever friends. Thirteen hours I drove, my cup overflowing with the love of Jesus and a childlike excitement for being again behind the wheel of my beautiful, nine-seat SUV. Andrew wasn't there this time to bring me coffee, but it didn't matter—the Spirit of God was so alive in me, I felt I could sprint in circles around the earth and never tire.

The commute passed in seconds, and the worship service sped along even quicker. Almost as soon as I had arrived, I found myself back in my car, mentally preparing for another thirteen-hour trek across the desert. Speeding along the main highway, I replayed over and over the fellowship I'd just enjoyed, rapturously studying the faces of my brothers and sisters: those bright and cheerful, loving faces that took hold of my heart the moment I beheld them, and had brightened all the more upon hearing of the Americans from California who had answered the great commission. Having not slept a wink since hopping in the car the first time, this joyful reflection was a beloved source of energy, and I rested contentedly in thoughts of the Lord and His great works, as the endless highway passed beneath me.

A single instant changed all that.

One moment, I was racing down the road; the next, my car had come to a dead stop, all four doors were ripped open, and a sea of hands flooded in from every direction, clasping onto me and stubbornly pulling in its own way, each wrestling with the others, seeming savagely intent on ripping a piece of souvenir flesh from my body.

A single set of hands, clamped onto the lapels of my shirt, finally prevailed, and I was whisked from the car like a ragdoll and thrown violently to the ground like a bag of sand, my face pressed hard into the dirt, as if the hands overpowering me were trying to bury my head without a shovel.

Angry shouts erupted all around, and I heard the frantic jingling of chains scurrying from somewhere behind me; I was handcuffed, and iron shackles were clasped onto my ankles.

Hoisted from the ground like a skewered hog, I was thrown into a car and taken to the Central Department of Criminal Investigation, where I was dragged into a small room, no bigger than a common bathroom, tossed into a chair, my dazed head aimed at a camera, and my picture taken. The photographer then sped out of the room and I was fingerprinted.

No offense had yet been declared to me.

I could not tell left from right or up from down; the world had become a chaotic maze spinning like a top, with me staggering in its midst.

Then, a large officer thundered into the room.

Drawing a lion's breath, he snorted a burst of flame and growled, "What is your purpose here?"

Shock had momentarily robbed me of speech; I could not remember how to work my tongue to form words.

"We've been watching you," he snarled. "Your pattern of crossing into Dubai—what is its purpose?"

Don't lie, I screamed to myself—but be wise!

"I come on the weekends to see my friends," I answered, after some labored mumbling.

Scorching my eyes with a fiery glare, the officer stepped forward, nearly pressing his nose to mine, and hissed, "We have cameras everywhere. Do you *really* think we don't know what you've been up to all this time?"

My eyes went white.

"You know where I've been?"

"Yes!" he snapped, his jaw clamping like a crocodile's, sending sparks shooting from his teeth. "And you," he spat with a derisive glower, looking me over, "a Saudi citizen! I don't think I need remind you what happens to deserters of Islam."

He didn't and did not; but the point was made—like a freight train colliding at full speed with my helplessly chained body, reality's bitter taste and arctic chill leached through me.

Death's noisome breath condensed along my goose-bumped skin, slipping slowly like a hissing asp over my shoulder as the interrogation continued. I answered quickly, briefly, or not at all, being careful not to lie, but also to prevent them from clasping definitively onto the very thing they suspected lay hidden within me.

Eventually, the officer seemed to grow weary and frustrated of my vague replies.

"Get him up!" he barked. "Let the doctor rest a bit while we check his schedule...see if he'll have any upcoming injections."

With a flick of his hand, I was dragged away to a tiny cell, where I was left to ponder the officer's last words.

Injection.

Surely, if they could determine I was a Muslim turned Christian, I would, in accordance with the Constitution of the United Arab Emirates (UAE), be put to death. I knew this well.

While the UAE Constitution does provide for some religious freedom, this is not broadly defined. A Christian can practice Christianity; Christians can even gather in places of worship; and it goes without saying that a Christian can convert to Islam; but no one can attempt to spread Christianity among Muslims, as Islam is the official religion. And anyone who converts from Islam to another religion is guilty of apostasy and will be sentenced to die by lethal injection.

Hours passed, and I prayed that God would calm my body, make it stop shivering; I didn't want to give the evil that possesses this part of the world a foothold because I was afraid. I prayed that someone would know of my imprisonment, and that they would visit me, just so I could see a Christian brother or sister, touch their hands, feel the warmth of their love, before my actions were uncovered by the intelligence officers wandering about outside my cell, leading to my departure from this world. And then, as I stared down my death, once again, I whispered a prayer of thanks to my Jesus for the time He had given me to preach His Word, after having wasted so much of my life expelling God-given breaths into the sand at the feet of a lie.

As I said "Amen," the world around me fell silent.

"Look, here," said a faint voice in the distance.

Something like shuffling papers followed, then a groan and a muffled expletive.

"They're all over—California, Pennsylvania, the capitol, even New Zealand and a host of other countries."

"It's risky," came another soft voice.

Some inaudible sounds danced around my ears in aggravating circles, reluctant to plunge into my eardrums.

More murmuring, then what sounded like, "Not worth it," stuck me like a needle.

I then heard words like "protests," "outcry," "global"—my face was smashed against the bars at this point, my cheeks sticking out a good six inches into the hallway. And I was so preoccupied with disentangling the sounds from the proximity and the static of the atmosphere that a sudden *clippety-clacking* sound registered in my brain as a strange new speech I needed desperately to decode; it was followed by a *clink* and a *clang*, and then an "*Oof!*" from me when the cell door was thrust open and I found myself at the feet of the officer and his men.

"We're going to make a deal with you," he said sternly, after I had been dragged back to the interrogation room. "Leave Dubai. Never come back—do this, and we will deescalate the situation."

Rather taken aback, I shot my eyes to the left and to the right, and then back at the officer, gazing intently at him to see if he was still flesh and blood, and this moment was present and not a dream.

"That's all?"

There had to be some sort of catch.

"Mark this document with your fingerprints," he said, thrusting a piece of paper before me, while another man approached me with an inkpad. "It states plainly that you will not attend any suspicious meetings."

Though the situation was grave indeed, my heart let out a chuckle as I reviewed the words printed on the page before me. A smile grew in my heart, and I happily pressed my fingers firmly onto the page—for what on earth is so suspicious about a Christian gathering?

Conscience clear, I wiped the ink from my fingers and asked, "Would you make a copy of that for me?"

"No!" he snapped, and then ordered my personal affects to be returned.

As God would have it, my phone was returned before the document was collected.

The officer turned to speak to someone; another officer looked down to wiggle his belt; yet another dropped something and stooped to pick it up.

The window had opened.

Snap!

By the time all eyes had returned to me, I had slipped my phone into my pocket—on it, a crisp and clear photo of every piece of documentation sitting on the table before me. I even managed to pull it out again and nab a few shots of my interrogators. And these evidences I yet possess to prove to the world that Dubai and the UAE boast of their freedoms, while underneath its citizens know none of them.

Upon my release, I immediately drove to the home of my Dutch friend Chris, who was living in Dubai at the time.

"Get in here!" he whispered sharply, as I scurried to his door.

"It's okay!" I exclaimed, trying to calm his obviously tense nerves, thinking I had alarmed him when I'd called before arriving.

Snatching my arm, he yanked me inside and slammed the door, and together we bolted to another room. There in the dark, he peeled back a corner of the curtain and motioned for me to peek outside.

At the end of the street sat an idle car, filled with silhouettes.

"You see it?"

I hummed my affirmation.

"Do you recognize it? Have you seen it before?"

The car was ordinary, but its presence infected me with a chill.

"I was watching through the window for your arrival. That car peeled slowly around the corner; very carefully it crept along—the moment you stopped, it stopped."

"Secret police," I breathed.

"They've followed you."

"I won't stay," I said, and quickly leapt up to leave.

"No!" he shouted, grabbing me by the arms. "I'm in no danger from man, much less *them*! Rest here a little while; I'll get you something to eat."

"My shift starts in less than twenty hours," I replied. "I've still got half a day ahead of me. I shouldn't have come."

"Nonsense!" he declared. "Where two or more are gathered in My name, says the Lord, there am I with them! We're two, aren't we? We're gathered. He's here. We're fine. Let's eat."

I stayed with him for another hour, telling him every detail of what had happened, and showing him the photos on my phone.

Taking my hand, he began to fervently pray over me for my protection and for the purposes of God to be worked through the evil that followed me.

Revived in body and spirit, I slipped back to my car and watched my rear-view mirror all the way back to Saudi.

"So, you'll not be coming back this week?" asked one of the leaders in the church of Dubai, whom I had called before the start of my shift to explain the recent events.

"Of course I'm coming back!" I blurted without a thought—how absurd a notion! "Do you think a piece of paper will stop me from worshiping Jesus? Not even the threat of death will stop me! Until God is finished with me, no man can touch me!"

"When you arrive," he answered, the gravity in his voice so weighty it nearly caused the phone to slip from my hand, "we'll be sure you're well concealed. There's a secret entrance; we'll bring you in that way. I'll call you later this week with the details."

***

What is normal in America is a fantasy in Saudi, and what is normal in Saudi is a waking nightmare; only, those lost in the darkness that is the grip of Evil, clutching by the throat my native land, are so deep in Deception's sleep that they cannot wake to see the horrors through which they wade; and those who yet have eyes to see remain locked in the shelter of lies, wherein they can enjoy the singing of the free birds in flight, deaf to the screams of my world. Just as I collided again with that reality—the grotesque atrocities that had been a common part of my once content and normal existence—so too must all who hear my story collide with the people; not just a religion or a government, nor the agents thereof; but rather the real flesh and blood creations of God Almighty, the everyday unsung wanderers, who suffer daily, endlessly, ignorant to the freedom found in Christ, trapped beneath the veil cast by the wickedness of this land, concealed by the overflow of black, liquid gold that bubbles from the ground to power comfort and affluence, deceived by denials and political correctness that paint with roses what has been stained with the human blood watering even now the sand of Saudi Arabia and every nation supping the venom of Islam.

I rounded the corner of the hospital, rubbing the sleepiness out of my eyes, when through the door burst a young woman, struggling with a great bundle draped around her neck and dragging along the floor beside her; we collided rather violently, as she was in quite a hurry.

Reaching forth to steady her, I noticed that my white coat had suddenly been dyed red.

My eyes focused intently upon her, and that's when I noticed that the bundle was breathing; it had an arm draped over the young woman's shoulders—that arm was dripping blood all over the floor, mixing with the beads of sweat falling from the ends of the young woman's burka onto her tattered and bloodied feet; she had certainly covered on foot whatever great distance she'd come.

"Help," she panted, barely able to speak. "Mother."

Emergency personnel had already been alerted; they zipped past me even before she'd finished speaking.

As they carefully placed the young woman's mother onto a gurney, I pulled her aside.

But we did not speak.

No questions had to be asked.

For I'd seen her mother before, as I'd seen many like her; and their stories are all the same.

There on the gurney, the woman convulsed as blood bubbled from her forehead; her eyes rolled about in their sockets, scurrying every which way; streams of blood trickled from her mouth; and as her jaw chattered and moaned, screaming terrified nothings at ghosts swirling about her, pieces of teeth broke off and danced across the floor.

All at once, I was whisked away to my time as an intern, on a day when, as part of my training, I was assigned to an emergency response team.

A neighbor had made the call, reporting a disturbance—shouting, cursing: a great commotion of war-like sounds.

"Stand back," said a police officer, when his knocking had received no answer.

Heaving a battering ram, the door broke free of its frame, and I followed in immediately after him.

As the dust from the blasted door cleared, I perceived in the dark room before me a large man. Framed on the one side by the white light streaming in through the veiled window behind him, half of his face was painted black; a silvery outline ran along its edge. Of the other half of his face, I could see eyes of red, around which had been sprayed a speckling of crimson. His teeth were born, wide and gangly, at the horde rushing through his door; those fangs secreted feral juices over his mouth as his lips snarled about them. His shoulders hunched forward, he growled with each long and heavy breath. His hands were clenched in tight, stark white fists; the ends of his knuckles dripped with blood. Shattered glass lay scattered at his feet; lamps, vases, and other blunt household objects were strewn about the floor. As the police approached him, I followed a puddle of blood flowing quickly toward the entrance; it was thick and dark; clumps of hair floated lazily with the current.

There at the end of the crimson pool I found her.

She was unresponsive.

The hue of her skin was black, blue, and purple—only small patches of her natural color could be seen. Her nose was twisted, her eyes puffed and sealed; she trembled as blood gushed from her face and out of her mouth, mixed with gruff and labored sounds from a crushed windpipe.

What else but a savage animal could have reduced a woman to such a state?

As my team and I worked to stabilize her, to pull her back from the brink of death, my eyes looked up to see the giant man looming in the corner of the room.

A police officer stood beside him as the man wiped his fists with a cloth.

Not a word was spoken.

No question was asked.

No one said anything to him.

We all knew the Hadith—as such, the hands of the authorities were bound, their lips sealed.

But my heart would not be silent.

As I worked frantically to bandage her wounds, I prayed, pleaded, beseeched God, as my heart bled into my chest.

"God in heaven! Look upon this woman with mercy! She will find no justice in this place, oh Christ!"

In our care the woman remained until she recovered.

But the day of her discharge was no cause for celebration.

Indeed, I praised God for His miraculous work in sparing the woman's life, for stopping the power of her wounds from ushering her unto death; but there in the lobby stood her husband, the animal who had painted his hands with her blood, as I knew he would do again.

God gave me a little while with her—oh Father, grow the planted Seed of Your Word!

I never saw her again.

But many like her came after her.

In droves they would come—all of them just as she, and worse.

And there would be no justice for any of them.

Not here.

I walked along the hallway, following the trail of blood left by the young woman's mother as she was wheeled down to an operating room.

As I stood outside that place, I laid my hand against the wall and prayed.

Though appalling had been this scene, not one among us was shocked.

Some looked upon it as one would a scraped knee on a child.

It was a common cold, a runny nose, a stubbed toe.

My feet carried me slowly to my car that night.

No sirens had marked the day.

No media coverage had swept the nation.

No outcry had roared from the public.

It was silent.

All was as it had ever been, here, in the darkest of the dark.

I was no longer in America.

I was home again.

***

"You're sure you want to do this?"

"I'm leaving tonight, no matter what! Man will not intimidate me into neglecting meeting with my brothers and sisters in Christ! I'll be there bright and early, as always! If you would," I added with a chuckle, "be sure to have a freshly-brewed pot on hand."

"Okay," my church friend said with a sigh. "As I mentioned before, it would be best if we took you by the secret entrance."

"That's fine with me. What do I do?"

"Listen carefully, when you get off the main road, take a right—"

His voice suddenly halted.

Another, fainter voice emerged.

I could hear only muffled whispers.

"Ahmed," said his voice, returning suddenly, still locked in a whisper and trembling. "When you were arrested last week, did they take your phone?"

"Yes, of course. Why?"

The word was breaching my lips when the realization hit me.

A silent phone slid slowly down my face.

Rushing to my window, I scanned the area.

Everything looked normal—but normal in Saudi does not mean good.

I knew something was out there, lurking in the shadows of the falling night, waiting for me.

Dropping on my knees, I prayed, "Dear God, the eyes of the evil one are upon me; his ears are keen and have heard much. Whatever happens," I said, "whatever plans lie in wait to work evil, may it all be worked for good and Your glory."

I hit the road.

Taking my usual route, I kept an eye on the rear view mirror, watching for any headlights that seemed in favor of following the trail I blazed. All around me the world was in darkness; even the moon was veiled.

Speeding along the highway, several hours into my drive and fervent praying, I began to feel comfortable that no one was following me; I was the only set of lights on a long, dark, and dusty road. Another handful of hours passed, and I was sure my tail was clear; but the UAE border lay only a few miles ahead. Surely, they would recognize me; my name would be linked to the document I'd signed—even if I was allowed to pass, someone would no doubt then start tailing me.

"Carry me through, Father," I prayed, as I cut through the blackness of the night. "Where You would have me go, there take me."

I drew a deep breath to steady my rapidly beating heart.

The border was close at hand.

Onward I sped through the moonless night.

A streak of black painted the way before me.

The last thing I saw was the reflection of my headlights bounding off of something large and metallic, followed swiftly thereafter by the sound of crunching metal, all instantaneously replaced with the stillest of silences and a blinding white light.

17
Outcast, Part Two

WHEN after a glorious eternity, wherein I had been gifted to walk outside of time, treading endlessly in the purest light, which made the days of earth look like a pool of pitch darkness; light so clean and cleansing—wading through it as through an ocean, soaring in its midst as on mighty wings, ascending up it as on a mountainside, and letting it dance through my fingers like the sand of a desert, one home to countless grains, each bearing a likeness wholly unique, resembling not a single other grain in any way, but that each was filled both to and beyond its capacity in a paradoxical harmony with such delights and wonders as my mortal mind will never again enjoy as it did, until I pass from this life and into the next; once released from this eternity, I awoke to find myself in the midst of a jungle of tubes and machines, all connected to my body, flashing and *beeping* and *booping*, each in its own way.

"Wh...what happened?" I said aloud, searching for my legs and hands that I might rise. "Where am I?"

Just then, a team of doctors rushed into the room.

"Welcome back to life!" cried one.

"Amazing!" exclaimed a nurse. "It's like one miracle after another!"

"Indeed!" chuckled the doctor beside her. "When you told us he was awake, I almost didn't believe you."

"What happened?" I asked again, wincing as my head throbbed.

"I am Dr. Adeel," said one, stepping forward. "You were in a serious car accident, two weeks ago."

"*Two weeks* ago!" I exclaimed—a searing shock then burst through my face.

"You've been in a coma ever since you arrived here. I must say, far more than luck seems to be on your side."

"Dr. Adeel," I breathed, blinking as the pain in my face sluggishly subsided, "I am a doctor myself—tell me everything."

"Rather bizarre," he said, stepping nearer to me, while the rest of the doctors and nurses stood huddled nearby, marveling and chattering amongst themselves. "You slammed into a tanker truck at full speed—but it's how the truck ended up where it was that's puzzling. It was just sitting there, abandoned, lights off, not running, stretched across the road; just sitting there like, well...a roadblock, I guess you could say."

My lips tightened.

"The authorities have yet to discover where the truck came from, who it belongs to, and what it was doing there. So strange," he said, his eyes widening as he shook and scratched his head. "You'd think that if someone had experienced mechanical trouble, they'd have left the truck on the side of the road, right? Not stretched like a barricade *across* the road. I don't know," he sighed. "Maybe he was trying to turn around and the thing died halfway into the turn, or something. Even still," he argued, seeming to pick up an internal debate he'd been hosting for the past fortnight, "why not just walk to the UAE border? It wasn't far from there! Amazing the border agents hadn't been alerted, you know?"

I drew a deep breath and nodded slowly.

"Anyway," he said, expelling a long breath, "you collided at full speed. I'm sorry to say, your car is a mangled mess— but, hey, what's that to being alive, no? And aren't you lucky to be! The tanker, you see, it was carrying acidic material; thankfully—*incredibly*—it didn't burst. Still, it's a miracle that you were pulled out without a single broken bone."

My eyes burst wide.

"Not *one*?"

"Not one."

"May I see the medical file?"

"Absolutely!" he declared, handing it to me.

The report noted numerous skin lacerations and a host of extracted foreign bodies; also among the laundry list was a severed facial artery, for which, given the number of stitches recorded on the page, it seemed they must have hired a tailor to put my face back together.

I raised my hand and softly tapped the area around my eye and cheek.

"Careful!" Dr. Adeel cried, snatching my wrist a moment too late.

Every facial muscle twitched nervously at my touch—a sensation like a set of jumper cables attached to my cheek jolted through my face, searing the nerves along the surface of the skin, and racing in both directions to the back of my skull, where the two streams of pain collided in an explosion of white heat that filled my head and sent shockwaves through my limbs.

"You have a shard of glass resting directly on your facial nerve," he continued, carefully lowering my hand. "Smiling, chewing—any sort of muscular movement, really, in this region," his finger, standing just away from my face, circled about the wounded area; "it will be rather painful."

Rather painful?

There were no words for this pain!

He said it was a shard, a tiny flake of glass—but I was sure there was a red-hot steel I-beam covered in acid sticking out of my face!

"When can I have it removed?" I asked, doing my best to utilize the fewest facial muscles as possible.

"*Remove* it?" he exclaimed, as if there had never been a more absurd request. "No, no—we're not removing it."

"*What?*"

"It's right on the nerve!"

"I *emphatically* agree!"

"Right, but if I go in and try to remove it, there's a great chance I'll sever the facial nerve and leave your face paralyzed! No, no," he chortled, shaking his head; "it's out of the question. You're welcome to find someone else to attempt the procedure; but I don't think many will be willing to take the risk. Leave it there," he said, speaking in what I assume he felt was his most reassuring, comforting tone. "Learn to live with the pain."

I closed my eyes and prayed to God for calming.

Relaxing my face as much as possible, I looked back at the medical report.

"My heart stopped."

"Yes!" Dr. Adeel replied, expelling a note of astonishment. "I don't know how they found you so quickly, the paramedics; but it's a darned good thing they did. That severed artery was bleeding profusely; another minute or so, and you may not have responded to CPR."

Leaning over me, he pointed to a note about blood transfusions.

"Look at that number!" he exclaimed, vigorously tapping the paper. "You sure put a dent in our blood bank! Seems Death itself had kissed that cheek of yours, given all the blood that spilled out of it."

Dr. Adeel and I chatted for a little while longer before I was left to rest and ponder all that had happened in what had seemed like both an eternity and an instant. But it wasn't until I arose from my bed, shortly before my discharging, and beheld my face in the mirror that I saw the whole situation with better clarity.

Something like a large cheese grater had pressed viciously against my face and pulled with violent vim, ripping the flesh all around my right eye and cheek into deep trenches capped on the rear-most ends with bunches of shredded flesh. I could recognize only half of the face staring back at me, and not at all. These scars run deep; they remain to this day: an ever-present reminder of the cost of following Christ: a mark all men can see for themselves, no matter where I am or what I'm doing. Mine is a face strangers stop to regard with a double take—and let them look! Let all the world see my face! The praises of Christ and His Gospel will ever pour forth from these unstoppable, untiring lips, proclaiming the significance of the scars attached to them and the invaluable worth of the stripes Jesus carried for the sins of the world! I bear on my body the marks of Jesus, the cost of loving Him! If anyone yet doubts my story, my faith, let them look upon my face! See these marks! And may Christ's holy name be praised forever and ever and evermore! Amen!

***

"Hey! What are you doing here?"

I whipped around to see a police officer running toward me.

Beholding my thoroughly bandaged body, he stuttered for a moment in his stepping, then proceeded.

"What do you think you're doing?" he persisted. "Rooting around for spare parts?"

I turned again and pointed to the pile of twisted metal before me, dumped among a parking lot of other cars seized or being stored by the local authorities.

"This is my car, officer," I said.

His eyes widened so quickly and broadly that his sunglasses toppled off his face.

"What?" he muttered. "This...this is...*yours*?"

I nodded.

"I'd thought for sure the poor soul who'd driven this heap had been pulled out in a million pieces!" he declared, then quickly ran to the car and began examining the driver's side, appearing to look for some reason as to why I hadn't been swallowed into the impressive wreckage.

Running his fingers along the metal and leather interior, which looked as though a huge bucket of red paint had been thrown on it, he shot his cue ball eyes back at me and said

306

breathlessly, "You're alive? How is it possible? How could one survive such an accident?"

Though I had a thing or two to say about the employment of the word "accident," I shook my head with genuine awe and said, "My God may yet have something for me to do."

Stepping slowly toward me, he looked me squarely in the eye and asked, "And who is *your* god?"

"There is only one," I replied calmly. "From the right hand of the Power was I upheld by a pierced hand. Remember today."

Then, after signing some necessary paperwork, I went on my way.

I arrived home later than afternoon and was visited by my California friends, who had been very busy spreading the Gospel across Saudi Arabia.

"Why don't you leave this place?" suggested one, upon seeing my wounds. "You could seek asylum in the United States!"

"As long as I can," I replied, "I must remain. These are my people—how can I abandon them?"

"Think of how effective you could be at preparing people like us to take your place! Go to the States, where it's safe."

"This world is not my home," I said. "As such, there is no safe place for me to lay my head. My passport is stained with the blood of Jesus; I have already been granted asylum in the Kingdom of God, and there shall I make my home, when all the work Christ has yet for me to do has been completed."

A few weeks passed, and I found myself back to work again. I attracted many a gawk and pocketsful of gasps from doctors and patients alike, as I waltzed around the hospital. Those who had heard of the crash watched me closely, as if thinking I were some sort of apparition, or a sign that they had been working too long and were in need of another cup of coffee; some even approached me with poking fingers, to test whether I was truly flesh and blood.

"What on earth happened to you?" bellowed the head of my department.

He had gotten word that a mummy in a lab coat had been wandering the halls treating patients, and called me into his office to see for himself what was the truth behind this odd report.

"I was in a pretty bad car crash," I replied.

"*PRETTY* bad?" he shouted, his head all eyes. "Why, what sort of crash leaves a man looking like this and still *walking*?"

"This kind," I said, holding up my phone, showing him a picture I'd taken of my car while at the police station.

Snatching the phone from my hand and pressing the screen against his face in disbelief, he eyed me carefully and said, "Speak. Let me hear you say a full sentence."

"Like what?"

"Give me a definition of neurotrauma."

"Neurotrauma," I began: "An injury to the head or spine, caused by a sudden, traumatic event, which can include concussions, traumatic brain injury, skull fractures, spinal—"

"Okay, okay!" he said, expelling a relieved breath. "Just wanted to make sure you didn't have anything like that. No fogginess? No speech problems? No trouble breathing?"

"Aside from an aching facial nerve, nothing, sir," I replied.

"Incredible!" he declared, shaking his head as he reclined at his desk. "I can't even count how many crash victims I've seen in my time—you've probably seen a good deal of them yourself."

I nodded.

"Never—and, I mean, *never*—have I seen a car like *this* carry any survivors." As he handed me my phone, he looked to the ceiling and cried in Arabic, "God has given you a new life! It's like you've been born again! Recreated by God!"

I will never forget these words, nor misremember them.

He said exactly this.

How odd for a Muslim to say such a thing, I thought, gazing at him from beneath a knitted brow. Such words are not found in the Quran, nor are they a part of Islamic theology or culture.

A *Muslim* could look at me and say of me "born again," while I was hard pressed to find Christians who would do the same?

How else could such a man speak as he did, employing the words that he did, unless Jesus had used my scars to reveal the truth of new life to him?

I couldn't help myself.

"I was protected," I said, my heart flexing hard with boldness and zeal. "The true God held me in His hand, shielding my life from Death, as my car was chewed to pieces all around me. I know He protected me, for, when it happened, I was on my way to worship Isa, the true Messiah."

I wasn't done.

"No amount of good works can earn or purchase anything for us in heaven, nor wash away our sin. God is holy," I stated, eyeing him squarely, "and nothing defiled can enter His presence. Only one who is holy can cover our sin, wash it white as snow, and present us holy before God. Isa is the Word of God," I persisted, carefully plucking words a lifelong devotee to Islam could understand, "and He is *one* with God. Isa died for all sinners, so that we could be forgiven, reconciled to God, and have eternal life!"

In just ten seconds, I had uttered all the critical contrasts and abominations to Islam.

Together, we endured ten days of stunned silence.

Then, in about the time it took me to blink, the man had sprung from his chair and rushed at me, zipping so quickly and coming so near to my face that I nearly toppled over, out of my seat.

"HOW DARE YOU!" he screamed, molten saliva raining over my face. "LEAVE! GET OUT! I'LL REPORT YOU FOR THIS! LEAVE MY PRESENCE AT ONCE!"

As he'd vehemently commanded, I did; and it wasn't long thereafter that I received a call from the general director's secretary.

"You are hereby informed," she said, very politely, "that your position at this establishment has been suspended indefinitely, effective immediately."

Not long thereafter, I was summoned before a review board of the highest medical authority in all of Saudi Arabia. The investigation and analysis of my case went on for months—session after session, interview after interview; and, eventually, I was called once more to stand before the board.

"After careful consideration of this case," said one among the members, "we have determined that you did indeed suffer severe psychological brain damage in your car crash, leading to your wild, incoherent ramblings."

"There is nothing wrong with my brain," I answered, calmly.

"We *insist*," snapped another, emphatically, "that there is no other explanation for this outburst of yours. Therefore, we are offering to commit you to a psychiatric institution, until your brain has healed and you are well enough to return to work."

"I appreciate your concern," I replied, "but my mind is perfectly sound. What I told my supervisor was and is the truth: Jesus Christ is my Lord and Savior. My faith is in Him, and I am not ashamed, nor am I afraid."

Sitting back in their chairs, the members of the board regarded one another quizzically, some casting helpless glances, others throwing frustrated frowns.

"Can't you understand?" sighed one at length. "We're doing all we can to preserve your career and livelihood; but you're stripping us of any power to do so."

Their motives were good, but I simply could not affirm that my faith in Jesus was due to brain damage; such did I say to a line of disappointed faces.

"This will end up costing you everything," said another. "You understand that, don't you? Everything you've worked for, all those endless days of studying and training and working grueling shifts—*gone!*"

"You're breaking the code of ethics for healthcare practitioners."

"No Muslim can become a Christian! It's apostasy— against Sharia law!"

"You will be cast into poverty! What money you have now will dry up like a puddle in the desert—no one will give you work if you are terminated for such an offense as this!"

"Think of your future wife! Your children! How will you provide for them?"

When they had exhausted all their arguments, I took a deep breath and said, "I have kissed Death and returned to life. Next to what I have in Christ, my career is rubbish; to die and be with my Savior is gain. I stand firmly by every word I have spoken, with full understanding of the consequences. My words are true and honest; I have kept my integrity before the Lord."

"You're throwing away honor and security! You're casting your life into the dust! You'll have nothing!"

"I will have my God! And my God is *not* money! He is the one who made and owns the hills and the cattle that graze thereon! I look to the birds and the flowers and see how their needs are met—so too shall mine be, for my Father holds me in higher regard than them! Surely, I will never want for anything!"

"Enough," said one, shaking and lowering his head. "Go home. We will deliberate and summon you again before us when we have reached a decision."

Having absolutely no clue how God would show up in this situation, I spent the next few weeks praying and laying myself at the feet of His will.

"Father," I said, "You have carried me through much. These years practicing medicine have been a blessing, an honor and responsibility bestowed upon me, an open door, through which you've led me. I give it all to You. I go where You lead me."

At long last, the call came, and I found myself once again standing before the review board.

Stepping forth, the secretary handed me the judgment.

"Your position as medical doctor," announced one of the board members, "is hereby terminated. Effective today, your license is revoked, and you are disbarred from practicing medicine in the Gulf States region."

I read the paper in my hands, on which his words were inked in formal language.

Looking up, I saw a row of somber faces.

I smiled and turned away.

Then, the moment my foot touched the road outside, I galloped into town.

"Sir! Hello, sir?" I bellowed breathlessly, as I skidded into a local shop. "Sir! Yes, hello, thank you—sir, I would like this framed, please, thank you," and immediately, as would a child presenting to his father a picture he'd drawn in school, I held up my official letter of termination and disbarment.

Indifferent to its content, the man kindly set the document into a nice frame, which I then hung proudly upon my wall, right next to my medical degree; and how that document did fill the room, outshining the credentials hanging beside it, for here was a certificate of graduation with highest honors, a testament to true value, in that all I had lost and will yet lose for the sake of Christ, and in the pursuit of knowing and being known by Him, is gain.

***

The year 2016 had just begun; how different this new beginning looked compared to the springtime in New Zealand I'd known nearly six years prior, when the door of my heart had been thrown open to Jesus, making all things as bright and colorful and bursting with new life as in the world around me. I stood now at the peak of winter: jobless, living off of only a small medical pension, as the government had frozen all my bank accounts following the crash. Without a car, I was grounded; grounded, I could not make the trek to Dubai; outside of Dubai, I could find no Christian fellowship to welcome me; and with no Christian fellowship, my soul was quickly starved.

But my forever family is a strong, tightly knit unit, and it wasn't long before I was connected to a lovely Christian woman named Nicole, who worked at the American Embassy in Saudi.

"I'm head of security," she said when we finally met in person. "I've heard your story. It's just incredible! And now I understand you're looking for Christian fellowship."

"Yes, indeed," I replied, eagerly. "Do you know anyone who would take me?"

"I sure do!" Sliding open a drawer, she extracted a piece of paper on a clipboard and penned my name onto a long list. "There," she declared, presenting it to me.

"What is this?"

"Your name has been added to the list."

"The list?"

"Yup! You are now approved and recognized as an individual welcome onto U.S. Embassy property. I'll take care of the official filing, but this is the quick reference list. We hold a Christian church service and fellowship once a week—be here Friday evenings at seven."

"*REALLY?*"

"You bet! We also hold prayer nights and gatherings at various times throughout the week. Meet here and the group will shuttle together to Freedom Hall."

"I'LL BE THERE!"

And I was, without fail! God had made a way for my transformation into the image of Christ to continue, and joy abounded every second of every day as a result. However, with all this joy and happiness came a great deal of smiling, and with smiling came searing pain; that shard was four months scraping my facial nerve, and I was no more used to the pain than a fish is used to walking about dry land on his fins.

Day and night I prayed for deliverance from this never-ending agony, which had been robbing me of sleep and making food bitter. I asked everyone I knew to pray; and, every prayer night, with my new Christian friends standing all around me, they did just that.

As I rose to leave one evening, my heart overflowing with the rapture of the Spirit and my eyes leaking tears of torment with every involuntary smile and laugh, an Indian man, new to the group, stepped before me.

"The Lord has heard your prayers," he said, gazing down upon me with large, commiserating eyes. "My name is Dr. Alexander; I am a general surgeon consultant. Come to my clinic, and I will do whatever is in my God-given power to relieve you of this anguish."

For the first time in four months, I felt no pain as a smile bigger than any I had dared attempt in some time stretched widely across my face.

Arriving bright and early the next day, Dr. Alexander and I bowed our heads in prayer, asking God to guide his hands and work healing upon me.

"In Jesus' name," he said, gazing deeply and resolvedly into my eyes, "you will be healed this day."

My body lay down across the operating table.

Dr. Alexander placed a hand on my shoulder and called upon Jesus' name once more, committing his hands to the Great Physician.

I breathed deeply and slowly drew the shades over my eyes, as a blessed numbness trickled through my face.

"The anesthetic should be wearing off now," he said. "Have you any feeling in the area?"

Raising my hand, I gently, timidly tapped my cheek.

Then, I cautiously pulled back a smile.

I puffed and wiggled my cheeks, twitched, yawned, pulled, pushed, punched—I could feel it all, but there was absolutely no pain!

"HALLELUJAH!" I screamed, leaping from the table. "It's a miracle!"

Smiling warmly, he held out his hand.

"Let us never forget."

In his palm, smeared with blood, sat an ever so tiny shard of glass.

Carefully, I took it from his hand.

"As this stained shard of glass is foreign to your dying flesh," he said, "so too are you foreign to the world with which that flesh will perish; and you can be sure that he who lords over what will soon pass away has felt your presence scraping the nerve of his power by the sword of the Word that lives in you." Leaning closer toward me, he spoke in a grave tone, "He will ever seek to extract you."

My eyes fell again upon the shard.

Even something so small, I thought; and I have not forgotten.

As I tried to find words grand and worthy enough to thank him as he deserved, my mind was suddenly struck by a terrible thought.

"I haven't any money!" I declared, horror seizing my bones. "I'm so sorry! Forgive me! The government froze all my accounts—what little I have surely won't cover the cost! Please, tell me what I—"

Dr. Alexander gently held up a hand to silence me.

"Your bill," he said softly, "is paid in full."

As the sun continued its rise over the Saudi sand, I became increasingly involved at the U.S. embassy, befriending the guards and even serving as a volunteer to shuttle people from the embassy gates to a place called Freedom Hall. Liberated from my persistent pain and well fed on the meat of the Word, I no longer walked to get around; rather, I skipped fifteen feet off the ground, clicking my heels and dancing merrily among the clouds, singing a sweeter tune than the birds flitting about me, and raining over all in my path the love of Jesus. It was in this manner that I sauntered once again into the embassy to see my good friend Nicole and participate in another glorious fellowship.

Only...

"Who are you?" I asked, taken rather off guard by the new face behind the desk.

"Dean," said the man sternly. "What do you want?"

His eyes snarled as they looked me up and down; his face was like stone.

"I'm, uh...I'm here for the Christian fellowship."

"Ha!" he bellowed and then returned to his work. Gazing back up at my perplexed face, he said, "You can't be serious. What kind of game is this?"

"Is Nicole here?" I asked.

"Nicole? You know her?"

"Yes! She's a friend of mine."

"I *seriously* doubt that," he snapped. "Now, hurry up and tell me why you're here."

"But I have! I'm here for the Christian fellowship!"

"That's ridiculous! Besides, no one is allowed on these grounds without proper security clearance!"

"I know! I'm on the list!" I cried, beaming; a childlike impulse beckoned me to start jumping up and down, but I resisted. "Nicole put me on it!"

His brow furrowed as he snatched the security file.

Slamming it down on the desk before him, he threw a finger on the list and barked, "Name!"

"Ahmed Joktan." I took the liberty of pointing to my name on the paper. "Right there—second from the top."

His eyes widened and his body drew backward.

"Identification—now!" Having examined my ID, he eyed me curiously and said, "And you're a Saudi citizen?"

"Yes!" I cheered. "And a Christian!"

"No, no," he mumbled, snatching his phone and dialing quickly. "No, this is ridiculous. Yes," he said into the receiver, "please come to the gate for a moment."

We stood there in silence until one of the elders of the fellowship arrived.

He and I embraced gleefully.

"You mean he's been attending these meetings?" cried Dean.

"Of course!" the elder replied. "Is there a problem?"

"Is there a *problem*! He's a Saudi!"

"So?"

"Absolutely not!" he shouted, expelling such astonishment it was a wonder he didn't suddenly pass out from the shock. "I don't know *what* you did to Nicole," he barked, throwing a finger in my face, "but you are no longer allowed on these grounds."

"WHAT?" cried the elder. "But he's a Christian! He's been attending for months!"

"That doesn't matter!" Dean clapped back. "He's a Saudi! He is no longer welcome!"

"Well, praise the Lord!" I cheered.

It was as if the cord fueling all the sound in the world had been suddenly yanked from its socket.

Both Dean and the elder turned slowly toward me with dumbfounded stares.

"Ahmed," mumbled the elder at length, "what are...aren't you...how can you say, 'Praise the Lord' at such a time as this?"

"I will always be joyful!" I said, quoting 1 Thessalonians 5:16-18. "I will be thankful in all circumstances, for this is God's will for all who belong to Christ Jesus—and I *do*!" I added, turning to Dean with a beaming smile. "I need not a list to confirm that."

Later that evening, I called one of the pastors of the church in Dubai and told him the story of my expulsion.

"Looks like I must go elsewhere," I sighed. "I've got my U.S. visa and just enough still on hand for a ticket there and back. I was thinking about making my way through the Midwest."

"I know a great pastor out there," he said. "His name is Mark; he heads a solid, Bible-believing church in a small suburban town. Here, write down this address."

Having done so, I packed my bags and readied myself for another trip to the States.

Before departing, I walked back by the embassy.

"Hello and goodbye, my friends!" I said, shaking the hands of the guards stationed at the gates, with whom I had become rather close. "I'm off to the States!"

"We'll miss you," said one, tightening his lips as his eyes began to redden.

"We already miss you," said the other. "It's just not right, any of it."

"All I want is to freely worship my Savior in the land of the free. And this is U.S. soil, is it not?" My eyes were heavy with the bleeding of my heart. "I do have a visa," I said, rummaging through my bag and extracting it. "This is U.S. land—won't you let me enter to worship with my Christian family one last time before I go?"

The guards turned to one another.

Parting his quivering lips, one said, "I'm sorry. But your name is no longer on the list. I...I have to ask you...to leave."

As I took a step backward, he reached out quickly and took my hand, shaking it firmly.

"God be with you," he whispered, then resumed his post and posture.

Of the forty nationalities that had comprised the fellowship from which I was now barred, I had been the only believer of local blood—for no other reason than this had I been banished from what should have been free soil. But the Muslim influence is strong, so compelling, that even freedom cowers in its presence. The great nation of the West was here no more than a tortoise sucked up into its shell.

And, so, I went on my way.

Just then, I ran into Dr. Alexander, who was walking casually to Freedom Hall.

"You're not coming, I take it," he said, nodding toward my bag and journeyer's posture; my name being removed from the list was not unknown to him, but he had been praying, along with the rest in the group, that God would open a door somehow, so that I could again partake in the fellowship of believers.

"They still won't let me in," I replied, heaving a heavy sigh. "It seems my expulsion is irreversible."

"That makes two of us."

"They've banished you too?"

"Not the embassy. My hospital."

"*What?*"

"I've been fired," he said, ever so blithely that I hardly noted the severity of what he'd said.

"No! I'm so sorry! Why?"

"They found out one of my patients didn't pay his bill."

My jaw fell into the sand.

I could find no words, nothing sufficient for an apology; no word that would not have shattered with inadequacy beneath the weight of my guilt, nor burst in utter failure to hold the outpouring of anguish I felt for the man and what his act of kindness toward me had cost him.

"Just like your glass shard, my friend," he said with a smile. "Extracted from this place, but not in accordance with the will of this world's prince—how impotent are the Devil's little triumphs, for my God is sending me to scrape Satan's nerves elsewhere. And, so, I shall."

With that, he bade me farewell with a brotherly embrace, and continued on his way.

"Smile often!" he called over his shoulder. "Smile for God, and remember me!"

And I, turning toward the setting sun, lifted my eyes to the heavens painted in hues of scarlet, violet, and blazing orange, there to marvel and offer my silent tribute of praise: a smile worn without a trace of pain, and worn even today as then, as ever it will be.

18

Refrigerator Rights

"HONESTLY, I think he's afraid you'll blow up the church, or something."

Her name was Anna; she and I met in the States.

"Do you know Mark?" I'd said, when I'd learned she went to the very church about which my friend in Dubai had told me.

"Yes," she'd replied, "but he's not the pastor anymore. He went to plant another one and left this church to a new pastor. His name is Matt."

"Bible names."

"Indeed! And Matt's great—he's very much like Mark: a devoted follower of Jesus. I really think you'll like him, and I *know* he'll like you!"

That was then.

After calling Matt to tell him about me, that emphatic "*know*" carried a much difference emphasis.

"I *know*! Crazy, right?"

"Did he actually *say* that?" I asked.

"No—he didn't say 'blow up' or 'terrorist,' or anything. But he very firmly and sternly warned me that Muslims cannot be trusted—said their religion permits lying to gather converts. He even wagged his finger at me!" she added with a chuckle.

"Well," I said, chuckling along—by now, this kind of response acted on me no differently than discovering sand under my fingernails, "did you tell him I'm *not* a Muslim?"

"All I had to say was 'Saudi' and he shut down the discussion. 'He's tricking you, using you!' he scolded, and then proceeded to tell me something about a story or a movie he'd read or seen once about a woman and her daughter being duped into leaving America for the Middle East and there being held against their will. I think he's got the impression that you might be trying to trick me into marrying you for a visa, or that you're intent on kidnapping me and hauling me back to Saudi."

Shaking my head smiling, I let out a sigh and prayed a little prayer for the man.

"Would you ask him again? Tell him I'd be happy to meet in public. Why not at the Starbucks down the road? Do you think he'd be willing to do that?"

"Wear a thin, white shirt."

"Why?"

"So that, if he does meet you," she said, raising her eyebrows and tilting her head toward me, "he'll see right away that you're unarmed."

It was a hot summer day when at last Matt agreed to meet me. Sitting beneath an umbrella on the outside patio of the Starbucks, I waited anxiously for him to arrive. Unsure what sort of coffee he might want to drink, I'd purchased two iced coffees and a hot, black coffee, which I kept in reserve, just in case he didn't fancy his brew on the rocks. But as I gathered an armful of cream and sugar, I realized he might be disinclined to take anything from me, thinking that I might have poisoned his drink.

I seemed to recall a fellow who'd once had a similar trepidation.

"Oh, well," I sighed with a shrug, "two iced coffees on a hot day is not exactly suffering."

I sipped.

And waited.

And sipped.

And thought.

Anna had told me that she'd recited my whole story to this man.

I was glad.

This meant he'd have had the chance to digest it a bit.

Sure, it seemed not a bone in his body believed a word of it; but at least we could start our conversation a little ways from the beginning. What he hadn't been told yet was the part about my dream.

"*That'll* be interesting," I muttered aloud.

Sipping still, getting so near to emptying the cup of its refreshing delight that I secretly hoped Matt would take his iced coffee for poisoned, I watched the cars whiz on by, one after the other, on and on, going as their master's went. And what was driving them? So many people, I thought—Lord, will many be saved?

"You Ahmed?"

My head whipped around to see the source of the query.

A long, bespectacled face leapt back in alarm.

"So sorry!" I blurted, using as non-threatening a voice as I could muster. "Yes! I am Ahmed!"

The man stood cemented in the spot to which he'd leapt.

His eyes refused to blink, even as he peeled away his glasses.

Slowly, his jaw began to drop.

His gaze would not be broken.

But he was not looking at my eyes.

A tingling of self-consciousness danced about my scarred cheek.

"I—I'm sorry to have startled you," he stammered, fumbling around for the chair opposite mine, his eyes unwilling to help him find it. "I'm Pastor Matt."

"Coffee?" I asked, when at last he'd found his seat. "I have both hot and iced."

I slid both to him and he set them aside with thanks.

"Anna told me a lot about you."

His left and right side seemed incapable of cooperating with one another to sit as one on the chair—back and forth he shifted as the war raged.

"And I've been told a great deal about you, as well!" I replied. "I understand you've known Mark for quite some time."

He affirmed the point, but he seemed disinterested in talking about himself.

Answering quickly, he went right into a fiery test of my faith, laying hold of it to be touched by the all-consuming flame of the Bible.

I very much appreciated this.

As I spoke, declaring first the deity and resurrection of Christ, forsaking the Qur'an, forswearing its commands and the life seeped in sin and darkness I had once lived; as I testified to Christ's saving power, the salvation by which I am justified before the Father, the faith that held and holds me fast in Him amid tremendous, torturous persecution, and the hope that leads me onward and compels me to proclaim the Gospel to all the world; as I professed my deep and passionate love for Jesus, my awe at the unconditional, eternal, and transformative love by which He first loved me, and my unworthiness to receive even the finest misting of His grace, given the false god I had served, the evil I had supported, the violence and destruction I'd craved, and the hostile position I had taken to His outstretched hand; as I detailed the glorious moment I had beheld the one I would soon call Savior, here in this temporal realm, standing in my midst as pure, radiant light, exposing what was and had ever been the deepest of darkness I'd called my life; as I spoke these things, my eye could not help but watch the iced coffee standing idly beside him. How solid had been the ice therein, so densely packed together, forming a large block. But as he listened to my answers and testimony, that block began to weaken, the ice to dissolve, and the cup containing it to weep. After quite some time spent conversing, the man's face mimicked this cup—streaked red it had become, stained by great streams funneling from watery eyes, pooling among the growing puddle.

"Jesus, the Son of God," I said in conclusion, "in His infinite grace and mercy, chose one who had not chosen Him to be a servant proclaiming the salvation found in Christ. Whether man trusts my faith is of little concern to me. My mouth testifies to this, as does this face," I said, pointing to my scars, "as does this body."

Speaking thusly, I turned and began to lift the back of my shirt.

"From now on," I said, speaking Paul's words from Galatians 6:17, as the sunlight painted slowly the emerging, mangled flesh, "let no one cause me trouble, for I bear on my body the marks of Jesus."

"Stop," he said in a voice soft and sharp.

He placed a trembling hand over his mouth and looked away into the passing traffic.

Taking the melted iced coffee before him, he raised it to his lips and sipped.

He gagged and jolted; the lukewarm coffee spewed from his mouth.

His head fell slowly backward; his eyes squeezed tightly.

Then, raising his weary gaze to me, he whispered with what power his speech had left, "It's true. No Muslim could speak the way you do, nor endure such things as you have endured, if not for...I want to believe you, Ahmed," he continued after a pondering pause, his face contorting, looking as though his brain were throwing its weight against an immovable object in his head, "but I have to pray about this. My God," said he, as his eyes turned heavenward, "can I really believe this man?"

That last question sounded as if it were meant for him.

His eyes turned away to bore deeply into the ground.

"I need time to pray about this," he said again; then, after hesitating a moment, he lunged forward and wrapped me tightly into his arms.

My instant reaction was more akin to that of one taken suddenly by a boa constrictor; and the twitch I gave in response might have been the prevailing action, had not he whispered through streaming tears, "I *will* pray—I truly, *truly* want to believe you."

That twitch instantly relaxed, and my arms soon found their way about him; then, offering a parting salutation, I watched him lumber slowly away to his car.

All night I stayed up praying, begging God to take away any fear or doubt plaguing the man's spirit, to soften his heart, to show him the truth. For some reason, I found myself rather drawn to this brother—how my friend in Dubai had picked out this man's church, right in the middle of a small town in what seemed no more than a random place in the Midwest, was rather astonishing to me.

No, I thought; there was nothing random about any of this.

"God," I prayed, "I sense there is some great work to be done here. Show me to Your opened door."

"I haven't slept all night!" exclaimed Matt, ushering me into his office.

Getting his call had been surprising enough; being asked to come to his office was mind-blowing.

Sitting opposite him, I closed my knees and placed my hands atop them, my shoulders back and head straight, with wide eyes charged with demonstrating my attentiveness, set above a toothless smile—this was my best attempt at looking harmless.

"It's like being born again, *again!*"

I would have asked for elaboration, but he kept right on going.

"Your story cut right through me! What profound joy did it pour into my very soul—overflowing! But that's just it!"

If those words and their presentation, I thought, were setting up the relating of an epiphany, he surely did well conveying the power thereof, as in speaking thusly he lunged forward with a finger extended upward, coming so near my face I just about toppled out of my chair.

"Listening to you speak yesterday—I was weeping with immeasurable joy! For I beheld in you the power of God as never I had seen it! My faith was being held to the flame; my eyes being enlarged to see *God*—to *really* see Him! Not this fits-in-your-pocket, Americanized version—I didn't even know I'd been viewing God so small! No! To see Him in all His glory, in all His majesty! To marvel at His tremendous might, to swim through the depths of His bottomless love and mercy! To bear witness in the flesh to the darkest mire through which He extended forth His hand to save! Those words that speak of Him in the Scriptures—glory to God, they're bursting in living color before my very eyes and shooting sparks through my heart!"

He was like a tank of compressed air with the nozzle struck off, and one could but wonder how much pressure yet remained to be expelled.

"And you're not the only one!" he declared.

"The only one?"

"The only Muslim to have had a dream pointing them to Christ! I'd heard about this sort of thing before; but I've spent the last however many hours—days, weeks, *whatever!*—looking into these cases! It's all over the place! Hundreds! Thousands! Tens of thousands! Practically everyone speaks of a 'Man in White!'"

His words fell so quickly from his lips; their every syllable met my ears as if it had just broken through the sound barrier.

Throwing a quaking hand to his desk, he clamped down upon a tall thermos and chugged three monstrous gulps.

Having been breathing only the air of coffee-breath he'd sent in a whirlwind about the room since my arrival, I timidly asked, "How many cups of that have you had?"

"Doesn't matter! Lost track after five, anyway—that was hours ago. Point is: this is a pattern. Muslims all over the world have been snatched out of Islam through dreams! Look at this case, just a couple of years ago: Nabeel Qureshi. He had several dreams! And this goes way back! Bilquis Sheikh in the seventies—she from an affluent Muslim family in South Asia, called to Christ through a dream. It's just amazing! God is choosing to reach into the darkness by way of dreams!"

"He is the same yesterday, today, and tomorrow," I said. "Many times the Bible talks of God's work through dreams."

"That's not all I learned!" he continued, spinning in his chair, snatching a stack of papers, and spinning back around to face me, doing it all in a single, circling swing. "I did some research on you too!"

"Oh?"

I was really starting to like this guy.

"Everyone in your story—I called them! The tall man in New Zealand, the people at YWAM, your friends in Dubai who know Mark—I called them all! Look at all this!" he cheered, waving the stack of papers. "My notes! A whole tree's worth of chicken scratch! It's all here: every word you'd said—confirmed! Please!" he begged, throwing the stack back on his desk, "Forgive me for having doubted you! Won't you please speak to the congregation on Sunday? Would you like some coffee, by the way?"

A gigantic smile exploded onto my face.

"Yes to all!" I exclaimed.

***

Matt and I packed two decades of conversation into a single afternoon. Coffee really is an amazing thing. By the end of it all, he and I were locked in the firm embrace of brotherhood.

"This story has absolutely slain my heart!" he declared, wiping tears from his eyes. Holding me at length before him, he proclaimed, as his gaze studied me carefully, "It's like I'm looking at a ghost! By all I have ever believed to have known about the world and Christianity, here in my sheltered Western world, a man like you shouldn't even exist! No! Stories like yours are almost unheard of in the West! We must tell everyone! Come, speak to the congregation on Sunday!"

Some narratives might require a great many chapters and back-and-forthing to produce between two characters a transformation from hostility to brotherhood—but God's narrative, in this instance, required relatively no time at all.

"My faith has skyrocketed—clear over the *moon!*—even more since hearing your story! We American Christians are asleep to God's work in the world beyond our back yards!" he cried, having in the previous breath confessed that he had been deeply afraid and sinisterly suspicious of me. "Are we really *seeing* God at work? We gather and pray and put offerings in the offering plate, take bread and wine, sing songs—this is all good and right; but how can we be so comfortable in our fortresses of pacifying pleasure when people are suffering and stumbling around in the dark? Please! Speak to the congregation! We'll hold a special evening service! I'm telling you, not one person here has *ever* encountered anyone like you, or any story like yours! It's a foreign world to them—they need to know the darkness that exists and see the power of the God they claim to serve! Please! Speak to the congregation!"

"I will, gladly!" happily agreeing to the engagement for about the fiftieth time.

"Good! And come to my house tonight for dinner! My family simply has to meet you!"

And, so, I did, that evening and many days thereafter. Our bonding was instantaneous! The joy of that household rushed forth from its entrance as if from a mighty, inexhaustible fire hose, drenching all passersby.

Matt introduced me to his wife and many children, and I got to know them all extremely well in our short time together; I was instantly adopted as a son and brother. Such hospitality and unexpected love had not been felt in some time—Matt even took it upon himself to arrange a living situation for me.

"I wish you'd just stay here!" he said, as he and I carried out to the car a mattress he was giving me.

"Yours is such a large family!" I argued, tying the mattress to the roof. "You're already busting at the seams of the house. I'll have my own room in which to sleep, rather than occupying your hallway."

"But you're my brother! I want you to stay in my home!"

"This is more than generous," I reassured him, tightening the rope. "Please know that I am extremely grateful."

"And I want *you* to please know," he exclaimed, walking around the car to me and looking me dead in the eye, both hands clasped like bear traps around my shoulders, "I am your family now, just as you are mine! Whatever you ask of me, I will give it! Any time, day or night—whatever you need, no matter what, I'll *always* be here for you! And don't you *dare* knock when you come to the door! This is *your* home, now; you have refrigerator rights—we're family! And, as such, I expect to see you here on birthdays and holidays! American Independence Day is coming up—you're not welcome; you're *required*!"

I would come to learn an amazing thing about Matt: that even without coffee, he speaks in all exclamation points, a language of his own I've come to call Exclamatory English.

Ours became a bond that endures and continually fortifies, even unto today; and I've exercised my refrigerator rights more than a few times. And while it seemed I had found a great blessing from heaven in Pastor Matt and his family—and, I had—I could not have conceived in those days the blessings God had yet to bestow through the bond He'd created.

***

Sunday evening finally arrived, and I stood before a host of wide eyes and gaping jaws—the dropping of a pin was the crashing of moon-sized cymbals. Some people were visibly shaken; a few even wept. Where some churches had seen rousing replies, I found here a great deal of solemn reflection, a host of people very seriously and sincerely pondering and absorbing this new world, so suddenly unveiled before them. I felt as though I shook every hand and heard every voice of those in attendance that day. One by one they approached me to inquire further about my story and to thank me for extracting them from the comfort of their present lives. And these people, I found, were not to be impacted for just a day—they are a force of serious, Bible-believing and loving Christian warriors, who strive daily to hear the call of the Savior and leap into action at the sound of His voice. Matt even called for a special offering to pay my way back to Saudi—and, boy, did that blessed congregation give!

But there were some who doubted.

"It's unbelievable!" complained Matt when we met later that day. "So infuriating!" Flashes of red streaked across his face. "Who do they think they are to deny the work of Christ?"

"It's their job as elders to be careful about those who might influence the congregation," I said, employing an even tone to try and calm him. "Just be careful not to sin in your anger. You know, I seem to recall a man from around these parts who *also* didn't believe me at first."

"I *know*!" Matt plopped down in his chair and grabbed his head. "But they've heard your story now! Just wait 'til they see all the evidence I've compiled about you! Page by page, I'm going over it with them! I won't stand for any more doors being slammed in your face! If that doesn't convince them, what will?"

"The power of God."

And for that power Matt and I immediately prayed; on our knees we would pray daily for that power to move through the church, to remove the doubts of the elders, and to raise up people to answer the call to go to Saudi Arabia and spread the Gospel.

"We need to get organized!" shouted Matt one day.

"How so?" I asked, raiding a sandwich from his fridge.

"Your ministry! Let's form it into something concrete, something established! An international organization aimed at bringing the Word to Muslims in Saudi Arabia and all over the world! We'll form it here in the States, where there won't be any governmental interference—no concerns about being shut down or having our website blocked! We'll utilize American freedoms to reach those living in darkness!"

"How do we do that?"

"We just do it! Got a name?"

"Mphm hermnfph pfrmph."

I had just taken a large mouthful of turkey and cheese on wheat.

"Okay, we'll come back to that—as of now, it's only right that you be Director and CEO."

"And you're my Vice President!" I exclaimed, spewing a few crumbs.

"I'll dive into any certifications or licenses we might want to get, and I'll reach out to some resources from my time as a missionary in Spain to see what kind of support or insight we can gain!"

We worked the rest of the night, laying the groundwork for an organized ministry. Eventually, our labors produced a solid foundation on which to begin building.

It had been a most fruitful time, but the sun was quickly setting.

"Matt," I said, as we reclined with an evening decaf, "I'll be going back soon."

The balloon of gaiety that had been inflating throughout the day quickly deflated into a set of hunched shoulders supporting a curved neck and hung head, bearing a most broken and despondent haze over drooped lips, where only moments before had been bright, bursting sunshine.

His voice low, Matt lifted heavy eyes and muttered, "Are you sure? Brother, I...that tanker truck incident was no accident. They're not done with you. I just know it—if you go, I'll never see you again."

"I have to go," I replied delicately, as this was not the first time he'd begged me to stay, even before his calling for the offering that had purchased my ticket. "My visa is about to expire."

"There must be another way! We can appeal for an extension, or something! Please, brother! Don't go! I know I was the one who called for the offering, but..."

"Christ calls me to be a light in a dark world! As of now, there is yet work to be done. Unless God provides a way for me to stay, I must trust that He wants me back in Saudi—for what reason, I don't know; but I have to go."

"Then, let's pray!" cried Matt. "Father," he pleaded, "stretch our Your hand and bar my brother from returning to that hostile land! He surely will die if he goes back! Open a way for him to stay here, where it's safe!"

He prayed every day in this manner, even as I stood before him at the airport, ticket in hand.

"Don't worry, brother," I said, laying a commiserating hand on his shoulder; his eyes were red and his chest quaking.

"Put your trust in God. I am His witness, and as such I am part of the greatest witness protection program known to man."

We shared a laugh, threw our arms around one another, and whispered our final goodbyes.

As the plane soared into the heavens, I lifted the voice of my heart unto God, thanking Him for the bright horizon He had painted for me in the States; and when at last my foot hit the Saudi sand, I turned my eyes to the skies and asked, "Where now goes the story, Father? By what means will You use me this time to call the lost?"

A hand readied in the distance.

A piece of paper was set into place.

A drop of ink hit the page.

19

The Letter

SETTLING back into my former groove of evangelism via video apps, I shared the Gospel with atheists, agnostics, people of various religious beliefs and backgrounds, even Christians struggling with sin—but my primary focus was still Muslims; and I never missed an opportunity to weave the love of Jesus into a conversation—or any situation, for that matter. I continued thusly for quite some time, being as wise as I knew how to be, that I might fly beneath the eye of the Saudi government.

But this glass shard had been scraping a very large nerve for quite a while now.

One day, while I was out running errands in my new car— a tiny, silver-painted, manual-transmission, Chinese-made coupe I'd managed to procure for what little I had left in my finally unfrozen bank accounts—I pulled up to a speed bump. Taking it at no more than two-and-a-half miles per hour, knowing this old, tattered car was a pothole away from its frame falling off, a car rolled up hastily beside me and screeched to a halt.

A cloud of dust enveloped it slowly from its wake.

It sat quietly.

At long last, the cloud passed.

Down rolled the window, and from the shadow within sluggishly emerged a leering head. A long, crooked nose kissed first the daylight, while a thin brush began painting away the streaks of black staining the face's many crevices. The ends of a wide, mouth-splitting smile folded over the ears, while strings of blood leeched from cavernous cracks along lifeless, chapped lips and oozed from broken gums clinging to mangled, blackened teeth; a vale of thick, knotted eyebrows cast a grim shadow over it all. As if cowering in caves, the eyes sat deep within two dark sockets—their gaping pupils glowed like spotlights. Thin was the flesh stretched over his veiny skull; patches of rot, like rust on metal, chewed away at the features, some joining with one another on their corrosive paths. The head began to tilt, its eyes remaining fixed, and a hyena-like chuckle trickled off a wet, waggling tongue. It started slowly, winding up in the pits of his mouth, then grew steadily in speed and volume, becoming a wicked, wide-eyed cackle, intercut by wheezing gasps and a raspy rattling in the throat.

Rather concerned, I rolled down my window.

"Are you all right?"

Screeching amid his swelling laughter, quickly becoming hysterical as his red-eyed face peeled backward with a wide, unnatural-looking grin, the face screamed, "YOU ARE AN ACCURSED *INFIDEL!*"

My blood turned to ice and all the air in my lungs instantly dissipated.

Mouth dry, I gaped at the wild sight before me.

"Do...do I know you?" I asked.

Pulling the skin of his face down over his laughter, forcibly reforming his appearance, he sniggered as the wicked glee, still boiling, bubbled to the surface, barely trapped within him, and pointed slowly to the back of my car.

"Your window," he tittered, and then leisurely rolled away, his laughter released in full to fill the heat of the day with its bone-splitting sound.

Throwing my car quickly into park, I tossed my head every which way, and then turned around to see the window. Its angle and the glare from the sun falling against the layer of sand washed over it produced nothing for my eyes to see; so, I carefully exited the car and walked to the back.

No sooner had my eyes fallen upon the window did a fault line in the Saudi sand open up at my feet. There on the window had been spray-painted the Arabic letter "N."

In the runny, red paint, I could see the martyred Christian, framed in the pane of my childhood, hung on a crane high above the city, wearing this very symbol.

Without thinking, I snatched a tire iron from the car and smashed out the glass, before sprinting back into the car and speeding to the nearest repair shop for a replacement.

On my way back home, I grabbed my phone and began to dial.

"Matt! I don't have much time! Please, pray for me!"

"What is it? What's happened?"

"The government has made its move—I'm going on the run!"

"Wait! Wait! What's happened?"

"They'll be hunting me, Matt! They marked my car today with a symbol of death! Just pray!"

Quickly hanging up, I screeched into a space outside my apartment, ran up the stairs, and gathered as many necessities as I could carry, left my last payment on the counter, then took off into the distance without looking back.

In Matthew 10, Jesus tells his disciples that when they are persecuted in one town, they should flee to the next. I did just that, settling in a work camp three hours away. And there I hid myself for the next few days.

But the Saudi eye is long and wide, and persistent above all things.

Walking back to my car one evening, I perceived a large envelope taped to the driver's window.

It was bulgy and terribly heavy.

Had I parked in the wrong spot?

Was this a ticket?

What kind of ticket weighs as much as this?

As my fingers traced the bulging, I feared this had nothing to do with parking.

My breathing hastening, I looked both ways and all around, and then carefully began to peel back the seam.

A flash of gold light cut across my eyes.

My throat sealed.

My feet went numb and my hands shook violently.

Tipping the envelope, three gleaming bullets fell into my palm.

Their noisome perfume of death filled my nostrils.

I clenched my fist and hurled them into the sand; and as tears streamed from my eyes, my cold, quaking fingers extracted the accompanying letter.

DOG of Jesus——you will stop speaking in the name of Jesus and turn again at once to Allah and Muhammad his messenger. If you do not return to Islam, your blood is ours. YOU HAVE TEN DAYS. You can run, but we will find you. We will hunt you down. WE WILL KILL YOU.

If there was one thing of which I was absolutely sure, it was that I did not have ten days.

20

Dictation

SPEEDING along the highway, my eyes scoured the empty blackness for a cell tower. I desperately needed to make a call.

"I think this is it, Matt," I whispered, crouched in my car and carefully surveying the night. "I won't be able to outrun these guys forever, but I'm ready to graduate and be with Jesus. Matt," I said, forcing my words past the lump in my throat, "this may be 'goodbye.'"

"Don't you say that!" cried Matt. "I won't believe it! Until God takes you from this dying world, I know you and I still have work to do!"

"What can I do now? I have no money for a flight to the States—or anywhere, for that matter! And I'm on the run!"

The line went quiet for a moment.

"Tell me your story," said Matt, his voice peeking out of the silence. "From the beginning—tell me everything!"

"Why? What good does it—"

"If you're going to die out there, the least we can do is write down every detail of your story, preserve it, and spread it across the world! If they kill you, your story will live on; they won't be able to touch it! Now!" he shouted; I could hear papers rustling in the background. "Start spouting!"

"Where do I begin?"

"Your testimony—let's get that down first! We'll record all the meatiest parts up front; then, if we can, we'll pack it in with all the fixings, fortify it with as many other details as we can! Let's go! Hurry!"

For the next long while, I recited what amounted to a bulleted list of facts; the next day, I expounded on those bullets with a hasty version of what I would usually speak to congregations. With every subsequent day I was gifted, the story became richer in depth and detail.

Matt stayed up, hour after hour and day after day, waiting for me and taking dictation, in what we came to call out "Red-Eye Meetings."

He never missed my call.

I drove into town under cover of darkness to buy food and supplies. My tiny car rolled silently into an alley, and I crept to a local store. Having procured the necessities, I scurried back toward the alley; and then, out of the corner of my eye, through a great cloud of dust, I saw a large mass of black, darker than the night surrounding it, barreling down the road, racing toward me at breakneck speed.

A burst of light caught my body, rooted in the middle of the road.

Turning, I beheld a gigantic SUV, bounding over the uneven road, as if careening over a long row of trampolines. And from the passenger window popped the figure of a man, who quickly drew a rifle.

It had not yet been ten days.

Before I could react, the sound of popping popcorn kernels as projected through towering, surround-sound speakers began exploding all around me.

Throwing my items into the dust, I sprinted to my car and screeched across the street to the next road. Bullets littered the driver's side, pelting the metal like hail on a tin roof; my window burst into a million tiny pieces and the whiz of hungry rounds zipped past my face.

Only by God's grace did I manage to maintain control as I burned the clutch through gears like I had never been even remotely capable of doing. Up and down streets, cutting corners, swerving dangerously close to buildings and other obstacles—I raced until I could no longer hear the sound of the rifle, at which point I cranked the wheel into a tight, dark, and well-concealed corner; and there I waited, watching until every grain of dust I'd kicked up in my wake fell to the ground.

No one came.

It was silent.

I crept out and quickly covered my tire tracks, then scurried back to safety.

There would be no going back to the work camp.

The hunt was on, and my hunters were greedy for blood.

Once satisfied that they had been shaken, I dove into my car and took off into the blackness, seeking dark corners or alleyways in which to hide. I stayed in one place no more than two hours at a time, covering the most distance at night, leaving my car only to buy food or gas, and never in daylight. My tiny coupe was my new mobile home. I had no means by which to clean myself as the days progressed, and I hardly slept a wink. All I could do was pray and ask God to carry me through to the next sunrise, to provide what food and water I would require to survive.

Now, more than ever, I knew I needed to get the full story to Matt, complete with every minute detail about myself, my journey, and the cruel history and nature of Islam. To do this, I needed to emerge from my dark, desolate places to locate those cell towers. They were not all that easy to find, and I was never at ease speaking beside one—believing I had lingered too long in one place, I would quickly end the call and seek out another tower. I could not risk an open line for extended conversations.

With the core testimony wrapped up, it came time to offer the details from my childhood: my upbringing, my familial connection to the 9/11 hijackers; my father, the mighty, Meccan Mufti; memorizing the Qur'an; rituals and devotions and punishments; my training as a jihadist, my lust for American blood—all these were things about which Matt knew regarding my past, but I began to expound in far more detail than ever I had, dragging him deep into the thorny weeds of my existence. Faithfully, patiently, and diligently he wrote, even as the tale waded neck-deep into vomitous swamps of depravity—Christians murdered, crucified, and hung from cranes; women beaten near to death by husbands, violently raped by prison guards exercising rights granted them by Muslim authorities; people thrown from buildings, dismembered and beheaded in the streets; and all the barbaric means by which I had been tortured.

Onward he wrote, tirelessly, enduring the endless revelation of a foreign world, wicked and terribly lost beyond his comprehension.

Many times I could hear him weeping on the other end.

"The American church is so deeply asleep," murmured Matt during one of our dictation sessions. His speech was slow; his mouth was an opened grave. "I just don't understand it. Why aren't people opening up to this story—I asked my small group this very question last night! All this resistance I keep getting over here—I don't understand it! Are we all blind?" Tears as audible as his words began to leak through the phone. "I'm so weak," he confessed breathlessly. "God has called me to this task; yet, I have not the strength to bear this cross! And here am I: the one merely taking dictation! What have I suffered?"

His sobbing filled the line for the next few minutes.

I spent those lying prostrate before the feet of Jesus, my friend held high in my hands.

"I'm shattered," he cried. "My wife sees it—she sees how broken I've become; and what an undeserved blessing is she to hold and encourage me in this time. My elders see it, too—they keep raising concerns. Oh, God! Help me! Give me the strength to bear this burden, without becoming a burden myself!"

He and I spent the last of the hour in ardent prayer.

"I'll be taking a long road tonight," I said. "My plan is to cover a great deal of ground and hopefully put some unexpected distance between me and anyone trailing me. I don't expect I'll come across a cell tower until later tomorrow."

"Call as soon as you find one," he replied. "I'll be waiting. I love you, brother."

Every time we spoke, Matt would urge me to get out of Saudi Arabia; but I was rather reluctant to do so—Muslim kindred were still in the dark. I desperately needed to find a place hidden from the government eye in which I could continue God's work.

"That place is the U.S.A.!" Matt exclaimed.

"Maybe so," I argued, "but I can't get there! I don't have the money!"

"Pray!" he cried. "Right now! We're praying! I'm praying! Father God, if it be Your will that my brother should leave Saudi Arabia, reach down and miraculously rescue him from that hostile land! Leave no doubt in his mind that You are calling him to flee!"

God did not wait long to answer.

I looked up all available flights. No passage to the U.S. was available in any short window; the only flight leaving almost immediately to a safe haven was the next day to New Zealand.

But the cost was steep, more than twice the price for a plane to the States.

Heaving a sigh, I said, "Well, Lord, this doesn't look promising. Please, show me Your way."

I called my bank to inquire about my balance.

And that's how my steering wheel became dented—the number they recited was slightly more than exactly the cost to fly to New Zealand. Rubbing my forehead after the shock had sent it careering toward a bruising impact, they said the balance had just been updated from my most recent contribution. That deposit was almost precisely, to the penny, the cost of my ticket.

As God would have it, and Matt would later relay, it had been one among the doubters, an elder, who had wired the money.

The message was clear.

I hopped into my car and set a course for the Dubai airport in the United Arab Emirates.

Long, dark, and dusty was the road; best of all, it was remote—if the terrorists caught wind that I was fleeing, the hunt would intensify. The problem of crossing over into Dubai still lingered, but God's provision had been so clear that I actively blocked out any doubt and just kept repeating to myself as I drove, "Trust in the Lord. Trust in the Lord, for He is good. He will provide a way."

My headlights could barely penetrate the thick darkness.

Sand blowing through my empty driver's window scraped my face and pricked my eyes.

My tires hummed as they swallowed the ground beneath them.

Deeper into the night I sped. And then, softly but suddenly, and swelling by the moment, I started to hear over the whirr of my tiny engine a great rumbling; but, looking up into the sky, I could see only the glow of the moon and billions of glimmering stars, speckled across a tranquil, clear heaven.

The thunder rolled.

I looked into my rearview mirror.

Nothing.

Just a cloud of dust painted red by my taillights.

My foot pressed a little harder onto the gas.

The growling of a turbulent storm intensified.

I looked back again.

The cloud of dust had been painted white...and it was quickly getting whiter.

Suddenly, a set of headlights burst forth with a furious roar.

Rushing along side of me, bellowing into the night a full-throttle, reverberating battle cry, there appeared a gigantic, black SUV.

Time slowed to a near halt, trapping the world in slow motion; the tumultuous sounds of the road faded into nothing.

Like a minnow frozen beside the path of a ferocious shark, I watched as the black beast glided ever so sluggishly alongside my car. In perfect synchronization, the windows reflecting my horrified gape began to descend, revealing two dark figures set therein—their limbs moved as if submerged beneath several hundred feet of water, and each lifted slowly an automatic rifle; then, from the roof emerged another figure, this one raising something like a sniper.

Sets of red eyes glowed in the darkness; their hungry breaths gnawed at my ears; and the sound of fingers tightening against triggers echoed through my skull.

The first trigger clicked.

My next breath could be heard around the world.

Time abruptly snapped into light speed, as a storm of fiery rain poured into my car and the SUV raced forward, jerking into my path.

I swerved and hit the gas; the salivating shark rounded again, its jaws born wide.

A barrage of bullets blasted through the windows and doors; shards of glass filled the air, mixing with the red-hot lead dancing about the cab. Their rounds exploded all around me, each impacting with the force of a screaming asteroid; I felt as though all my bones were being repeatedly pulverized to dust.

Throwing the car into the next gear, I kicked the pedal to the floor, skidding around the SUV to gain some distance.

Within a second, they were hot on my tail again.

Bullets bounced off the road ahead; sparks blossomed from the asphalt, leaping off the dusty earth, while tiny volcanoes of sand erupted along the highway.

The SUV rumbled to my right and again jerked toward me, their tires squealing. I slammed on the brakes and then cut to the left, swerving behind them, before pounding the pedal so hard my foot nearly broke through the floor.

As if attached to a rocket, my little car screeched ahead— the RPM gauge nearly made a complete circle.

I exploded past them.

But they would not be shaken.

Again, the raging beast rumbled along side of me; the earth trembled and cowered beneath its towering, rubber hooves. Widening its mouth, bursts of flame roared through my windows and tattered the car's fragile frame; its ire was more fierce and bloodthirsty than ever—the heat of its breath skewered my eardrums; the mighty beating of its ponderous wings tossed my car about the road like a leaf in an autumn gale; its jaws snapped faster and hungrier than before; the fumes from its venomous saliva filled my head, throwing the world into a disoriented jumble, turning seconds into eternities, and thoroughly convincing me that every frantic breath I drew would be my last.

For over thirty minutes we raced along the barren wasteland; smoke billowed from my burning tires and the car heaved a death rattle every time I cranked the clutch; but their weapons would not expire, and there was not a moment my bones were not filled with their sinew-splitting screams.

I wrenched the wheel this way and that, my eyes scanning the pitch black nothing before me, with one eye ever glancing at my fuel gauge, hastily falling.

Just then, amid the chaos there erupted through my shoulder something like a vicious stab from a searing knife. I let out a feral yell and threw a hand to my arm; at the same time, a bullet sailed clear through the hole in my back window and exploded in my dashboard.

Tightening my grip on the wheel, I swerved again into another patch of darkness; any pain I'd felt was instantly gone.

I was running out of ideas; the SUV was biting hard on my tail, and their unquenchable fury bustled all around me.

Suddenly, my car bounded into the air, the rear wheels coming completely off the ground. I skidded on the front tires at a perilous rate of speed, as the back end began to drift through the air; and when all four tires again hit the road, I found myself in an uncontrollable spin, whirling round and round so fast that I couldn't lift my arms against the force to grab the wheel, which was itself twirling to the point of popping off.

"THIS IS IT!" I cried, as the car raced away into the night. "I'M GOING TO MEET JESUS!"

SLAM

The whirlwind world that had taken hold of me suddenly vanished; peeling my face from the dashboard, I looked up and saw that my car had crashed into a sand dune.

Unsure whether I was dead or alive, I threw open the door and bolted out at top speed into the Arabian Desert, deep into the Empty Quarter.

I could sense that my soon-to-be killers were hot on my heels; but the vast expanse of sand, I knew, would absorb the sound of their approaching; there would be no telling how close they were until they were right on top of me. All I could do was run and wait for a bullet to rip through my skull.

Gulping gigantic mouthfuls of sand and frozen air, I sprinted until I could no longer breathe, until my lungs burst through my ribs like a balloon squeezed between two sets of fingers, and I collapsed face-down, a lifetime of strength spilled in my wake over the silent sands of the Rub' a Khali.

My will pressed and fiercely berated me to keep running, but my lungs had flattened, my legs had become limp and worthless strips of flesh; my throat was stripped to pieces and coated with a thick layer of sand.

Not a single shred of power remained.

I was helpless to continue.

Burying my head deeper into the ground, I prayed, "Lord, You commanded me to flee, and I did so."

My eyes sealed tightly, bracing for the viper of death to clasp his fangs about me; I did not want to see his face.

"God," I breathed into the sand, "I shall soon behold You! Let me not pass from this world afraid. Take me gently into Your arms, dearest Jesus—how I have longed for that sweet fellowship!"

A cool, peaceful breeze slipped through the grains covering my face and slowly began to inflate my flattened lungs. Life trickled back into my limbs; my strength began to rebuild.

Eternity passed, and still my heart did beat; the serpent's tongue had not its life devoured.

Turning over ever so carefully, I surveyed the empty desert painted a silvery glow beneath the blazing moon.

Silence suffocated the air.

Stillness saturated the land.

Though my tracks were clear in the sand, my hunters were nowhere to be found.

Like vapor, they had vanished into the wind.

The serpent's hiss had been choked; his venom stopped, and his fangs broken—for tonight, he was wayward and blind; and I, the only soul in a vast wasteland of pulverized stone, rested firmly, not alone, upon a mighty rock.

Rising to my knees, I surveyed the endless expanse before me. In the distance I could see a light; its rays crowned the peak of a dune, adorning it with a glorious shimmer. And I turned my eyes to the heavens, there to behold another expanse, unobstructed by the hand of man, and filled—bursting, overflowing!—with more glimmering bodies than could be paired to all the grains of sand stretched out from where I knelt. From vast and far away lands their light did shine, each filling the deep darkness that surrounded them with what that void could not comprehend, nor suffocate: a lamp, forged by the very breath of God, proclaiming His glory in the darkest of places, immune to the miry stains through which it turns; and every body bearing that glory within set firmly in place, there to complete its work and by its death shine all the brighter, calling and compelling all to behold the great transformative wonders of the Almighty and feed the lights that remain, until the final day.

My eyes sealed tightly, and I wept.

"Will You not take me?" I cried, arms stretched wide, like a child reaching for his father to be lifted and held closely to his breast.

My soul beat against the gates of heaven.

I had again tasted the presence of Death, but had not been given over to cool his black tongue; as such, my longing to behold the beautiful face of my Savior, to clasp hold of His glorious body, and in His love forever find rest—this consuming fire, which burned all the more with every brush against the hand of Death, burned as never before, its flames scorching those already ablaze.

Yet, in the midst of my yearning, Christ again extended His mighty hand of mercy and grace, and took me up in His palm, holding me closely against the hole through which the nail had been driven. And there I heard His sweet voice, whispering ever so tenderly to my spirit, enjoining me to endure but a little while longer, for He had yet some purpose to weave into the grand story, in the telling of which He had lovingly chosen me as His instrument.

Peace consumed me, and I remembered the love I had not forgotten for my kindred, for Muslims all over the world living still in the darkness from which I had been rescued. Perhaps this was the reason for my constant striving to outpace Death, even though I could not wait to meet Jesus in His kingdom.

My feet were given new strength, and I rose from the sand.

Climbing to the apex of a nearby dune, I gazed over the emptiness to the sunrise that was the shimmering crown in the distance.

It was my car, lights still burning and bearing into the sand.

I could see for miles in every direction.

Not so much as a tuft of sand from the feet of my pursuers could be found.

They were gone, as if they'd never been.

Having carefully and for a great long while surveyed the desert, I slowly started down the dune to the one in which my car was imbedded.

The *bing* of the opened door chimed away into the night.

Stepping cautiously around the dune, I beheld my tattered car, riddled with bullet holes and face buried in the sand.

As I inspected it, a host of amazing things came to light. Firstly, not one tire had been blown out during the one-sided highway melee; each was perfectly intact, without so much as a needle's puncture. Secondly (and this one gave me quite the chuckle), the car had been turned off. Though I'd abandoned my keys, it seems that even with my brain spinning as if in a washing machine, and Death nipping at my heels, the ol' reflexes were firing still on all cylinders, compelling me first to switch off the car before running for my life. The simple fact that the body of the car had not been machine-gunned off the frame was enough to warrant a jaw-drop; but it was the choking, sputtering, and then igniting reaction following my turning of the key, bringing this beautiful, busted bucket of bolts to life, that really took the cake—and through the Rub' a Khali echoed a full-chested, joyous, "HALLELUJAH!"

Using the floor mats, I scooped away much of the sand burying the tires, then fixed them beneath the rubber for traction to roll the car free.

As the sun rose slowly over the approaching border, my thoroughly chewed up ride hobbled into a parking lot outside a nearby convenience store. Gazing ahead toward the crossing into Dubai, I pondered all that could go wrong. There was me, first of all; my ID card would certainly light up my recent run-ins with the authorities. Then, there was this car—few people, I assumed, would have no questions for a man driving a chunk of Swiss cheese. Border crossing is always a cavity search, and I was wearing my rotted teeth on a necklace.

"When all seems hopeless," I muttered, watching the heavenly fire spread through the clouds. "Lord, please make a way."

I entered the store and began gathering food and water to appease my screaming hunger and rather ticked-off thirst.

As I went, I passed by a stack of fresh pastries.

Strange, I thought—what's this doing here?

Reaching forth into the midst of the stack, my fingers coiled about a roll of duct tape.

"Not much of a donut!" I chuckled to myself, and then turned to put it back where it belonged; but before my first step fell, my mind walked directly into a solid wall of realization, rising suddenly out of nowhere.

"SILVER!" I declared, drawing a curious look from the shopkeeper.

I sprinted to the counter.

"This is silver!" I shouted to the man, pointing eagerly to the tape.

He didn't speak; the lids of his eyes merely disappeared behind his eyebrows.

"I'll take it!" With that, I happily slapped it down before him. "Oh! And these too," I added, running back to gather the food and water I'd chucked down the aisle in my excitement.

The shopkeeper must have been the top cashier among his peers; he had me rung up and out the door in seconds.

Thanking him profusely, I glided through the door and bounded to my car, while the shopkeeper drew the shades and boarded the entrance; he watched me carefully through gaps in his barricade until I'd departed.

My hand reached into the bag and extracted my prize.

Silver! How wonderful!

And now for the payoff—tossing the food and water onto the passenger's seat, I scurried to my door and held up the tape to the body of the car.

Silver and silver—an absolutely perfect color match!

Well...good enough.

Darting around my car, I patched every hole, punched out what glass remained of every shattered window, then filled them with tape.

Now, it was on to the border.

"Jesus," I prayed, tossing the roll into the back seat and walking around to the driver's side, "I feel as though I must have crossed paths again with one of your angels. However it happened, You have made a way—now, I ask again, make a way, for I go now to cross a treacherous line. Be my ever-present help in this time of need!"

I hopped in, bore white knuckles over the steering wheel, and then heard a tapping on the tape window I'd made. Peeling it away, I beheld a border agent holding out his hand.

"Identification," he said, appearing either very tired or disillusioned.

It had been a swift trip; Dubai lay just inches before me. I took a deep breath and handed him my UAE identification card. But as I moved to open the door in anticipation of his asking me to step out so that he might conduct his routine inspection, the man heaved a sigh and yawned deeply.

"All right," he said, rubbing his eyes and handing me my ID. "Move along."

My ID-clutching hand remained unmoved; my eyes stood frozen, fixed wide upon the spot he'd just vacated.

What just happened?

Did he—?

"Let's go!" he shouted.

Snapping my head forward, I saw him impatiently waving his arm for me to pass through the opened gate.

A one-hour border inspection was the sign of a good day—but a mere ten seconds?

"Twice ordered was more than enough!" I declared to my friend upon reaching his house in Dubai. "I tell you, Leonard, I charged through that God-opened gate!"

"If I didn't serve so great a God," he exclaimed, finally dropping his hands from over his gaping mouth, "I'd say it wasn't even possible! No one gets through that crossing with only an ID check!"

Just then, his wife, having just returned home, burst into the room.

"Ahmed!" she cried. "Your car! It's absolutely destroyed!"

"Hi, Hannah!" I cheered, whipping around to see her. "I know! Isn't it amazing?"

"He was just telling me about it!" chimed Leonard. "I've yet to see it myself."

"See *what*? It's a pile of twisted metal! How *ever* did you get here?"

Chuckling, I took another bite of the sandwich Leonard had fixed for me upon my arrival.

"I should really send a testimonial to the manufacturer! I'll bet people would come out in droves to buy that car if they saw how it fared in a literal war zone!"

Hannah suddenly rushed forth, clasped mine and Leonard's hands, and marched us outside.

Pointing eagerly to the underside of the car, she shouted, "Look at that! Look at all that stuff hanging down! Look what you've done to the road. Look how filthy the interior is—that smell! It's like a wild animal has been living in it for months!" She suddenly let out an ear-splitting gasp. "LOOK AT YOUR ARM!"

In the order she'd advised, I looked. Numerous parts I could not name, and which I somehow had not seen while taping the body, were indeed dangling freely from the belly of the car; they were black from their recent intimacy with the road, which, as I perceived, hadn't fared too well either—a long black line, as from a giant crayon, traced the street all the way to where I was parked. And there *had* been something like a wild animal living in that car for months: me. The smell and filth in which I'd dwelt for so long had ceased to affect my senses. Thanks to Hannah, I gulped a great mouthful and pungent olfactory sample of what I had become while on the run.

Then, I looked at my arm.

My shirt was saturated red at the shoulder; the pain suddenly returned, stabbing me as it had during the chase—I could even hear the gunshot.

Ushering me toward the house, Hannah barked indignantly back at her husband, "How did you not see this wound while you were talking?"

Leonard didn't answer. He had been struck dumb at the sight of my vehicle; his upper and lower jaws had become distant strangers. But of all the automotive carnage before him, his astonishment seemed to have honed in on a single spot.

"Wait a minute, Hannah," I said softly, taking her by the elbows to slow her advance toward the house. "Wait a minute." My eyes looked over her shoulder at Leonard. "I'll be right back."

Leonard was leaning in the back passenger window on the driver's side.

I stepped slowly toward him.

His hand rested gently on the driver's seat; his unblinking eyes held it in a death grip.

"Leonard?"

"Look," he whispered; and, ever so steadily, he touched a small, dark spot on the back of the seat.

He stepped back.

I took his place and examined the spot.

My knees very nearly gave out from under me, for there, burned into the back of the seat, was a bullet hole, positioned directly behind where my racing heart had been fixed throughout the chase. And my knees did finally meet the ground when I inspected the other side of the seat, where I found the glint of the golden tip of a marksman's round peeking through the leather.

I crumbled into a heap in the midst of the dusty driveway, sobbing uncontrollably and praising the mighty hand of God, which had held me fast against the viper's fangs—the very hand of God had stood between me and certain death! More mercy than ever I could dream to receive had been lavished upon me—and me: so sinful a man, whose hands had longed and trained to squeeze the very triggers now forged against me! It was no new revelation, that God had spared me from the very jaws that had been my own; but it was nonetheless heavy this time, as even it is today.

Bearing me in their arms, Leonard and Hannah sat me down against the car, while Hannah worked to patch me back together.

"This is no rogue group hunting you," came Leonard's grave voice. "No, this is the government; I'm sure of it. And they'll soon follow you here. I would not be surprised if Dubai cooperates with Saudi—they'll both be coming after you."

At every turn, a shadow seemed to loom, like a towering tidal wave rearing to crash; the mist from its dark crest fell over my face as I sat there, my body heavy with the weight of the impending wall ready to descend upon me.

"You must go. Now."

His words were calm, but direct.

"Hannah," he said, "you must leave, too."

Her face ran white.

"W—what about you?"

"They'll soon learn of our connection to Ahmed—that black streak in the road will surely help. If they come here and find no one, they'll suspect both of us."

"If I'm not here they might suspect he's with me!"

"I'll tell them where he is! But not before that plane leaves the ground! I'll tell them everything: that I fed him, helped him, and where he's gone; just don't tell me where you're going, so I don't lie when I say I don't know!"

"But, Leonard!"

"Hurry!" he snapped. "They're probably on their way now! Go!"

I sprang to my feet.

"Wait, brother! I can't ask you to—"

"You don't have to, and I won't let you! Pray now with me! Father," he said, "You've carried my brother this far—carry him now to the airport; confound his pursuers; and bring him safely to a land blessed with freedom! Now, *GO!*" he shouted, shoving me into the car. "And God be with you!"

In a mechanic's graveyard near the Dubai airport, I bade farewell to my faithful car, then sprinted inside, only to discover a line going out the door with people waiting for boarding passes. Time was running out; my flight was soon departing, and this line had missing that flight written all over it.

"Anyone going to Auckland, New Zealand?" shouted a voice from the front of the line.

"ME!"

The entire airport snapped startled heads toward the sudden, feral scream. Even I was surprised by the sound; it was a rather involuntary exclamation, rather like the call that had beckoned it from me.

A pleasant looking man jogged toward me, took me by the arm with a smile, and walked me to the immigration line, which consisted of only me.

"And here's your boarding pass, sir!" squeaked a tiny, very friendly young woman. "Enjoy your flight!"

Just like that, I was nuzzled into a seat, flying high above the clouds, bound for New Zealand.

"You did it!" I cried aloud to my Savior, as my hands danced through my hair, rubbed my face, pinched my cheeks—I simply didn't know what to do with myself!

Throwing my head back in my chair with a hand clasped over my forehead, I hurled from my body on the wings of a sigh all the recent stress that had like Velcro attached itself to me; the tail end of it chuckled as it gracefully tumbled over my lips.

It's over, I thought.

I'm finally free.

I'm finally safe.

Wrong on all counts.

21
Land of the Free

"I wish I had better news," said Matt, who'd called shortly after I'd touched down in New Zealand; something like a coffin nail had popped his usual bubbly personality. "Leonard and several others have been arrested."

My hand fell against the terminal wall.

"Hannah is beside herself; she could hardly tell me what happened."

Lower and lower I slid toward the floor as he spoke.

"They took him the day you left, then stormed the church and dragged off some others suspected of being close to you. I don't know anything else as of now—I'm sorry."

Several people walking by stooped toward me.

"Are you all right, sir?"

"Shall I call for a doctor?"

But I could make no answer; such news as I'd just received could not be born. And with its weight driving against my shoulders like the descending plate of a hydraulic press, I stumbled through the airport until I found my friends John and Reena, in whose arms I collapsed and wept bitterly.

Several days later, and all that time spent on my knees praying in the spare room of John's and Reena's home for those persecuted on my account, I received another call from Matt.

"PRAISE GOD!" he cried, his Exclamatory English back in full force. "They've been released without charge! And what a story!"

I sprinted into the other room, gathered my hosts, and put the phone on speaker.

"Leonard tells me the Dubai police arrived at his home within five minutes of your leaving—they tore the place apart, he said, looking for you; but he told them nothing! After a fierce interrogation, they dragged him to prison, there to be questioned with the others. Leonard kept an eye on the time; when he knew it would be too late for them to catch you, he confessed to your whereabouts. And they *were* too late! He overheard them shouting at one another on the phone—apparently they couldn't find you in the records of any passenger lists because you'd used your passport, rather than your UAE ID!"

"What does that matter?" asked John.

"Saudi is not as advanced in these things as Westernized nations," I explained. "Using a UAE ID to enter Dubai and a passport to exit it makes me temporarily untraceable, as the identification numbers exist in different databases and are not linked."

"IT'S AMAZING!" shouted Matt. "Leonard said the officer at the jail lost his mind when he got the news! Apparently his men stormed your gate just as the plane had left the ground! They literally got to watch you ascending into the heavens toward freedom!"

"Are they all right?" I begged. "Leonard and the others?"

"A little worse for wear, but they could offer the police nothing more and were released after three days; no charges have been filed! PRAISE GOD!"

By all accounts, it seemed that was that: the final trial had been passed; I'd escaped Saudi Arabia, my friends had endured and been released without charge, and I was again free to roam about the ends of the earth, preaching the Gospel to the lost. And so I did, going here and there, speaking and teaching, but always and first of all demonstrating the love of Christ, however I could—even volunteering to wash dishes at a restaurant owned by a Muslim man. I scrubbed and chatted away about my Savior and the Good News, day after day; one time (because, how could I *not* have done?) I used the cleaning of dishes as an analogy of our sins being wiped away!

Indeed, this story of dishwashing evangelism would make a great little anecdote to wrap up this grand tale.

But the world was not through with me just yet.

"Word has been traveling through our chain of friends," said John one morning, pulling me aside before breakfast. "Don't expect anyone to make a direct call—the religious police have entered Dubai."

"*What?*"

"Dubai has agreed to cooperate with Saudi," he continued, walking about the room shutting the shades. "That black money of theirs! A bounty has been placed on your head. I've just gotten word that an international notice of extradition has been issued; you're to be handed over to Saudi Arabia to face execution by beheading."

"New Zealand won't honor that, though!"

"Don't be so sure," he whispered, returning to me after having darkened the room. "The love of money is a compelling force."

Excusing myself, I sprinted to my room to make a call.

"What if I apply for asylum?"

"Don't do that!" shouted the tall man. "Ahmed, *promise* me you won't do that!"

"Why? I don't understand! They would hand me over for *money*? I thought this was a land of freedom!"

"Listen to me!" he snapped. "I've already lost someone that way!"

My mouth ran dry.

"The situation was very similar—they applied for asylum and were snatched away, right here on New Zealand soil, even as they placed ink to paper in a government building! That was years ago, Ahmed; and I've found no trace of them since. They're dead; and I won't allow you to fall into the same trap."

"But...this place," I whimpered, watching a dark cloud roll over and turn to ash what I'd long known only as a green and growing land.

"This place is full of men," he answered gravely. "And some—government officials, men and women alike; they will turn a blind eye for the love of money. Ahmed, you are no longer safe here."

"If they want to take you," declared Reena, slamming her fist down upon the table, "THEY'LL HAVE TO GO THROUGH *MY* DEAD BODY!"

"*Quiet!*" John hissed suddenly. "*Get down!*"

All of us hit the deck and watched with bated breath as two dark silhouettes passed very near the drawn shades.

John crept toward the window.

Reena's razor-sharp whisper slit the eardrums: *"GET BACK HERE!"*

"I've got to see who it is!"

Sliding his belly across the floor, he slithered up the wall next to the window and carefully peeked behind the curtain.

"Who is it?" Reena whispered. *"John! Who is it?"*

"Don't know," he answered at length. *"Never seen them before. Tall men. Dark suits. Sunglasses. They look like undercover cops. Whoever they are,"* he continued in a low tone when he'd crawled back to us, huddled under the kitchen table, *"they don't look friendly."*

"I'm leaving," I muttered, inching toward the back door.

"DON'T YOU DARE!" shrieked Reena.

She was very much like a mother to me, Reena; and, as mothers do better than anyone, she shot at me a glare that shrunk me down to the size of a pea.

I relented, but only for the day. Leaving a note on my bed, this little pea leapt from his window and darted through the night to find another pod in which to hide. For several days, I bounced between this place and that, to and fro between houses of Christian friends, keeping always a step ahead of the police, who left not one corner un-snooped.

There was no end in sight to this chase.

"Jesus," I prayed, "I can run about this tiny island until they drive me to the sea, never again getting to share Your Good News—except, perhaps, to the fish I pass as I sink into the belly of the Tasman. I will face this danger. Please, walk with me, or bar the way."

My legs weary from the run, I crept slowly into the street, whereupon the corner stood two tall men in dark suits, each with a large set of sunglasses perched upon his nose.

I slid my back along the storefront behind me, eying them as I went.

Their darkened gaze surveyed the branching intersection before us.

"Gentlemen!" I cried, after several failed attempts to speak more than a wheezing cough.

Both men snapped quickly around. Four eyebrows jumped up from behind four dark lenses, and two large feet stomped forward; another two readied to spring.

"Don't come any closer!" I shouted, backing toward the door of a local shop, hoping the public setting might dissuade them.

Those feet stepped no further.

"You're looking for me!"

They nodded.

"What crime have I committed?"

No answer.

"Do you seek to arrest me for a crime?"

Silence.

"Would you question me?"

One head nodded slowly.

"Then, I will hear you! But only on these terms! We meet in a place of my choosing, with witnesses of my choosing."

After a great pause, one set of tight lips parted.

"Where?"

I pointed to the residential area nearby.

"There," and I gave them the address.

Both turned slowly, following the direction of my pointing; then, their faces returned to me.

After a moment of silent staring, they turned again and started toward the houses.

I followed at a distance and extracted my phone.

"*John,*" I whispered. "*I'm coming back.*"

"Really? That's great!"

"*I'm bringing some undercover officers with me.*"

"*WHAT?*"

"*We'll be there soon.*"

"How...*what?* Are they...what did you do?"

"*I'll talk to you in a minute.*"

John's eyes made a full moon look square when he opened the door to see the officers, even more so when he saw me waving at him from across the street.

The situation explained, he agreed to offer his home as the meeting place, invited us in, and led us to the sitting room.

I took a chair directly across from the officers.

"Are you a Christian?" barked one, his sunglasses peeled and his dark eyes boring into mine.

"What kind of question is *that?*" yelled Reena.

"Is Christianity a crime?" I asked, having only narrowly caught myself from falling out of my chair.

"Is New Zealand no longer a land of religious freedom?" asked John, readjusting his jaw after it had plummeted to the table.

Thoroughly washed by the barrage of voices hurled at him, the officer sat back slowly in his seat, rubbed his face, then looked at me through squinted eyes, while his face battled against his cheeks to pull them into a smile.

"Of course it is—and, no, Christianity is not a crime," he said, sounding as if his jaw had been screwed in place. "You needn't worry," he proceeded, sounding like a man reassuring a child that candy lies just inside his van. "We won't tell the Saudis. Now, are you a Christian?"

"He doesn't need to answer that!" barked Reena. "His beliefs are his own and none of your business! Anything else?"

"Just a few more questions," said the other, his eyes even more attentive to me than his partner's—they were so attentive and unblinking, that I could not help but study him in return.

In doing so, I noted that one arm was sliding very slowly backward, and then inching forward again.

"Fine," I replied, leaning back in my chair and folding my arms. "What would you like to know?"

As I leaned, my scope of view broadened.

I could just barely see under the table.

"When did you arrive?"

I turned my head and let out a cough; looking down and away, I used my peripherals to scan the underside of the table; and there I caught a glimpse of a cell phone.

The officer was trying to subtly record the conversation.

"Behold," said Jesus in Matthew 10, "I am sending you out as sheep in the midst of wolves."

"A few days ago," I replied.

"Why did you come?"

"To visit friends."

"How long will you be staying?"

"I haven't decided just yet."

"How many friends would you say you have in the area?"

"More than I deserve."

"What sort of activities have you been engaged in here in New Zealand?"

"Visiting."

"Anything else?"

"Landscape admiration...and jogging."

"What is it you want?" snapped Reena when these questions had run on for some time. "He's a godly man! He's not a threat to anyone! You can take my word to the bank! I'll testify to this before any court in the land! He's done nothing wrong and you've presented no crime he is suspected of committing! Explain yourselves this *instant*! Why are you interrogating him?"

One officer looked at the other.

Sighing, he took up his sunglasses and rose to his feet.

"We'll be in touch," he said, and then turned toward the door.

His partner rose, as well. Taking a step, he stopped suddenly; then, before I could react, he whipped around and snapped a photo of me.

"*HEY!*" screamed John, as the officers hurried out of the house. "This is my home! That's illegal!"

"Let it go, John," I said softly, placing a hand on his chest. "We'll have to let it go."

Word would be delivered to me that the Saudi government was prepared to strike me a deal. In full knowledge of my poverty, they put in writing that they were willing to "generously" provide me a scholarship to a university of my choosing, along with a monthly check—all in exchange for my silence about the whole "unfortunate" matter and my pledge to cut all ties with and renounce Christianity.

I took out a pen and etched my reply.

"Nothing, not even your worthless money, can separate me from the love of Jesus Christ, the one true God."

Signed.

Sealed.

Delivered.

"Now, there's an idea!" declared the tall man, as I stamped the envelope containing my reply. "There's a different kind of visa for which you can apply—a student visa. You won't have to go through the same process as the other one; it's quicker and could leave you less exposed. We've got to try to obtain whatever legal padding we can get, really. Only problem with this one is you'd have to be accepted into an English Language Institute."

He and I went to one and inquired, but there was no way I could cover the fees.

"Is there anything you can do?" I begged the receptionist.

"*I* can't," she replied. "But I can connect you to the director. You can appeal to him, if you like. He's a very nice man; I'm sure he'd hear you out, at least."

The director corroborated her analysis of his character and the supposition of his response to my inquiry.

"Welcome!" he chuckled, opening his door with a great big smile, while the color of his nature bubbled over the rims of his shimmering personality, completely enveloping everything before him. "Please," he said, motioning to a set of chairs in the center of the room, "take a seat!"

His office was as warm as his company; the very air we breathed was a delightful concoction of Eastern spices. A bronze glow painted the atmosphere, and all around the room were Buddhist decorations and symbols, delicately garnished by the sound of trickling water mixed with soft, string music.

"So!" he giggled, plopping himself into his chair and gobbling up the tall man and me with his eager and friendly gaze. "What can I do for you?"

"My friend here doesn't have the money to cover the cost of admission," said the tall man. "Is there anything you can do for him?"

The director's wide and glimmering eyes were quickly veiled behind two slits; his bushy brows furrowed, and his smile contracted into a puzzled pursing.

"Are you not a Saudi?" he asked me.

"I am, sir."

"How is it then," he continued, scratching his chin, "that you haven't the money to pay? All of my Saudi students come from inordinate wealth. Of the problems they call their own and bring to me, never have I fielded one related to—or even involving!—finances." Leaning forward, he eyed me from a cocked head. "Why are you so poor as to have nothing to put toward tuition?"

"Of all my possessions," I replied, gazing straight back, "money is the least of what the Saudi government has taken from me."

He sat back slowly in his chair.

Several silent breaths passed, as the water's chortle echoed about us and the strings continued to pluck out their tune.

"Why?"

His speech was carried on a soft exhale, released very slowly.

"I am a hunted man, sir."

His eyes widened again and his arms folded.

"Tell me everything."

And when I had finished, the raging river flowing from his eyes had replaced the sound of the chortling water, and the plucking strings fell defeated beneath the weight of his wails.

"My dear boy," he cried, laying a hand on my arm, "whatever it is, however I am able—I promise, I will help you."

The tall man and I stayed up through the night discussing the events of the day, marveling at the way God had moved in our meeting with the director.

"And in this we see again the power of Christ!" he declared. "That He'd bring a Buddhist into our path to hear and be moved by the story of Jesus working through you!"

"It really is amazing! Every fee waived! Praise God!"

Just then, the tall man's phone rang.

"Hi, Jeff! What can I do for you?"

The tall man's face suddenly fell, dragging with it all the light and color in the room.

"Okay," he said breathlessly. "Tha—thank you, Jeff."

"What is it?"

"We have to go—now."

"Why? What's happened?"

"That was an old friend of mine," he said, hastily throwing on his jacket and scrounging for his keys. "He's pals with a man in government: Greg, a Christian. I'd told Jeff about you and what you've been going through since your return. He must have relayed that to Greg—c'mon!" he barked, ushering me out the door. "Though he didn't have any specific details," he continued, once we'd jumped into the car, "he said Greg tipped him off that the government has put you in the crosshairs."

"What about the visa?"

"Doesn't sound like we have any more options. Greg had Jeff call and tell me to bring you to him. That's where we're going."

It would be a long, tense drive through several hours of darkness.

All the while I watched carefully as New Zealand sped past my window; I wanted to make as many memories of a land I feared I would never see again.

This place had been for me open arms of welcome; how quickly it had become a deadly snare.

"You must leave New Zealand at once."

The tall man and I could but gape at Greg; his tone was low and grave, and he'd spent no time on pleasantries.

"Have you a travel visa to another country?"

"I have my passport," I replied.

Greg's lips bunched.

"I guess that will have to do. But it won't be enough."

"What's happened?" asked the tall man.

"The government has agreed to cooperate with Saudi Arabia; they will soon apprehend Ahmed and forcibly bring him to the Saudi embassy on the orders that he must fill out some official paperwork to get his visa."

"Okay," I said, a bit puzzled. "But, that's a good thing, right? I need that visa."

"Listen to me." Greg's words were as sharp as spears and as heavy as anvils. "Agents of the Saudi government have already been dispatched. You will not leave the embassy in the same way you came into it—instead paperwork to file, there will be blood to mop."

A thick, balloon-like silence grew in our midst, inflating and pressing hard against each of us.

"What must I do?"

Greg took me by the arms.

"Pray," he said, looking me dead in the eye, "and get your-self a ticket to the United States."

"It's not working!" I called to the tall man after two hours of trying to select a seat online. "Look! Every time I click on a seat to reserve it, I get this error message! Every seat is de-clined!"

"Try that phone number," he said, tapping on the screen.

Having done so, I called to him again.

"They said I have to come in and consult with someone at the airport."

The tall man looked at his watch.

"Let's go, then," he said. "We've got only a few hours until takeoff."

Gathering the nothing with which I'd arrived, I scamp-ered to his car and together we raced to the airport.

"I'm very sorry for the wait, sir," said a pleasant woman behind the service counter. "We're unusually busy this morn-ing. How can I help you?"

"I logged onto your site and tried to reserve a seat on this flight—but every time I clicked one, I was denied."

"*Hmm.*" Her lips pursed and shifted to the right. "Let me see, here. Do you have your passport? Wonderful, thank you."

After a protracted period of *tap-tappidy-tap-tapping* on the keyboard, she drew back as though someone had pulled on her torso with a rope, smiled brightly, and said, "Oh! I *am* sorry! It looks like we've already allocated for you a seat!"

You could have driven a freight train through the hole in my face.

"Let me get my supervisor to confirm."

A lanky, balding man lurked to her side, peered at the screen, and then lifted a set of droopy eyes to me; they remained fixed on my face for what seemed like half the morning. Then, without saying a word, he punched a key on the keyboard, slunk to the printer, and handed me a ticket, before turning away without a sound.

I watched him until he vanished around a corner, and then dropped my eyes to the ticket.

There was my flight number and destination, along with the letters SSSS.

"Ma'am," I said, looking up again, "what is SSSS?"

"Secondary Security Screening Selection," she replied through broad, pearly teeth. "Enjoy your flight!"

"What is that?" I whispered to the tall man, as we walked toward the gate.

"If I had to guess, and I will," he said, "you'll be getting to know the security team a bit more intimately."

My mind began to race.

"What's happening?" I begged, stopping dead in my tracks. "What's God doing? Why did He even bring me here if I'm only to remain on the run and have to escape again! Why this giant detour from Saudi to America?"

"It wasn't a detour! Look at me—Ahmed," he replied, clasping my arms, "it *wasn't* a detour. God had a purpose for your being here. You may find it small in your eyes, but He used you to touch the lives of many, who will in turn touch the lives of countless others! Just think, there are people on this island that no man could reach, other than one formed by God as He formed you. Think of the Muslim restaurant owner! Would a man like him have opened up to me as he did to you? And the Buddhist director! Who among our Christian group could have gotten an audience with that man and so preached the Gospel to him, as you were able to do? God has gifted you this unique path. You are His workmanship! And an answer to my prayers!"

I eyed him curiously.

"What prayers?"

Tears welling in his eyes, the tall man tightened his grip on my arms.

"I was a missionary in Saudi Arabia for many years."

"How did I never know that?"

"God laid before me a great deal of important work to do here in New Zealand," he continued; "but a large portion of my heart remains buried in those sands, bleeding for the people there. For weeks, I fasted and prayed that God would bring me a Muslim from that land, even just one person I could lead to Christ—He brought me you."

My mind immediately raced back to the pallid, gaunt, and gangly man I'd met in the house of white pillars.

"He brought me you!" he cried again. "And He gave me the blessing of having you in my home—I stayed outside your room all night," he said, tears falling over his cheeks; "on my knees outside your door, I begged God to take away your fear, to lift the veil from your eyes, and to break through the darkness that had so long held you in bondage. I'm telling you this because I *know* your journey doesn't end here. Whatever lies beyond that gate," he said, pointing toward the security check at the immigration department, "God will walk through it with you. He has even greater things yet for you to do."

My arms clasped about him; my heart commissioned them to pull him directly through my chest that he might stay inside of me always—and those arms were determined not to let go until they had fulfilled their task.

"Father," he whispered as I held him, "I leave my dear friend in Your mighty hands! Watch over him, use him, and bring him back to me someday, whether on this earth or in Your kingdom!"

Walking toward the immigration department, I whipped out my phone and frantically began to delete all text messages, phone numbers, photos, *everything*—wiping it clean, so that not even a fragment remained to compromise my friends.

"Whereabouts are you headed today, sir?" came a folksy and charming voice.

I looked up to see a tall, blonde, and burly woman smiling down at me from beneath an aura like a midday sun.

"The United States of America!" I replied, handing her my passport and trying to match her gigantic smile.

"Well, now!" she beamed, scanning my passport. "Doesn't that just sound—"

Her speech ground to a halt.

Her smile disappeared.

That glowing aura over her towering head was extinguished, and her pupils dilated.

Swallowing hard, she robotically turned her head to the side, her eyes unblinking and fixed upon the same horizon as they moved. Her hand slowly lifted and took up a phone; she whispered into the receiver. Then, spinning her torso slowly on her waist, as if being turned by a remote control, she faced me and slowly inched an unsettling, wide-eyed smile onto her face.

But before I could inquire after what certainly appeared to be a grave and novel medical condition someone in my former profession might wish to examine, three sets of hands swarmed and snatched me from all sides; and I hovered, feet dangling freely over the marble floor, all the way to a tiny room, where I was hurled into a tiny chair for a tiny talking-to.

The room shook and a portly officer entered the room, slamming the door behind him.

"What's your business here?" he snarled.

"May I speak with a lawyer?"

"SHUT UP!"

"Answer the question!" barked another officer.

"I'd like to speak to a lawyer."

"I'll bet you would!"

"This is international soil, bud! Here's a list of your rights!"

A hand slapped the table and turned over an empty palm.

A dark smile grew upon the lead officer's face.

And that's when the hail of missiles began to fall—questions, spat from all sides, rained down upon me, hour after hour, breaking against my bones like wrecking balls and beating my eardrums as if they were a part of a jazz musician's percussion set.

"What makes you so special?" hissed one of the officers.

"I believe in Jesus."

"Since when does a *Muslim* believe in Jesus?" expelled another, vomiting his derision all over me.

"All Muslims believe in Jesus," I replied calmly. "But I believe He is God."

Thinking I was but moments away from being handed over to the Saudis, I took the opportunity to share my testimony, telling them everything about my faith in Christ and what my journey had been up unto this point.

To my surprise, they actually listened.

The hail-fire ceased.

Their mouths were stopped; I hoped their ears were opened.

Having recounted a quick but meaty version of my story in just a few minutes, I looked around at the stone-faced officers.

Then, I shot a quick glance to the clock.

My flight to freedom would be departing in minutes.

The lead officer turned his head slowly toward the clock, then slowly back to me.

"You've been profiled as an extremist Christian," he growled. "You are no longer welcome on New Zealand soil. But," he added, following a deep sigh, "you have not broken any of our laws; we'll honor that."

At the wave of his hand, two officers took me up by the arms and dragged me to the boarding gate, down the bridge, and along the aisle to my seat, where I was deposited between two Samoan marshals. Bookending me in place, their massive, muscular shoulders compressed my lungs with enough force to rupture a pair of weather balloons; and, for twelve hours, these gargoyle-like statues did not move, not even to use the washroom—which, in turn, meant I didn't get to use it either. There was an empty seat beside one, which would have allowed some breathing room for their muscles and my lungs. But, alas, they elected the Ahmed-sandwich seating arrangement; and though I never saw those men again, their crushing presences left an indelible (and, probably physical) mark on my heart.

When at last we touched down on American soil, the Samoan marshals peeled me away from their rippling biceps and tossed me into the airport.

Having finally, fully filled my lungs and emptied my bladder, I skidded toward the U.S. immigration line, while the feeling slowly came back into my legs.

"How are you today?" asked a bright and cheery face with a voice like an explosion of birthday confetti.

Having a human Picasso standing before her seemed not to faze her in the slightest; I guess stranger things than Samoan-compressed Christians come in and out of airports.

Bracing for another tackling and trip to the tiny room for an interrogation, I handed her my passport; and with an honest tone of uncertainty on my tongue, I replied, "Fine."

"Fine is good in my book!" she exclaimed. "Now, if you'll please place your fingers here," she added, motioning to a scanner; "we need your fingerprints."

As one reaching into the mouth of a crocodile, I placed my hands on the screen.

A flash of red burst across my fingers.

I gasped and jumped.

Then, with a *FLIP, BOOM, BAM*, my passport was flung open, a stamp was inked, and my passport stamped.

Bearing her teeth between a set of widely parted, rosy lips, the officer handed it back to me and cheered, "Welcome to America!"

I froze, passport in hand.

"*Seriously*?" screamed by brain, as my eyes darted from left to right, hoping to catch a glimpse of the imminent surprise attack. "You're just going to let an *extremist* Christian like me waltz in here without at least knocking him over the head a few times?"

A burst of warmth jumped through my arm.

My eyes rolled about in my head, then snapped on the image of the officer, touching my hand and looking up at me with a soft smile and a twinkling eye.

"Sir," she whispered, "you're free to go."

Patting me on the shoulder, she smiled again and motioned with her head for me to move along.

"THANK YOU SO MUCH!" I squealed, and then scampered down the hallway, my knees bounding off the ground, meeting my eye level with each step. "I'VE MADE IT! I'M HERE! PRAISE GOD! THE LAND OF THE FREE!"

22
Home of the Saved

"THAT'S wonderful news! So glad to hear you made it!"

"By God's grace alone! Jesus carried me safely from the jaws of the enemy!"

"Please, Ahmed, let's not do *that* again."

"Jesus is my life, Jamal—*that* is the truth. He is the only way."

"So you've said. Look, I'm not interested in your new-found version of Jesus, all right? I'm just happy to hear you've bested those guys. Things must change, and you can be a tool in this fight. Saudi must return to the way it was, reject these hardline Wahhabi traditions."

"I agree Saudi is a dark place."

"*Dark?* Ha! With the oppression of women, people like you dragged away for speaking their minds, not being able to believe whatever they want! Don't get me wrong, I think you've lost your way in abandoning Islam; but with all the government has done to you, I can't say I blame your stead-fastness in clinging to Christianity."

"I clung to Jesus before my family disowned me, before the government tortured me, before losing all my worthless material possessions and going on the run as a hunted animal.

And I cling to Him now all the more, not out of compulsion from the oppressive acts of the government, but rather because Christ has opened my eyes to see what powers are truly at work in this world. Jesus commands me to bring light into the darkness; He compels me with His love, which He has placed in my heart; and no matter what, I'm going to proclaim it. Jamal," I said very directly, "Jesus loves you too, and I will pray for you always."

"I appreciate your kindness," he replied. "But Isa, may he be blessed, is not who you claim him to be; so, I will pray that Allah will liberate you from this deception before Isa returns to free you by force. Furthermore, I will pray that you'll join me in this fight. Yours is a story that could change the political and cultural landscapes of our homeland."

"Let the story Christ has written for me first change hearts and minds, and point our kindred to the way, truth, and life that is Jesus. I will fight for a Saudi free of the darkness that binds it, but I serve the imperishable kingdom. Nations will crumble; evil men will arise; where one man of darkness falls, two more shall take his place. I look to the true King, already enthroned above the earth; and to all nations I shall be a voice calling in the desert, 'Make straight the way of the Lord!'"

"And may the mercy of Allah be upon you! Now, I must be getting back. Tell me, where do you go from here?"

"I think I'll hang in California for a while and continue my evangelistic work; some old friends have graciously given me lodging."

"What kind of visa did you get?"

"Six months."

"Will you apply for asylum?"

"I think so."

"I would. Get a lawyer and as much support as you can. You have friends all over the world, right? Do you think they would be willing to sign affidavits testifying to your Christian faith and the certainty of death that awaits you in Saudi?"

"Many are eyewitnesses to those facts!"

"Don't waste any time. I'm glad to hear you're safe—now, *stay* that way. I'll be in touch."

"God be with you, Jamal."

"Who was that?" asked my friend when I hung up the phone.

"A journalist at The Washington Post: Jamal Khashoggi. He's originally from Medina, Saudi Arabia; but he has no love for the government, whatsoever. He has been doing a great deal to affect change, but I fear for him."

"Do the Saudis seek to kill him, as they do you?"

"The government ever seeks to silence all dissidents with a bullet. But I do not fear those who can kill the body—Jamal will one day have to stand before God, and if he is not covered by the blood of Christ...so long as he has breath, there's still time."

For the next several months, I went about California preaching the Gospel—I spoke in churches, evangelized on the streets, and maintained a robust online outreach. But, with only a six-month visa, time was not on my side; so, I quickly hired a Christian lawyer.

"We've got twenty signed and sworn affidavits," he said, stacking my case files, "and there's another on the way. Plus, I was able to use the Freedom of Information Act to secure the

Saudi government's international request for your extradition. I think we've got a pretty solid case for asylum, here," he sighed, throwing his hands on his hips and admiring the over 400-page mound of evidence we'd compiled. "Eyewitness testimony, sworn statements, videos, photos, audio, on top of the precedent set by the Saudis in regard to their dismembering treatment of people like you! Now," he said, clapping his hands together and rubbing them furiously, "this will take a little while; and this is where it could get hairy for you."

"What do you mean?"

"Well, the government is not exactly quick about these things—don't get me wrong, I'm going to do all I can to ensure this is expedited; it's a good thing you didn't wait until your visa had expired. Some cases I've seen can take three—even five—years to be heard by the USCIS."

"*Five years?*"

I could feel the Saudi sword rubbing against my neck.

"Let's pray you don't have to wait that long!"

"Good idea—let's pray now!"

We did, and my application was submitted on Good Friday, 2018.

And then we waited.

About three weeks later I got a phone call.

"Ahmed, it's me," said my lawyer. "I have some very unusual news for you."

His was so monotone a voice, I could not draw from either the well of joy or dread.

"What is it?"

"Homeland Security has scheduled an interview for you in the first week of May."

"That's incredible!"

"I've never seen anything like this."

His vocal cords were tightening like the strings of an overly tuned piano.

"You sound tense—what's the matter? Isn't this a good thing?"

"Could be," he said softly. "Could be *very* good...or, it could be very bad."

"Have faith, my friend! God works *all* things for our good!"

"I agree," he said, speaking very slowly. "Just be wise. Be on your guard. I'm not sure what we're up against, here."

The day quickly came.

My lawyer and I arrived bright and early, our arms filled with every scrap of evidence we could gather, proving in overwhelming fashion that to be sent back to Saudi was to be sent to die.

"Ahmed Joktan!" called the immigration officer.

"*HEY!*" my lawyer screamed. Scurrying up to the officer, he hissed in sharp tones, "That's a gross, negligent, and *dangerous* violation of privacy! This is a public space, and you just announced his full name right out in the open! Right here in the lobby!"

The officer's stone face stared back into the beet growing atop my lawyer's neck.

"What good does being angry do us now?" I said, walking up to them. "Can't take back what's been done, can we?"

Having been escorted to the interview room, another officer stepped in, mumbled a salutation, and plopped himself down in a chair opposite me.

"I'd like to begin with this video evidence of my client's Christian faith, which—"

"Immaterial," grumbled the officer, picking at a spot on the table.

"*Excuse* me? This evidence demonstrates that my client is a professing Christian—praying in Mecca to Jesus Christ, evangelizing in His name!"

"So?"

The officer still had not even looked at my lawyer.

A firestorm of sentences seemed to form on my lawyer's lips, but none could manifest into sound for quite some time.

"We can plainly demonstrate," he said at length, "that a professing Christian, converted from Islam, as he is known and documented by the Saudi government to be and have done, is condemned to die under Saudi's apostasy laws. I *insist* you permit me to present this evidence."

"And *I* insist you move on to something else," snapped the officer. "I say it's immaterial—you're wasting my time."

Snatching one of the files set before me, the officer began to thumb through our evidence.

"Let's see: disowned by your family, living on the streets—oh, here's a good one: *tortured*!" he spat with a scoff. "Something here about missing teeth, some scars—what's this?" he giggled, holding up a photo of my bullet-riddled car. "You brownies don't know how to drive, or what?"

My lawyer was boiling.

"Have you no respect for the task at hand, officer? Is this some sort of game to you?"

Slapping the file closed, the officer sneered at my lawyer.

"We'll see." Turning to me, he heaved a *humph* and groaned, "What's your story?"

"Did you review none of the evidence we provided beforehand?" my lawyer interjected. "Have you studied *any* of the evidence we submitted?"

"I wasn't talking to *you!*" the officer barked, then motioned to me with a flailing hand to start talking.

Though rather off balance, I started at the beginning, offering a concise account from childhood to conversion to the present.

"And my father brought me several times into town to see these executions. I've witnessed countless Christians have their heads cut off or be crucified and hung from cranes, high above the city."

"I don't believe it."

"What?"

"That's a load of garbage," chuckled the officer, shaking his head and folding his arms. "But please," he added, jerking his head forward in a taunting manner, "continue."

Taking a deep breath, I proceeded.

"They would beat me, day and night, and then rub salt in my wounds."

"Yeah, sure," said a pair of wide, rolling eyes.

"In the envelope were three gleaming bullets and a letter telling me that they were going to kill me—*this* letter, here."

"Your handwriting, eh? Nice work. What is this, crayon?"

"They chased me for thirty minutes along the Rub' al Khali, pelting my car with a barrage from rifles and automatic weapons."

"Oh, get real! What is this, some corny action movie plotline? You're just making this up so you can stay in the country!"

"How *dare* you!" cried my lawyer.

"You're not *really* a Christian!" screamed the officer, throwing a finger in my face. "Admit it! You're not a Christian, are you?"

His words were like the lash of my imprisonment; his vehement hostility was like the ignorant silence of the world as the cries from those enduring unspeakable evils in the dark cells and concealed corners of my homeland spills over their palms from the black money placed therein.

"I am," I replied, thoroughly crushed but calm. "By Christ my Savior, I am."

"I've had enough!" the officer snarled, rising quickly to his feet.

"*Sir!*" called my lawyer, leaping from his chair and rushing toward the door.

Spinning quickly, the officer snatched my lawyer's hand and pulled him near; he began to whisper.

The door then slammed behind him.

Turning slowly, my lawyer glided trancedly back to his seat.

He settled in it like an autumn leaf falling from a tree; then, after staring into the void for a few minutes, he slowly and carefully began to pack up all the materials we'd brought for our two-hour session of cruel mockery and derision.

"What did he say?" I asked.

He straightened his neck, fixed his tie, and cleared his throat.

"In his own *choice* vocabulary, and in so many words," he answered, his lips pursing and eyes reddening, "he expressed to me that you are the worst liar he's ever encountered, and that I have been duped by you."

There was no point in discussing the issue.

"We're to come back in two weeks," he continued. "We'll learn the status of your application then. C'mon; let's go."

Homeland Security's reply was both swift and sluggish; it came suddenly but took forever to arrive. And I wasn't at all surprised to see their verdict.

Application for Asylum – DR. AHMED JOKTAN

Applicants for asylum must credibly establish that they have suffered past persecution or have a well-founded fear of future persecution on account of race, religion, nationality, membership in a particular social group, or political opinion and that they merit a grant of asylum in the exercise of discretion.

For the reason(s) indicated below, USCIS has not granted your application of asylum:

PAST PERSECUTION

Applicant has not established that any harm experienced in the past, considering incidents both individually and cumulatively, amounts to persecution.

FUTURE PERSECUTION

Applicant has not established that there is reasonable possibility of suffering persecution in the future.

VERDICT: ASYLUM DENIED

I did not recover quickly.

"I'm about to explode!" cried Matt on the other end of the line. "Whom do we serve? God or government? And here I am fielding pressure from Christians, telling me this denial *proves* you've been lying all this time! Someone told me that I should trust the knowledge of the government, that *they* know more than we do and therefore rejected you because of some hidden darkness you've harbored to trick people like me into helping you!"

"I don't care if not one soul on this earth believes what I say!" I wept, barely able to speak amid the breaking and grinding of my heart. "If all should cast me out, so be it! I have a mightier friend, from whose side I will never be cast away! Oh, dear Lord!" I prayed, my words bellowing each upon its own gasping breath. "Vindicate me! Jesus, vindicate me; for I have told nothing but the truth!"

Matt and I burned the midnight oil, praying as never before that God would work His mighty purpose through this trial, that He would give us peace, pave for me the way I should go, and in the end use it all to cast from the eyes of many the veil of darkness.

God was not slow to answer.

A few days later, I received a referral to a lawyer in Washington D.C., a specialist in immigrations cases such as mine.

"This is a clear demonstration of bias!" she declared upon reviewing my evidence, the manner of my interview, and the outcome thereof. "Anyone can plainly see the crushing persecution of Christians in Saudi Arabia—the penalty of a Muslim converting to Christianity is carved in stone!"

"Indeed, my first lawyer and I felt the same way. But, even with this clarity, I was denied—as you say, it looks like bias. So, what can I do? If they wish not to believe me, how can I be believed?"

"This is still the land of the free," she said, "and still the brave make this their home. Reach out all over the nation to every single friend you have—ask them to be brave, to stand with you, and contact their elected representatives. We must use the power of the people to put pressure on the government, overwhelm them, compel them to hear us, and leave them not even a ledge on which to maintain a hold of this unjust rejection."

"Does the government still consider the voice of the people?"

Wiping a hand over her face, she sucked her lips into her mouth and sighed.

"We must put our trust in something higher than men of worldly power."

"She wants all my friends to write to their congressmen and women so we can drum up support. I've been calling people all day—will you write to yours?"

"I *will*." Matt's voice sounded the way a wince looks. "It's just, his politics don't quite align with support for Christianity and its values. Still," he continued after a long pause, "you might actually be in the perfect position!"

"How do you mean?"

"Bi-partisan support!"

"Is such a thing even possible?"

"God, not government, makes mountains to move; His tools are often the most unlikely of instruments! I can see this case appealing to an extreme on either side! No matter which part about you they might oppose, you have something each party blindly supports for political positioning: Christianity and immigrant!"

"I don't get it."

"I won't attribute motive to anyone; the parties have established their voting values. One has shown previously that they would likely blow their trumpets for having saved a Christian from the evils in the Middle East; the other would probably sound the gong for uplifting the downtrodden immigrant! God can turn the evils of our time and the folly of man to work for His good! Not the least of which is this: those same people who have been gnawing my ears about how the government knows more about your being a liar than what my 'blind' eyes have been able to see—they don't trust our senator for a second. If he sides with you, I think they'll finally see the power of God at work in your life! I'll get my pen!"

And so he did, along with friends and friends of friends from all over the nation—they bombarded congress with letters beseeching their representatives to act; and it wasn't long before I got my first letter.

Dr. Joktan,

Numerous constituents in my state have written to me on your behalf. The message has been received, loud and clear. You have my support and my pledge to do all I can to help you in your time of need.

It seems that some things really do take an act of congress, for I was soon flooded with responses from senators and congressmen all over the nation, all pledging their bi-partisan support to work as one to see my case through to the end. And, just like that, a letter from the U.S. Citizenship and Immigration Services office appeared in my mailbox.

Mr. Joktan's file was requested back from the Office of the Chief Counsel and has been reviewed. Mr. Joktan has been scheduled for an additional asylum interview at the Asylum Office on the following date.

"I can't believe it came so soon!" cried my lawyer; I could hear over the phone the echoing *SMACK* of her hand slapping her forehead. "Congressional inquiries usually take *months* to arrive!"

"But we serve a great and mighty God!"

"I'm on my way!" she cheered, then hopped on a plane from Washington D.C.

Immediately thereafter I dialed Matt.

"Really! You want me to come with you?"

"Well, if you'll be too busy—"

Before I could finish the sentence, Matt was at my side, slapping me excitedly on the back and begging me like a child inquiring about the arrival of Christmas day when we would be going in for my interview. So feverish was he, so eager and bubbling over with electric exhilaration that, to this day, I'm not so sure he hadn't sprinted the whole distance on foot.

With my lawyer and several friends assembled, we piled into a car and sped along the highway to our appointment.

"I've called ahead and made a few demands," said my lawyer, amid her briefing the group on what to expect when we arrived. "There will be a security check at the door—have your ID handy, so that we don't waste any time; punctuality and efficiency will provide our team with good optics and, at the very least, give staff no cause for subconscious disapproval. I've been assured that the waiting room has been reconfigured to my specifications; our checking in will be done away from public eyes and ears. Finally, and best of all," she said, smiling at me, "I've secured a new interviewing officer. He is intimate with the case and our evidence, which will keep the interview running smoothly and allow us to hone in on every precise detail."

Shortly after checking in, I was called for my interview.

"Before you go," said Matt, catching me by my sleeve, "may I pray for us?"

"Please do!"

Huddling together and sealing tight our eyes, we all bowed our heads at the feet of Jesus and let our hearts bleed before His holy presence.

"We are helpless to move this great mountain, Lord," he prayed; "but You, our Mighty Warrior, You go before us this day—cast down the towering beast that stands in our way. Move Your thundering hand; let it be a ponderous sound that shakes the very foundations of the earth, dislodging the darkness from the eyes of the doubters and unbelievers. We are Your servants; this is *Your* story, and we are but poor players, unworthy of the stage upon which we've been placed, who can speak naught but folly from our own lips, who can naught but stumble in our own power. Go before us this day, oh Christ! Give us the words to speak; fortify us that we might stand! And shine! Oh, Jesus! Shine this day! Make us lamps set upon the highest hill, atop the soaring peaks; set us high in the heavens that all might see Your glory and turn to You! We ask in Your name this day and believe—Jesus, our God, we believe!—that You will walk us through the furnace, as You did your servants of old! Our days have already been written in Your book! Show us this day—show the whole world—what it is Your hand has already penned! Whatever awaits us at the turn of the page, we will praise You! In safety and in danger, we will praise You! Even on the threshold of death, we will praise You! For the battle has already been won! No power on earth can claim the victory! It is Yours alone! We go now, Jesus, into the unknown! Walk beside us, now and always! We commit ourselves and our dear friend, Ahmed, into Your hand! Praise be to God!"

And, all together, we cast forth a roaring, "AMEN!"

When my eyes regained focus of the room, I beheld an employee standing nearby.

Her eyes were lined red.

"May I add my 'Amen' to your prayer?" she asked, stepping forward an infant's stride, the tips of her fingers dancing about one another. "It was beautiful."

"Of course!" I cried.

"PRAISE THE LORD!" said Matt, expounding upon his usual earth-shaking enthusiasm.

"Praise the Lord!" she declared in return, a tear running the length of her cheek. "And may God be with you!"

And He was.

After two hours of testifying and presenting evidence to a very careful and caring officer, my attorney made her final statement and then informed me as we left that a miracle from God would be the receipt of a response within a year.

Mine came the next day.

From the treacherous sands of Saudi, God carried me to the land of the free, here, now to be shielded by the eagle's mighty wings and on them soar through the heavens of freedom, upheld by the breath and love of Christ.

What should have taken years took less than twenty-four hours. This land has become my land; this home has become my home.

It was and is nothing short of a miracle.

But God was not done.

He had yet another miracle up His sleeve.

23

A Forever Family

"**WELL,**" he sighed, pushing away from the desk, "it's finished. What do you think?"

Scooting closer to the computer, I took up the mouse and began to scroll through page after page, an ocean of words, laced with photos from my life and journey, and packed with every detail still vivid in my memory, along with a thorough history of Islam and its haled prophet Muhammad, presented for those who bear an ear to hear the call of Jesus lifting from the page, banishing the darkness of ignorance.

"'*From Mecca to Christ*,'" I read, arriving back on the title page. "Thank you, Matt. It's just wonderful."

"It's just plain awful," said the tall man over the phone.

No sooner had Matt and I wrapped production on the book—comprised of everything from start to asylum—did I eagerly send it to the tall man for his honest feedback.

And, boy, did he give it.

"You're not going to publish this, are you?"

"W—well, I...that was the plan." My head was still recovering from the blunt-force trauma of his honesty. "What's the matter with it?"

"Oh, Ahmed!" he cried, his words like those of a parent to a child oblivious to the dangers of walking into a busy street. "It's unreadable! This amazing story is just buried beneath a pile of choppy grammar, messy structure—there's no emotion in it at all! Just a lot of facts! This history of Islam is good stuff, but you've put it right at the beginning. Even if a reader gets through this history lesson, their reward will be only a stale narrative, on which they're sure to give up right away. No, you can't publish this."

"But I must! This is God's story! I want everyone to know the realities of Islam and life in Saudi Arabia, for Christians and Muslims alike!"

"Then, you've got to rewrite it."

"*What*? It was difficult enough putting together a *whole* book! I'm no writer! And neither is Matt! Surely, we couldn't do it *again*, much less better! What am I supposed to do?"

"Pray," he answered calmly. "I truly believe God wants this story told to the world, and that He has already raised up a writer for the task. Pray; God will bring you His pen."

"He's right," said Matt when I told him of the tall man's feedback and advice. "We're no writers. I still can't believe we managed to put most of this together over the phone!" Running his hands over his face, he groaned and said, "Yes, this definitely needs to be rewritten."

"But by whom? *We* certainly can't do it! This was our best effort! Is there a writers agency we can call, or something?"

Matt sat in silence for a few moments, his eyes dancing about the floor and a hand gently stroking his chin.

"There is...no," he winced, shaking his head. "No. *He* wouldn't do it."

"Who?"

Mecca in My Wake

"It doesn't matter. I do know someone who is a writer...but no; he wouldn't do this. Let's, you and I, pray about it. As the tall man said, God will bring us His pen."

We did so, and then spent the rest of the afternoon discussing plans for our ministry and missionary organization.

Before the midnight oil had expired, Matt returned to a topic he had broached a handful of times prior.

"I'm just saying, you'll need a helper! He who finds a wife finds a good thing, you know! And, let's face it, time is not exactly on your side—you're a spring chicken in autumn, my friend!"

"And I don't disagree! It's just...Matt, would any woman take me?"

"Your orthodontist has already given you a leg up—thirteen of them, in fact! With that new golden smile of yours, how could any woman resist?"

"But look at my face—could an angel love a disfigured wretch? And look at my history! Could gentleness make a home where there had once been violence, where danger yet looms? My family carried out the 9/11 murders! Could an American woman give her heart to such a man?"

Drooping his lips and shrugging his shoulders to his ears, Matt spun around in his chair, exclaiming, "Let's find out!" and quickly began to attack his keyboard.

"What are you doing?"

"Creating an online dating profile for you."

"But that's public! The FBI has cautioned me about such things."

"You're right," he said; though, his fingers continued their hoedown on the keys. "So, what do you want your name to be? Calvin? Rufus? Oh! How about Pierre?"

My eyes scraped the ceiling.

"Oh, fine! Let's go with Adam."

"Adam. Got it. What should we say about you in your bio?"

"How about, 'My pastor made me do it.'"

"Enticing. Did you steal that from a Shakespearian sonnet, or something?"

"Funny. Just write it."

"You sure you don't want, 'Rugged, Middle Eastern diamond in the rough,' or something like that?"

"Next!"

"Okay! Okay! Here—you sit down and write this. It's your bio, after all."

"I'd rather not. Why don't we just scrap the whole thing?"

"Do you believe a man should obey his pastor?"

"Well, sure, but—"

"And who's *your* pastor?"

"You...but—"

"Then obey me!" he exclaimed, with a twinkling wink in his eye. "Seriously, though; I truly believe your finding a wife will be a critical component, not just to your life, but to your ministry, as well. Just give it a try, and we'll see what God does, huh?"

"Fine."

"Good! Take a seat!"

"I don't know what to write!"

"Well, what sort of woman would pique your interest?"

"A Christian woman who's committed and serious about her faith."

"Good. Write it. Any specific criteria?"

"Maybe something about how I'd like to go about the whole getting-to-know-you process? How's this: I'll consider a date only if we each bring a friend and recite a favorite chapter of Scripture to one another?"

"Good! Bring friend, recite a favorite verse—"

"No—*chapter*."

"A whole *chapter*? Are you trying to sabotage your future marital bliss? How many people have memorized a whole chapter of Scripture?"

"A woman serious about her faith will do so. I really don't have all the time in the world to spend going on dates—this will thin the crowd significantly and tell me a great deal about her character."

"That's quite a request! But," he sighed, "what plans can we make to disrupt God's? Either you'll get no responses and then amend your standard, or we'll find ourselves a pearl with a head for memorization!"

My profile was published and we waited.

Matt inquired after it often; I kind of forgot about it.

And then...

"Adam!"

"Yes, mister Vice President?"

"The suspense is *killing* me! Let me see that profile!"

"Go ahead and log on, if you remember the password."

Hurling himself into the chair, Matt's fingers began to dance.

"Well, I'll be...aren't *you* popular!"

Dropping my preoccupation, I rushed to the computer and swiftly rolled Matt away from the screen; his delighted giggle filled the room in a vortex as he spun freely in his swivel chair.

I plopped my palms flat on the desk and gaped at the red number five perched ever so proudly atop the tiny, blue envelope icon.

My hand, like a wet sponge, flopped over the mouse.

From somewhere ten miles from my body, I watched the little black cursor sail toward the envelope.

Five names stood one atop the other—matches suggested by the service.

Matt snatched the mouse and clicked on the first name.

"No way!" he blurted before I could object. "Pass!" he cried, having reviewed the next and promptly deleted the name. "Nada! Hey, this one's kind of—*nah*, never mind."

Then, a *CLICK* like a sky-painting firework exploded through the room.

And there she was.

Something like the flying fist of a heavyweight boxer crashed into my chest.

The world around me melted into a blur of soft watercolors, and I floated suspended over a crystal pool, fed by a laughing brook, tumbling over stones with a sound like a chorus of whispering angels, their voices like the delicacy of their feathered wings. Though he tried, Matt could not pry my face from the screen; my eyes were affixed to it like a pair of suction cups.

"Matt," I mumbled. "She's...she's just...beautiful."

"She's a unicorn!"

"What?"

"A blue-eyed, red-blooded, American unicorn! Look at this profile! Have you ever seen such boldness, such radical and audacious faith?"

I gazed in stunned silence for a few moments more.

Slapping me suddenly on the back, Matt shouted, "*Well?* What are you waiting for, huh? Get typing!"

And, thrusting his chair under me, he bounded out of the room.

I hardly knew what to write—even if I did know, how could I with hands acting like they were watching an at-home fitness tape: shaking and sweating?

"Dear God," I prayed, using whatever breath my tightening lungs could spare. "I've never done anything like this. Send me to preach Your Word in the midst of a raging battle, bullets zipping overhead, and I will go with all confidence! But...*this?*"

Sealing my eyes, I took a deep breath and asked God for peace and something coherent to say.

"*Hello!*"

"*Greetings!*"

"*Fine day!*"

Getting worse!

"*Nice to meet you!*"

Without the exclamation point, maybe.

"*Nice to meet you.*"

Well, now, that just sounds disingenuous.

"How's it going in here?" asked Matt, leaping back into the office.

"Still working on the opening line."

"It's been over an hour!"

"This is not exactly the easiest thing, *okay!*"

"You're a doctor! You went to medical school!"

"And that was *light years* easier than this!"

"Move over!" he shouted, hip-checking me into the book-shelf. "Let the married man learn you a thing or two!" His fingers sashayed over the keys: "'*Hello! My name is Adam. I would very much enjoy the opportunity to get to know you better.*' Now get crackin'!" he shouted, rolling me back in front of the computer. "Tell her more about yourself, hash it out over the next few weeks, pray; and then, if all is going well, invite her to a group dinner! I'm your plus one!"

I followed that formula to a T, and it wasn't long before I had become so bowled-over impressed by this woman—to the point that I could allow no shyness or nervousness to hinder my asking—that I invited her to dinner with Matt and one of her friends.

Before the appetizer arrived, I found myself gazing as if into the sun at someone whose picture should have been ashamed of itself for how poorly it had captured its subject; this living, breathing vision parted her lips and spoke as the bluebird sings, "There is therefore now no condemnation for those who are in Christ Jesus." And so on she went, every verse on which I hung threatening to send my captivated face plunging helplessly to the table, until at last, concluding her memorized chapter of Romans 8, she said, "For I am sure that neither death nor life, nor angels nor rulers, nor powers, nor height nor depth, nor anything else in all creation, will be able to separate us from the love of God in Christ Jesus our Lord." Then with a tiny smile painted beneath twinkling, squinted eyes set neatly in frames of black, she added, "Amen."

It was then a touch of spice cut across that angelic mien.

Cocking an eyebrow and tilting her head forward, she let out a hearty, "Your turn!"

By the end of dinner, I was feeling myself hooked.

But marriage is no light matter, and marriage to someone like me requires even more care and consideration. For my sake, I could not let emotion rule the day; for her sake, I had to lay everything on the line with total transparency.

As we bade each other farewell, I handed her a copy of the *From Mecca to Christ* manuscript, printed from my computer.

"If you would," I said, "please read this carefully."

"Oh! Is this the book you told me about?"

I nodded.

"Read it *very* carefully," I urged. "As I've alluded, mine is a life that brings with it lots of baggage, some serious things from my past that must be considered. Everything is in here."

As Matt and I walked to his car, he threw his arm over my shoulders and said, "So, what made you choose 2 Corinthians 4 as your chapter?"

"It's short."

He and I looked at one another and broke out into a laugh.

"No," I said, wiping a tear from my eye; "the book I gave her tonight is my past; that chapter is my waking future."

When she had finished reading, she contacted me, and we set up another group date.

"You said when you gave this to me," she began, sliding the manuscript across the table, "that your life carries lots of baggage."

"I did."

Leaning forward, she skewered my eyes with her gaze and stated very plainly, confidently, "Jesus took away that baggage. The old you died out there in the desert. I'm looking at a new man, alive in Christ."

Matt's jaw and mine dropped right into the lobster bisque.

"And here I'd thought her just getting through that mess of a manuscript had been the amazing part," muttered Matt.

The flood gates had opened; she and I conversed constantly from that day forward, our discussions diving deeper into the depths of our lives through open discussions about Christ, who He is, and what it means to be His follower; we discussed Scripture, its blueprint for marriage, and what we believed the Word commanded us to do as husbands and wives. And we did this not alone—with our desires hastening quickly toward a canopy of white and a pair of "I dos," she and I each enlisted the aid of an accountability partner to help us stay focused, pure, and honoring to God as we made this journey together.

All the right pieces were falling into place.

There was one thing, however, we had not yet had the opportunity to do.

"My little girl says you're a reformed Muslim!" boomed the billowing bellow from the belly of a most boisterous human being when we sat down to dinner. "A Christian, says she! Well, son," he hemmed, "I'm afraid you'll have to prove that to me!" A gigantic smile then sprinted onto his face. "No Muslim eats pork, do they?"

"No," I replied; though, the word fell from my lips with a touch of trepidation, sounding like it should have carried with it a question mark.

"Waitress!" he called. "Two pulled pork sandwiches! The *big* ones!"

"Be nice, daddy!" said a pair of sharply raised eyebrows, set over a tight-lipped smirk.

"*Whaaat?*" he whined, shrugging with a broad and innocent grin. "He's got to pass the test!"

Before long, the waitress returned and slid before me a steaming, American-sized, need-a-forklift-to-pick-it-up sandwich drenched in so savory and delectable an aroma that I could have filled a pitcher with the saliva readying my tongue to sink into this beyond un-kosher, food-law-breaking delight. My eyes disappeared into the back of my head as the warm scent of a new, belt-busting adventure slipped through my nostrils; my stomach gurgled impatiently.

A large container of sauce had come with the sandwich; given that this was a test, I felt not a little pressure to perform well. So, doing what I assumed all Americans did, I emptied the entire container onto the pork and sunk my teeth into the magnificent, messy display.

No one told me the stuff in the container was ninety percent salt, ten percent sauce; so, when her father asked me after we'd finished eating to share my testimony, I called for another pitcher of water—I was three pitchers deep by the time I got to my childhood.

"You used to keep camels, you say?"

"Mhmm," I affirmed between glugs.

"Learned a lot from them, eh?"

I nearly spewed water all over him.

Chuckling, he looked at his daughter and said, "Boy, I like him!" And when all there was to tell had been told, he stood me up, gave me a great big hug, and declared to everyone at the table, "Okay! He's in!"

All at once I was taken into the arms of my new American family, embraced as a brother and a son; and from the hand of its head was I given on a glorious, sun-soaked day the hand of his most precious jewel: an incomparable woman, with whom, complete in Christ, I was bestowed the honor and accepted the responsibility to be her lover, protector, leader, companion, and friend; to spend the rest of my life caught up in the fascination of who she is and all the intricate, explosively wonderful details that are the handiwork of the Creator, with my only concern being that my life may be too short to explore, learn, and guard them all—but that won't be for a lack of trying.

"And they came from every tribe, tongue, and nation," said Matt, musing on the day as he and I took a rest from the wedding festivities. "From all nations—just look at them! I'd be surprised if there wasn't a representative from every country here today!"

"It's overwhelming," I said softly, my hand draped firmly over my mouth, and a tear teetering on the rim. "They all came, every one of them. You see her?" I pointed to a young woman conversing with my new father-in-law. "She flew in this morning from South Korea; she's here just for the wedding and is going back tonight."

So many wonders in so brief a time had come about, not the least of which was this moment: when I turned to look at Matt and found him surveying the crowd...speechless.

It was a short-lived wonder.

"God has used you to touch so many lives all over the world!" he said, the awe heavy on his lips. "And here they are, all gathered to celebrate with you! Did any man ever have such a family as this?"

I turned to him with a smile; and, placing my hand on his shoulder, I let the tear fall.

"A forever family."

24

His Great Commission

I remember well that October morning in 2018.
No sooner had the ground beneath my feet shattered into a million pieces over a cavern of nothingness did my phone start to buzz.

"Have you seen the news?"

I could hardly form a reply.

There was no breath with which to speak, anyway.

I could but stare at the bold, yellow text set ablaze against a churning river of blood, smeared along the bottom of the television screen.

JOURNALIST JAMAL KHASHOGGI CONFIRMED DEAD

What had been my dread had become a reality; the day he had been reported missing, I could feel in my gut that he was gone. And what cut deeply and further blackened the loss of a friend was the fact that he had been lured to his death in the same manner by which the Saudi government had sought to lure me. Having been directed to the Saudi consulate under false pretenses, he was assassinated upon arrival and cut into pieces—a U.S. journalist dismembered and mutilated by the authorities of his homeland, all because he had defied them and criticized their rule.

"Father, God!" I wept, falling to my knees, there in the midst of my darkened room, painted with the silvery glow of the heartbreaking news. "Oh, dearest Christ! Had I have been bolder! Had I have held him faster! Had I have loved him greater! Where, now, is my friend, oh God? What word did You speak when he stood before You? On what did his spirit stand that day? By what was it covered? What payment did he claim to satisfy his debt?" My sobbing intensified into a twisting, silent heaving; my insides all contracted at once, and I could speak only by the free-flowing blood of my heart, painting red the floor beneath me. "What more could I have done, oh God? How much time did I spend on things that rot? Would I have stayed up with him through every night, speaking truth from horizon to horizon, might he now know Your arms of love? Jesus...my Jesus—has this servant failed his friend?"

As my tears puddled about my head, pressed hard against the floor, there came under me something like a soft but firm cloud. Though weak and trembling was I, helpless in my grief, that cloud started to lift, taking me away from the darkened room, up into the heavens, there to be bathed in the water of a warm, comforting sunlight that wrapped me like a woolen blanket. And I heard this Word: that I, a bundle of fragile flesh, have not the power to save any man, not even myself; it is for all men to choose life, if he will, and to fall upon the salvation bought by Christ alone.

A foreign peace came over me, reminding me that I had been commanded to go, and I had; but salvation belongs to the Lord, and whether Jamal ignored the truth or let it penetrate his life was beyond my reach to affect or mold to my will.

"God," I whimpered, "Your love is a free gift. To that love I'd pointed my friend. Because You are love, You have honored his choice; You have not forced him to embrace You. If he'd chosen his own way, that is the way he has been granted the freedom to go. But the countless ways of man lead to destruction, though they seem bright to our mortal eyes. I am but a messenger, pointing toward the one and only way. And so shall I ever be, until You return or call me home."

The room returned, filling in slowly all around me.

I felt a tugging on my shoulders.

Ever so gently, I floated to my feet.

Turning my head, I watched as the news played clips of my friend, of the chaos in my homeland against which he'd fought, and of Saudi leaders yet insisting these reports were false and all part of a massive hoax.

My resolve had never been greater.

"Matt," I said, taking up my phone, "let us go into the fields."

"What do we call it?" he asked after we'd drained three pots of coffee putting the final touches on our outreach organization.

"Mecca to Christ International."

"I like it. When do we start?" he added with a wink.

Throwing back the last sip in my mug, I smiled and said, "Now."

And we did, blowing up phones, speaking from pulpits, sending out emails, and going door to door. With over three million Muslims holding a presence in all fifty states, and billions more around the world, it was critical that our message be broadly spread.

"But I've never even met a Muslim, much less tried to share the Gospel with one!"

"You're not the first to have this concern," I would say, practically every time I went out or composed an email. "First and foremost, Muslim evangelism begins with love; the love of Christ—His unconditional, sacrificial love—is a foreign concept to a life spent trying to buy favor."

"Muslims are dangerous!" said many.

"*Islam* is dangerous," I would calmly reply. "In fact, meet a Muslim on the street and he's probably not radical. Inquire about his faith and you'll most likely find his knowledge of the Qur'an is not extensive beyond the rituals he performs and the verses he has memorized for liturgical purposes. Inquire, and he'll likely refer you to his Imam—such men, almost all of them, being well versed in all of Islam's teachings, lean toward radicalism, which is the blueprint found in the religion's books. The Qur'an and Hadith command them to attack Christianity and hold to what the rest of the world might call 'extreme' beliefs."

"What sort of methods work best in presenting the Gospel to such people?"

"Thankfully, we need not *invent* any new and clever ways to speak truth! Nor does the Gospel require any editing or modification! Jesus' method is more than sufficient, is it not? Jesus was gentle, but bold; he gave of Himself freely, but He did not accept half-heartedness. If you would approach a Muslim as a challenge to mark on your scoreboard, or a check to scratch off your list, don't go at all!"

We garnered support from all over the country and quickly established a fully-functional Muslim outreach organization, through which we began equipping churches to minister to their Muslim neighbors and show them the love of Christ; we started utilizing social and print media, and even began developing the idea of my taking a team of medical professionals to war-torn areas of the world to spread the Gospel through healing. But our core remained and still remains evangelism, traveling to Muslim neighborhoods across the U.S. and organizing teams to go and spread the Word to the ends of the earth, even in the darkness that is Saudi Arabia.

"This is His great commission—to *go*! Jesus commands us to *GO*! Not merely to church or to Bible studies! Rather, to leave our comfort zones, to risk our wealth, our reputation, our lives—everything!—for the sake of the lost souls Jesus calls even now to come to the cross! We go as He commanded, to make disciples of *all* nations!" I declared, standing before a group of curious potential evangelists; it was my first attempt under this new banner to organize a party to venture into the Middle East. "It breaks my heart that asylum forbids me to return to my home—my father is there, my mother, my brothers; all my family and loved ones, whom I hold drear. I can't go back to them and share this Good News—but I can equip each and every one of you to enter the lion's mouth and be an effective witness for Christ. Will any among you answer the call to go?"

The room was silent for a moment.

Then, a man seated at the back of the room stood up.

He began to walk toward me.

My eyes burst wide when I saw that sandy blond hair, sun-kissed skin, flip flops, and rainbow-tinted sunglasses tucked into his pale-blue breast pocket.

"THOMAS!"

Before he had reached the stage, I sprinted forth and took him into a great bear hug.

Holding me out before him, Thomas shook his head with a sad smile.

"I treated you poorly when we served together with YWAM," he said. "I apologize. Let me be the first to accept your aid and answer the call of our Savior with Mecca to Christ."

***

I arose amid the darkness and stepped out onto the frigid sand. Its icy nip gnawed at the base of my naked feet; its breath washed over my toes. All the world was dark; the stars were veiled, and I could perceive nothing of its form or composition, other than what I supposed it must be. I dared not make a move, nor take one single step—here, firm in the frozen ground, I felt I could steal another passing breath and scour for the next, ignorant of the minutes, hours, and days to come. Then, my legs began to cramp; my spine began to twist. So long had I been perched in the darkness; my body could not last much longer—but what could be found in darkness on which to sit? With naught but my own power to uphold me, I hardened my joints, stiffened my neck, and cemented myself all the more firmly into place; here I would stand, and stand *I* would. If anything could be known, it was the chill of the shadow looming over me, unseen but known by the painful cold it inflicted; and in its midst, before its piercing gaze, I dared not quake and fought hard against the inevitable fall. I was breaking, though I believed my stone strong. And then, bursting forth for but a moment—on schedule, but not on my time—a shadow of light filled the darkness, undoing what the darkness had devoured.

The stains of overwhelming glory dazzled my vision.

Then, I began to see.

Above the treetops was painted a streak of thick, grey cloud; but just a breath over the tree line, slicing through the grey, was a long band separating the haze—it was a window, as wide as the eye could see, into a crystal clear morning sky, washed in a warm glow that was quickly banishing the darkness. And though the dense cloud cover did not permit me to see its coming, that glow, making the darkness tremble, proclaimed with a loud voice, which shook the bones without sound, the coming of that which soon peeked over the frayed and misty edge of cloud. The moment its head crowned into the tear in the sky, my eyes were set ablaze by the power of its fiery red form, and the world was awakened. Slowly it climbed, until it was at last pressed between the dual layers of blinding smoke above and below, giving light to all; and, for a little while, it and everything it touched were made plain to the eye, and I saw clearly the great divide before me: my feet buried in scorching sand, while a dew-covered grass lay just beyond the tips of my toes.

Dripping a red radiance over the sky, the blazing body stained the heavenly spectacle with its blood, casting over the heavenly canvas a mighty brush to paint a masterpiece, for which nothing on earth—no force of nature, nor intelligence of man—could create an equal. Then, swiftly, it soared into the atmosphere, disappearing behind the massive stain in the sky; but the world did not fall dark. Higher and higher it went—this I knew only by the light that continued to flood the world around me from a source that was ever present in only part of its total essence; and higher still it would go, by its reign laying all things bear.

Somewhere up above, just barely within my scope of vision, there lay a final break in that massive cloud, with no stain above to conceal that which, for a little while, passed behind it unseen. There, at the apex of the earth, it would dawn, reveal itself once more—breaking forth in all its glory, removing the last of the shadows yet clinging to the earth.

And as I looked, the great expanse of sand in which I stood began to shift, and from each grain there sprouted something like figures of men—grain after grain arose and transformed, until I stood amidst a sea of my sand-born kindred, covered in the dust of our homeland, with our eyes turned toward the sky.

There we watched for the glorious reappearance, the shower of resplendent beauty and everlasting peace and joy, promised to burst forth as it had in the beginning, returning this time with the fullness of its glory.

Once more, it would come.

I could but wonder when.

With my eyes set firmly upon the heavens, my feet stepped forth onto the cool, dew-covered grass, kicking beneath me, with a multitude of souls following alongside and all around, all of us washing our feet in the dewy newness of life, leaving the dust of Mecca in our wake.

Appendix

Translations from Memoir to Narrative

Here follows a chapter-by-chapter breakdown of the means and methods by which the memoir *From Mecca to Christ* was converted into the narrative form of *Mecca in My Wake*. Statements marked with an asterisk (*) should be assumed to occur across multiple chapters.

—

Chapter 1.   The ghostwriter, to better articulate and emphasize Ahmed's emotions during the scene, has interpreted some of Ahmed's internal thoughts into a narrative composition*. This has been done to make the character of Ahmed as flesh-and-blood as the page allows, to bring forth a deeper humanity not experienced in the recounting of facts as they happened.

Chapter 2.   The ghostwriter has interpreted and composed some dialogue, drawing lines and inspiration therefor from the events as they happened, as well as from the sentiments and beliefs held by the speaking characters*. [To demonstrate: A military general can be historically recounted as having given a rousing speech to his troops, speaking about courage and bravery, without the transcript of his actual words being recorded; thus, the ghostwriter fills in that dialogue with words articulating the factually-attached focus, means, and delivery of the historical character, attributing these to the character as portrayed in the narrative, and drawing from as many historical and real-life examples as possible to best create accurate speech].

Chapter 3.   *From Mecca to Christ* does not contain an account of Ahmed's observing men escorting their sex slaves from the tent following the meal. However, Ahmed confirms these actions are accurate, as he had often beheld them in his youth; thus, they were included here to better paint the world in which Ahmed was raised. Additionally, Ahmed's specific musings on the Qur'an were added to develop the narrative character of Ahmed and to demonstrate how the teachings of Islam shaped his life and the lives of all living in Saudi Arabia today.

Chapter 4.   The dream penned in this chapter is not one had by Ahmed. Rather, it is a poetic, metaphorical representation of a real event (recounted in Chapter 5) and a foreshadowing of the events to come. This was done, firstly, to introduce into the narrative the concept of dreaming, which is a critical component to the entire story; and, secondly, to change the pace of the narrative thus far in adding color and intrigue through mystery. Regarding the reflection of a man sitting on a curb, refusing the call to prayer: this story was composed from Ahmed's explanation of what happens to such people, and inserted here to make the narrative character of Ahmed a spectator to real-life events. Finally, Ahmed's musing on Qur'an 9:111 takes knowledge Ahmed had during this time and presents it to the reader in narrative reflection to reveal the Qur'anic justification for the 9/11 terrorist attacks.

Chapter 5. The story about Ahmed finding the harmonica is true; however, it was taken from its actual point in his history and placed here for plot structure purposes. The event with the Russian pilgrim is true and added here in flashback form to better serve the plot. Ahmed's witnessing of the executions in the town square is a composite event—it is an amalgamation of the numerous executions and punishments of various kinds he'd witnessed throughout his upbringing. Stuffing into a single scene a handful of these historical events keeps the narrative pacing tight and flowing, and better reveals the severity of something seen often and over a long period of time. Lastly, the image Ahmed sees out his window at the close of the chapter is a sight very common for the eyes of Saudi citizens; the narrative context in which it is presented was created for plot and character development purposes.

Chapter 6. The ghostwriter selected the actual verses from the Qur'an recited by Ahmed and the unnamed student.

Chapter 7. Ahmed was shown many beheading videos during his training; the specific video described here was one seen years prior by the ghostwriter, and drawn upon to convey the grotesque imagery. As with chapter 5, Ahmed's experience walking through the streets is a composite of several events seen over his lifetime; the beheading of the woman is a direct relaying of an actual beheading from a piece of video evidence provided by Ahmed and shown to the ghostwriter.

Chapter 8.   No amendments other than those identified with asterisks.

Chapter 9.   The lengthy discussion between Ahmed and the tall man incorporates the topics presented in *From Mecca to Christ*, with several additional topics and arguments added by the ghostwriter, based on the all-encompassing study performed during their meetings. All topics featured are confirmed by both parties involved to have been discussed during this time.

Chapter 10.   No amendments other than those identified with asterisks.

Chapter 11.   While under house arrest, Ahmed heard from the other side of a wall his father chanting the verses about Noah's son. The ghostwriter turned this event into a dream to articulate its emotion and severity in a more colorful manner, using metaphor and dream to better catch the imagination of the reader and tie the situation to events recorded in chapter 7.

Chapter 12.   The ghostwriter selected the topic discussed with the woman in the chat room. Also, Ahmed's finding the piece of Shiite artwork was created to paint the moment more visually he realized that he, a Sunni, would be baptizing a Shiite. In his talk with the tall man, some discussion topics were inserted to expose to the reader real events taking place in Ahmed's life at the time.

Chapter 13.   The religious police officer in the black boots was created to represent the cold authority carrying out the punishments of Sharia law. While in prison, Ahmed hears the screams of a woman. Though not recounted as part of his prison experience, it was added to expose to the reader the horrors female prisoners face; the acts, as written herein, as well as the quote from Muslim authorities justifying said acts, are factual and not exaggerated or misrepresented. Ahmed's threefold realization, as well as his falling on his tormentors and begging God to forgive them, superimposes onto the narrative character Ahmed's present posture toward those who inflicted evil upon him and others; it does not recount historical actions that took place while in his cell. Historically, these realizations and posture came afterward for Ahmed; they were inserted here for plot structure, pacing, and character development purposes.

Chapter 14.   Ahmed's vision with the long corridor of doors was created to symbolically demonstrate the struggle experienced at this time. The character Rashid was created as a representation of individuals torn between loyalties, as Ahmed searched for acceptance in a church body.

Chapter 15.   The mustached elder was created to represent the hostile pushback and dubiety Ahmed experienced when looking for a church. While Ahmed's memoir does refer to an event with one specific hostile elder, this character is meant to represent the totality of that hostility experienced from many individuals. Finally, the conversation had between Ahmed, Andrew, and the young man was created as a single manifestation of many such discussions Ahmed had with people regarding going to Saudi Arabia to spread the Gospel.

Chapter 16.   The character Vince was created to represent the many people with whom Ahmed worked during his time with YWAM, specifically those who stood by him, believed his story, and served to provide him with encouragement. Ahmed's encounter at the hospital with a victim of domestic violence was created to capture the countless victims of such violence he'd treated throughout his time as a doctor. The story of finding a woman unresponsive in her home is true and recounted in *From Mecca to Christ*; it was inserted here as a flashback to better punctuate the theme of the chapter and advance the plot.

Chapter 17.   No amendments other than those identified with asterisks.

Chapter 18.   The timeline of meetings between Ahmed and Matt has been compressed for the sake of pacing. After their first meeting over coffee, Matt mentions how the night after meeting Ahmed he had done extensive research on him and his story—this research was actually conducted a month later at the prompting of Matt's church elders, who challenged him to be sure about Ahmed's claims. Other conversations between Ahmed and Matt feature topics and quotes taken from the full breadth of their relationship during this time, compiled and compressed into single scenes.

Chapter 19.   The appearance of the man who did in actuality pull up to Ahmed's car has been recrafted in such a way as to depict in physical manifestation the twisted and ugly posture and position many in Saudi Arabia take toward suspected Christians.

Chapter 20.   No amendments other than those identified with asterisks.

Chapter 21.   The phone conversation between characters Ahmed and Matt, as well as one with John and Reena, ties together into a single scene the pieces of news Ahmed received through various channels over an extended period of time. The setting in which Ahmed confronts the undercover police officers puts him on a street corner to give the reader the sense of exposure and the open danger the actual event possessed. The character Greg was created to personify the warning Ahmed received through his various channels.

Chapter 22.   Ahmed was in contact with Jamal Khashoggi during this time. The conversation composed here was created by the ghostwriter to encapsulate a specific highlight of their year-long correspondence and to set up the reaction to Khashoggi's death.

Chapter 23.   Ahmed's marriage was moved to later in the narrative timeline for pacing and comprehension purposes. In actuality, Ahmed was engaged to wed during the time of his application for asylum; however, the ghostwriter made this change to keep the chapter regarding asylum-seeking free from containing two pivotal events, so as to prevent splitting the reader's attention between said events.

Chapter 24.   The death of Jamal Khashoggi did not coincide with the finalization of Mecca to Christ International, as the latter had already been established. This was a creative choice by the ghostwriter to pair the need for the ministry to a real event demonstrating that need. The character Thomas did actually come to Ahmed to apologize and seek help in getting to Saudi Arabia to evangelize; the scene depicting this event was conceptualized by the ghostwriter. Ahmed's final vision was composed by the ghostwriter from the inspiration of a personal experience watching a veiled sunrise, used here to illustrate Christ and His second coming, and more colorfully capture in summary the entirety of the narrative and the grander tale of which we are all a part.

In his kindness God called you to share in his eternal glory by means of Christ Jesus. So, after you have suffered a little while, he will restore, support, and strengthen you, and he will place you on a firm foundation. All power to him forever! Amen.

1 Peter 5:10-11

SOLI DEO GLORIA

Made in the USA
Columbia, SC
04 April 2021

35652822R00269